ADVANCE REVIEWS

"This book is a must-read for anyone who is concerned about the direction our country is heading toward. Our founding fathers based their principles and the constitution on religious theology from the Bible. The party in control is now rapidly turning away from religious and moral thinking. The epilogue sums up the books in a well-written chapter. The 24 observations are extremely good. The one that stood out to me was that you should never believe everything you hear and to test it to see if it is true. This is a principle that I adhere to myself. The book is about religion and politics and weaves the two together into an exemplification of what is going on in our world today."

★★★★★

"The author gives a huge wake-up call, if we weren't already wide awake from the destruction of the radical Left Dem Party today, to American citizens. As he shares, the Dem Party of just a few years ago, has been radicalized by the current crop of Leftists. The current Democratic Party has minimal resemblance from their party even 20-30 years ago. Open borders, anti-oil-independence, defunding of law enforcement, wokeness, cancel-culture, and the absolute derangement and hate of President Trump, are just a few of the radical ideas of the Democrat Party today. He shares many excellent quotes and verses to defend his position. He stresses the importance of the Sanctity of Life, the Sanctity of Marriage, and the Sanctity of Family, as being the foundation of which America was built upon and we must stand true in rejecting the push by the radical Left in destroying these foundations. Highly recommend."

"Well-researched book that connects the history of the United States with Christianity. The author believes the United States is on a dangerous path because of turning away from the principles the founding fathers had - directly from the Bible. While this is a controversial opinion in today's world, the author goes into quite a lot of detail on why he believes this. I suppose time will tell whether or not he has valid points."

★★★★★

"A very good read. The book does much more than identify troubles and trends in the Democratic party. In reality it identifies troubling conditions and issues that plague the USA. The author states that collegiality that existed between the political parties is gone. His purpose is to explain how that happened. He identifies ten warning signs that caused the divide and then elaborates on the data that supports his evidence. Highly recommended."

A PARTY IN CRISIS

THE RADICALIZATION OF THE DEMOCRATIC PARTY

DARRELL J. AHRENS
CITIZEN

A Party in Crises: The Radicalization of The Democratic Party

ISBN: 978-1629673066

Rev 25-0507

TABLE OF CONTENTS

PREFACE

The Fallacy of D.E.I. (Diversity, Equity, Inclusion)

The Democrat Party, or at least its radical wing, has a new party slogan - D.E.I., abbreviation for Diversity, Equity, Inclusion. These Democrats insist that D.E.I. must be the standard, the goal, of policies established by our political, educational, and cultural institutions, and for that matter, even the Church. Even many of our educational institutions, including Ivy League universities have gotten on board, considering D.E.I. as an intellectual capstone essential to the planning, acquisition, and employment of human resources, and the standard to be adhered to for all organizational rules, policies, and regulations.

Whenever a policy, rule, or regulation has far-reaching impact such as D.E.I., it is wise to examine it closely and in detail to determine its potential effects and whether it passes the test of reason, rationale, and common sense. So, let's apply this test to each of the components of D.E.I., starting with a definition of each component to insure that all who read this are considering it with a common understanding of the term.

First, "Diversity!" Diversity is defined in respect to how things differ. It emphasizes multiformity rather than uniformity, and the physical, spiritual, and social differences that characterize individual and collective identities. These differences are in the realms of race, ethnicity, religion, gender (male / female), age, economic status, social status, and other differences which characterize the human race. The radical promoters of D.E.I. insist that such diversity in the population is the source of our strength as a people and a nation. Therefore, concerning immigration, open borders and mass immigration are to be accepted since the more immigration, the more diversity, and the more diversity, the greater our strength as a nation. In this they are wrong.

Diversity is not our strength. Unity is our strength as a people and a nation. Diversity is good, desirable, and to be welcomed. This should be intuitively obvious since the United States has been largely a nation of immigrants from its very beginning. Over the years, for the most part, the rich dimensions of cultural, religious, economic, educational, and social contributions of millions of immigrants, combined with the foundational Judeo-Christian values and vision inherited from the Founding Fathers, has resulted in a unity of purpose, mission, and goals that is commonly referred to as the "American way of life," which is the envy of most of the world, and this unity forms the very core of the nation's strength. Among other great accomplishments, it was this unity of strength and purpose that enabled the United States to take the lead in building the international coalition that won the most extensive and global war in human history - World War II.

Yes, diversity can be very advantageous to an organization, community, group, nation. Nevertheless, diversity can also be very disadvantageous, up to a point of danger, to the institution involved. Diversity becomes a danger to a community's or nation's peace, prosperity, and security when a group or organization's policies, standards, and goals conflict with the foundational principles, values, vision, and goals of the majority of citizens of the host community, organization, or nation. This is the case today with the radical wing of the Democrat Party, who insist on the right to abortion, right up to the moment of birth, and even afterwards; who insist that political and educational officials know what is best for children more than the parents; who support school and medical personnel when they refuse to notify parents of information vital to their child's physical and mental health, all in order to advance a political agenda; who have supported open borders over the years, leading to the national security crisis we face today; who have supported defunding our law enforcement organizations, resulting in the alarming increase in violent crime in our cities today; who insist that the American taxpayer pay for sex-change operations for any transexual who wants one. One could go on and on identifying policies of the radical wing of the Democrat Party that contradicts not only the Constitution, but the principles, standards, and values of the vast majority of the American people.

As an aside, concerning the crisis of open borders and the influx of millions of unvetted illegal immigrants and the current national security, economic, and cultural crisis this has caused, numerous polls during the recent Presidential campaign, showed that immigration, along with the economy, were consistently the top two concerns of the American people, to which the Democrat candidate and the party consistently failed to give proper attention. They paid for this with a resounding and humiliating loss. Fortunately, the recent election results make it clear that these top concerns will be dealt with effectively, forcefully, and soon, all to the panic of the radical liberals who bemoan the lack of diversity to the nation and the violation of the "Inclusion" factor of their D.E.I. policy that closed or tightly controlled borders would entail. To bring some sense to the immigration issue, I think it would be beneficial for all citizens, and especially the radical liberals, to consider the immigration policy of a former President of the United States.

President Theodore Roosevelt believed that immigrants should assimilate into American society as quickly as possible, learn the English language, eschew hyphenated national identities such as "Italian-American" etc., and declare their primary national allegiance to the United States of America. In 1907, he stated: "In the first place, we should insist that the immigrant who comes here in good faith, becomes an American and assimilates himself to us, he shall be treated in an exact equality with everyone else, for it is an outrage to discriminate against any such man because of creed, or birthplace, or origin. But this is predicated upon the person becoming in every facet an American, and nothing but an American. There can be no divided allegiance here. Any man who says he is an American, but something else also, isn't an American at all. We have room for but one flag, the American flag. We have room for but one language here, and that is the English language…and we have room for but one sole loyalty, and that is a loyalty to the American people." Sounds like a pretty good and effective immigration policy to me!

To summarize diversity, it is not our nation's strength, but it contributes to the nation's strength when it is combined with the nation's foundational principles, thereby strengthening the core of unity of values, vision, and purpose bequeathed to us by our Founders. Diversity, without unity, ends in confusion, chaos, cultural conflict, division of effort, purpose, and goals, and leads to policies not beneficial to the nation and the common welfare.

Second in the radical Democrat slogan D.E.I. is the component "Equity!" Equity is defined as "the state, ideal, or quality of being just, impartial, or fair." Sounds wonderful, doesn't it? However, the equity in the slogan D.E.I., as applied by the radical elements of the Democrat Party goes much farther. It provides resources and provisions to ensure that all people have access to the same opportunities for personal, educational, and economic advancement, and identifies and removes barriers that cause disparities in people receiving those resources and provisions that provide such opportunities. Sounds good so far, doesn't it? However, the Achilles heel in the equity of D.E.I. is that it is an equity of outcomes, which is virtually impossible to achieve.

The fatal flaw in this reasoning is the immense variety, diverse talents, diverse intellects, diverse capabilities, and diverse interests involved in human nature. Therefore, there is only one way to achieve an equity of outcomes, and that is to reduce everything to its lowest common denominator, to a level that everyone can achieve. And the outcome of that would be mediocrity. It should be clearly apparent that no matter how unlimited the resources and provisions that are committed to achieve an equity of outcomes, the end result will always be failure because of the unlimited variety, diverse talents, capabilities, intellects, and interests of we humans who are "fearfully and wonderfully made." Therefore, I would suggest that the fantasy of an "equity of outcomes" be replaced by the reality of an "equality of opportunity."

Our Founders, in the Declaration of Independence, emphasized that all men were created equal and endowed by their Creator with certain unalienable rights, that among these are the rights to life, liberty, and the pursuit of happiness. That right to the pursuit of happiness entails a right to the equality of opportunity to pursue that happiness without undue favoritism, prejudice, or bias.

Some time ago, I read about a high-ranking Air Force officer being asked what some his primary personnel concerns were. He mentioned that one of his main concerns was the fact that some 80% of the fighter pilots were white males, and he wanted to resolve this inequity of outcome. Being a former fighter pilot, I was appalled at his comment. Apart from ensuring an equality of opportunity for all those males and females who possessed the physical and mental qualities essential to being a fighter pilot, just how did he propose to resolve this so-called inequity of outcome within the fighter pilot community. Was the answer to assign a certain percentage of diverse minorities to fighter pilot training, regardless of their personal preferences? That policy would most certainly end up with not an equity of outcome, but a catastrophic outcome.

In summary, the equity of outcomes desired by the radical wing of the Democrat Party fails miserably to pass the test of reason, rationale, and common sense. Only an equality of opportunity will produce the best possible outcomes.

Thirdly, the I in the radical's slogan D.E.I. stands for "Inclusion!" It is defined as "the act of including or the state of being included." The radicals expand on this definition by claiming that the "Inclusion" in their D.E.I. slogan entails removing bias, and prejudice based on race, ethnicity, religion, gender, disabilities, etc., and bringing traditionally excluded individuals and groups into processes, activities, decision-making, and sharing of power formerly closed to them. In short, creating environments where those formerly discriminated against would feel welcomed, respected, and supported, and where they can participate fully and experience the full sense of belonging. And here again, human nature rudely intervenes and exposes their idea of inclusion as a liberal fantasy. Not only that, but it clearly displays the hypocrisy of the radical liberal establishment. How so? Consider the following.

Let's assume that I, a strong conservative, pro-life, pro-Constitution individual wanted to join the Democrat Party and work to bring reason, rationale, and common sense back into their ranks. What are the chances that the Party leadership and even a majority of members would welcome me into membership and invite me to share in party activities, decision making, and policy development? How about zero to none! Or consider the fact that among a majority of our colleges and universities, especially our so-called Ivy League institutions, the liberal professors vastly outnumber the conservative professors. Sometime ago, I recall reading (I believe it was in the Wall Street Journal) that the average ratio was around 90% liberal and 10% conservative.

Wait a minute! What about the radical liberals' insistence on D.E.I.? Ninety percent liberal professors compared to ten percent conservative professors does not give a glowing picture of diversity. In fact, it represents a strong denial of diversity. In the same way, that 90% compared to 10% clearly represents a strong denial of equity and an equity of outcomes. And lastly, that 90% compared to 10% clearly represents a strong denial of inclusion. To what extent do you think those 10% conservative professors feel welcomed, respected, and supported by those 90% liberal professors or by an administration that allows such an inequity. Or to what extent do you think those 10% conservative professors enjoy a strong sense of belonging to the academic cadre? Little to none, I would say!

Let's consider a more recent example of the radical Democrat liberals' violation of their policy of inclusion. During the recent campaign for President of the United States which ended with Donald Trump elected President by a wide majority in both the popular and electoral votes, his Democrat opponent, as well as other Democrat officials, members of the party and the mass media, referred to Trump as Hitler, a Nazi, a Racist, a destroyer of democracy, an enemy of the working and middle class, and other derogatory names too numerous to mention. With his resounding victory, President elect Trump was invited to the White House by the current Democrat President, Joe Biden, who himself made some derogatory remarks about Trump during the campaign. Nevertheless, President Biden congratulated Trump on his victory, welcomed him to the White House, and insured him of his full cooperation and support to provide for a smooth transition of power.

So, it would seem that President Biden is complying with the D.E.I. policy of Inclusion. Good for him! No so, however, with many other Democrat officials, Congress members, party members, and, with few exceptions, the mass media that, contrary to their professional journalistic standards, are clearly biased in favor of the Democrat party and its policies. To no one's surprise, some governors, members of Congress, and members of the mass media have stated that they will continue to resist Trump as President, fight against his policies and legislation in Congress and the Courts, and strive to render his administration ineffective. It is my opinion that, since many of these officials swore an oath to defend the Constitution from enemies within and without, their statements and actions come dangerously close to crossing, if not actually crossing, the boundary of treason. As a minimum, their statements and actions clearly violate their D.E.I. policy of Inclusion and put their hypocrisy on full display for the public to see.

Full compliance with the Inclusion requirements of D.E.I. is well-nigh impossible due to human nature and how it translates to the collective nature of clubs, groups, and organizations. As individuals, we tend to include within our inner circle people who think and act as we do, who share the same likes and dislikes, who adhere to the same principles, standards, and moral code as we do. Clubs, groups, and organizations usually have rules, regulations, and criteria one must adhere to in order to become a member. Therefore, both individuals and organizations are somewhat exclusionary in nature. If I seek membership in an organization that has dress rules requiring coat and tie, and I insist on wearing cut-off jeans and t-shirt, I will not experience inclusion. If I lead a Christian Bible group, and an avowed atheist who seeks to turn people away from the faith demands membership, I will not offer inclusion to him. The bottom line is that the overriding criteria for inclusion is loyalty - individual loyalty and loyalty to an organization's principles, standards, rules, and code.

You may ask, "What about the Bible's teaching: 'You are to love others as you love yourself' (Matthew 19:19) and 'Love your enemies and pray for those who persecute you'"? (Matthew 5:44) Certainly, we are to offer Christian love to everyone - friend, enemy, stranger. Notice however, that the passage says we are to love our enemies. It doesn't say that we have to like them. I can show love to someone without liking them or including them in my inner circle of friendship. How do I show such love? By praying for them; by assuring them of God's love for them through Christ; by assuring them of my love for them; and by assuring them of my forgiveness of them for the hurt, pain, and sorrow they have caused me.

But what if the individual refuses to accept God's love and mine, God's forgiveness and mine, and continues to hurt, harm, and persecute me? A Scripture passage, Titus 3:10 gives the answer as follows: "Warn a divisive person once; and then warn him a second time. After that, have nothing to do with him!" In other words, do not offer him inclusion. Nevertheless, I can still continue to show him love by praying for him.

And so, in conclusion and in view of all the above, what can we say about the radical Democrat slogan D.E.I. - Diversity, Equity, Inclusion? Simply that it fails the test of reason, rationale, and common sense as summarized below:

1. Diversity alone, without unity, results in conflict, confusion, chaos, disorder, and divided effort. Therefore, diversity is not our strength; unity is our strength, and the richness of variety in race, ethnicity, culture, and background afforded by diversity adds to the ultimate strength of unity.

2. The Equity of D.E.I. seeks an equity of outcomes and can only be achieved by denying those who have too much and favoring those who have too little. This smacks of Marxist socialism and communism, systems that have consistently failed to provide for the common welfare of the people. On the other hand, equality of opportunity, which is a bedrock of our Democratic Republic and its Constitution, provides the liberty, resources, and training

to enable each person to maximize their God-given talents and capabilities, resulting in strong families, strong economies, strong communities, and a strong nation.

3. The fatal flaw of the inclusion requirement of D.E.I. is that it fails to recognize the crucial requirement for inclusion, and that is loyalty - loyalty as a friend to another person, and loyalty as a member of a group or organization. Without this essential quality of loyalty, inclusion is not only meaningless but can actually be dangerous to the well-being of an individual or organization.

Finally, the Democrat radicals would do well to replace their slogan of Diversity, Equity, Inclusion, D.E.I., with the slogan Unity, Equality, Loyalty, U.E.L. Come to think of it, that slogan fits perfectly with the values and virtues of our Founders and what they envisioned for the Democratic Republic they gave us.

Introduction

Do you recognize the individuals pictured above? They were all former legislators - Senators and two Congressmen who were also Speakers of the House of Representatives. On page one, top to bottom, left to right, their names are Senator Henry "Scoop" Jackson, Senator Hubert Humphrey, Congressman and Speaker of the House Thomas "Tip" O'Neill Jr., Congressman and Speaker of the House Sam Rayburn. On page two, we have Senator Daniel Patrick Moynihan, Senator John Glenn, and Senator Joe Lieberman. They were all Democrats, effective leaders and highly regarded by their Republican counterparts. In fact, one of them, Senator Daniel Patrick Moynihan, although a Democrat, also served as advisor to Republican President Richard M. Nixon. How's that for an honorable and superb example of bipartisanship?

As you survey the Democratic Party today, who among its leadership stands out as a politician and statesman equal to any of those listed above? Only a couple quickly come to mind. Why is that? Because the Democratic Party today is no longer the Democratic Party that existed during the time of those statesmen listed. Certainly, the gentlemen listed fought hard for their party's principles and policies, giving meaning to the saying: "Politics is a blood sport," but only up to a point! Those gentlemen also understood that, in the democratic republic form of government that the Founding Fathers had wisely established, politics was also the art of compromise, and for laws, regulations, and legislation to pass through Congress, bipartisan agreement resulting from compromise would be necessary. The Founders placed heavy emphasis on bipartisan agreement, their rationale being that bipartisanship would best assure that legislation passed into law would be in the best interest of the citizenry as a whole, or as the saying goes: "for the common welfare." The Founders also established a system of checks and balances to assure bipartisanship and prevent any political party from achieving total dominance over any other.

The political attitude at the time of those statesmen I listed can be summed up in a story concerning Speaker of the House "Tip" O'Neil. When asked why he was so hard and even insulting towards President Ronald Reagan, he responded: "That's only politics. After six o'clock p.m., we are friends, buddies."

That attitude no longer exists today. Or if it does, it is extremely rare and well-hidden. The collegiality that existed between parties up until a decade or more ago is, for all practical purposes, gone. And as far as bipartisanship is concerned, there seems to be no light at the end of the tunnel. According to the Democrats, the definition of collegiality and bipartisanship is when the Republican Party gives in and agrees with the Democratic Party.

In this book. I explain how that came to be, and in that explaining, I address both the political and the spiritual corruption that infects the radicalized Democrat Party today. When it comes to political corruption, we're talking about corruption of the Constitution. However, when we're talking about spiritual corruption, we're talking about corruption of God's Word, and that is sin, and sin is theological in nature. Therefore, due to its seriousness, when making such a charge, one better have the theological facts in order to support and justify the charge, and that requires specific theological discussion, explanation, and application in some detail to avoid misunderstanding. Furthermore, since our Founding Fathers emphasized repeatedly that they established this nation on a Judeo-Christian foundation, the theology herein discussed and applied in order to identify the corruption within the Democratic Party, is Judeo-Christian theology. And so, on that basis, and due to the supremely critical importance of the subject, I justify the many Scripture passages and extensive theological reasoning contained in this book and make no apology for it.

There are some in the Democratic Party leadership, as well as party members that say a person cannot be a genuine Democrat unless they approve of and support abortion, even abortion right up to the moment of birth. To them I say that there are many in Christian leadership, brilliant theologians, as well as many members of the Christian Church, who say that a person can't be considered a genuine Christian if they approve of and support abortion. Thus, both sides of the controversy claim that one cannot be a genuine representative of an organization when they deny a central doctrine, belief, and policy of that organization. Jesus essentially said the same thing In John 8:31 when He told the people:

> "If you hold to my teaching, you are really my disciples. Then you will know the truth, and the truth will set you free."

Again, the question, how can one claim to be a true disciple of Christ and at the same time approve of and support abortion which refutes and denies his teaching on the Sanctity of Life as our Creator and Lord. The central message of this book is you can't. If one pro-abortionist reads this book, seeks the truth, and turns away in disgust from the ungodly stain of abortion which is despoiling our country, the study, research, time, and work in writing it will have been well worth it.

Darrell J. Ahrens

CHAPTER 1
THE DEMOCRAT PARTY TODAY

The Democratic Party today is far, far different from the Democratic Party of yesteryear. Today, it is a political party consumed by an overpowering hatred and an unhealthy lust for total political power that is a sickness corrupting the whole body. What is the reason for this terrible hatred? One word - TRUMP!

When Donald Trump decided to run for President in the 2016 election, his candidacy was initially treated as a joke by both Democratic and Republican candidates. How audacious for this businessman with no political organization, no political experience, never having held public office, never even having run for high office, to think he could be elected President of the United States.

What his opponents, not just the Democrats, but even many Republicans failed to realize was that Trump's candidacy struck a chord with a vast number of the American people who were sick and tired of politics as usual, sick and tired of politicians failing to keep their promises, sick and tired of the United States being taken advantage of by other nations, sick and tired of an anemic economy, a weakened military establishment, and international treaties and agreements which had been entered into by previous Democratic administrations for partisan political purposes, but were in direct opposition to the best interests of the American people.

And then, candidate Trump demonstrated the height of audaciousness. He won the election and became the 45th President of the United States, which shocked not only the Democratic Party and the country, but the world. How dare he do that! Does this non-politician, this businessman, actually think he is qualified to enter the arena of national and international politics? And the seed of hatred was planted right from the beginning, and was nurtured by the Democrats throughout Trump's first administration and continues on today as Trump's second administration takes off like a rocket with its first week containing more than 200 executive orders, and President Trump announcing policies designed to correct the disastrous policies of President Biden and four years of Democrat rule which brought great hardship to the American people and seriously reduced American's standing among the international community.

This immediate and strong action of President Trump within a few days of his second inauguration affecting virtually every area of governance from border patrol, immigration policies, economic policy, military policy, energy policy, national security policy, foreign policy, to cultural and societal issues, has amazed the American public and brought strong approval and high praise from the majority of the citizenry, even a few Democrats, not to mention a gigantic sigh of relief that we again have a strong President.

As far as the all-consuming hatred that the radical wing of the Democrat Party has for President Trump is concerned, any Psychiatrist would confirm that such all-consuming hatred eventually impairs a person's capability for rational judgment, reasonable response, and wise discernment. I think the majority of Americans would agree that the past four years of President Biden's Democrat administration gave ample evidence of such impairment, combined with and exacerbated by a clear cognitive decline in President Biden's mental faculties. During the past nine years, the Democrats have lied to and deceived the American people on numerous occasions, corrupted government organizations that had previously been held in high respect by the American people, including the FBI, in their attempts to bring Trump down, used fraudulent documents to appoint a special prosecutor, conducted a two year investigation into charges of collusion with the Russians, which cost taxpayers millions of dollars, conducted other investigations into charges of wrongdoing, conducted two disgusting and purely partisan impeachment trials, and all to no effect. All the charges were baseless, with not one shred of hard evidence to be found to convict the President of any wrongdoing. Throughout this time, through their words and actions, the Democrats made it clear that they were willing to trash their integrity, their ethics, their honesty, their honor, and any claim to respect if it would help them get rid of Trump. They presented to the country and to the world a picture of a political party that had grown corrupt, disgusting, and pitiful, a party clearly in political and spiritual crisis.

Even before President Trump's first inauguration in January 2017, the Democrat leadership made a decision that they would say anything, do anything, and make every effort to destroy the Trump presidency and rid politics of this usurper.

In Trump's historic and overwhelming recent victory, the public has stated in loud and clear terms their condemnation and disgust for corrupt partisan politics, the weaponization of government institutions and the courts against political foes, the political, moral, and spiritual corruption in high places, the weak foreign policy, and the alarming decline in patriotism and love of country. Whether the radical democrats have learned anything from this remains to be seen, but their initial response does not appear hopeful.

To rub salt in the wound of the Democrat's failure to find any evidence of Presidential wrongdoing, President Trump rose to new heights of audaciousness with the most successful administration in recent history. He kept promises he made as a candidate, and he kept on keeping those promises throughout his term of office, which was a major paradox in itself. He retracted policies and agreements, both national and international, that were contrary to the best interests of the United States. He took the tepid economy the Obama administration had left the American people and turned it into a roaring economy before he left office.

President Trump took trade agreements the Democrats had negotiated to America's disadvantage, and renegotiated them to our advantage. He established economic policies that encouraged manufacturing companies to return to the United States. He took our military, which had been allowed to decline sharply during the Obama administration, rebuilt and modernized it into the most powerful and capable military force in the world. He established energy policies that brought us to national energy independence before he left office, something we had not been for decades. He raised the economic standards of our minority populations to the highest in history. He was the most pro-life President in recent history, emphasizing both our sacred and our Constitutional duty to protect life, including the lives of our unborn babies in the womb, and encouraging and helping those who were considering abortion to deliver the child and then give the child up for adoption. The tremendous success of the Trump Administration threw the Democratic Party into a rage and drove their hatred of him to even greater depths. It was Democratic Party policy to never, never, give Trump credit for anything, no matter how good his policies were for the American people.

It is not my intention to list all President Trump's accomplishments during his first administration here. They are too numerous for that. But I thought it important that the reader understand the condition of the country when President Trump left office, since the following Democratic administration of President Biden immediately began the process of reversing Trump's successes and pursuing a radical socialist economic agenda, replacing the nation's Judeo-Christian foundation with a secular progressive foundation, replacing our amazing history, tradition, and Christian heritage with a false, revisionist history, tradition, and heritage, and replacing our Constitutional freedom of speech and freedom of religion with a restricted and curtailed freedom of speech and freedom of religion. The radical wing of the Democrat Party, in pursuit of its socialist agenda, would have us turn from our Founding Fathers' values and vision for the Democratic Republic they were establishing, a Democratic Republic which became, and is, the freest, most powerful, most affluent, most benevolent, most generous nation on earth and in history, and turn to Karl Marx and his socialism, which is basically communism, which only enslaves people, takes away their God-given freedoms, destroys their spirits, dehumanizes them, and makes them wards of the state. In other words, the radical faction of Democrats would have us exchange the riches of freedom and capitalism for the rags of socialism and captivity to the state. As Winston Churchill said: "The inherent vice of capitalism is the unequal sharing of the blessings. The inherent blessing of socialism is the equal sharing of misery."

The key is to further equalize the blessings of capitalism through smart economic policies which grow the economy, providing more resources to equalize and expand the middle class, which is precisely what Trump was doing in his first administration and is now continuing to do at the start of his second administration. Socialism can't do this because it is essentially only a redistribution of other peoples' money, and as Margaret Thatcher said: "You eventually run out of other peoples' money."

The Democratic Party socialists condemn capitalism; yet, in all probability, made their fortunes using the tools of capitalism. I have yet to hear of any of them offering to contribute their fortunes to the socialist cause. One can only wonder why, if they are so unhappy living in a capitalist society, they don't move to one of their socialist paradises - Russia, China, North Korea, Vietnam, Venezuela.

The Democratic Party has always had its radical wing which has occasionally been put on full display. In the years prior to the Civil War, the Democratic Party was the party of slavery. The Republican Party was established during that time as the abolition party with its primary purpose of ending slavery. The Dixiecrats, the southern wing of the Democratic Party fought vehemently against the civil rights legislation of the 1960s to end segregation. They were unsuccessful in preventing passage of the legislation.

More recently, an indication of its growing radicalism and corruption was at the Democratic National Convention in Los Angeles in 2012. The question of whether or not to mention God in their democratic platform document was being discussed. The Mayor of Los Angeles, who was heading the platform committee, decided to put it up for a vote by the convention delegates. It would be a yes or no voice vote decided by the loudest response. The loudest response was clearly "No!," - not to mention God in the party's platform document - heard by all there and all watching on TV. The mayor was obviously in a quandary. To pass a vote denying any mention of God in the party's official document stating its ideology, would be a public relations fiasco which the Republicans would certainly take advantage of. So, the Mayor declared the vote to be "yes," allowing the mention of God in the party platform, even though it was clear to all there and those watching on TV that the vote had been a resounding "No!" Just one of the many lies and deceptions that have come from the Democratic Party.

The radicalized Democratic leadership today has made it clear that it is not interested in compromise or conducting the business of governing in a bipartisan manner unless the opposing side agrees with them. The Democratic leadership today is interested in only one thing - total political power, and it has clearly shown in its actions taken against President Trump, which I listed, that it will use any means it has to, whether constitutional or not, whether legal or not, whether ethical or moral or civil or not, to achieve that power. They have no problem with passing legislation on a strict party line vote without a single Republican vote. Now a legislator with some semblance of honor, integrity, and wise discernment would pause and seriously consider whether a piece of legislation that did not get a single vote from the opposing party would really be in the best interests of the country as a whole, and whether it would really provide for the common good of the citizenry.

In its lust for power, this concern for the common good of the citizenry is apparently no longer of importance to the Democrats. But they have a problem with being able to pass legislation on simply a party line vote. And that problem is the filibuster which requires 60 votes to pass in the Senate. The filibuster is designed to prevent such strict party line votes and insure that legislation has support from both sides of the aisle. The filibuster is an effective check on one party domination in the Senate. During the recent Biden administration, Senate membership was split 50-50. Without the filibuster, the Democrats could still pass legislation on a one party vote with the Democratic Vice President casting the tie-breaking vote. But again, in order to do this, they must get rid of the filibuster. And that is precisely what the Democratic leadership tried to do.

They were prevented from voting to get rid of the filibuster by two of their own members, two Democratic Senators who still retained a measure of common sense, good judgment, respect for the common good, and the critical importance of bipartisanship when passing legislation.

If unable to get rid of the filibuster, the only way to achieve a party line vote majority is to increase Democratic Party membership in Congress, and specifically in the Senate. And yes, the Democrats have a plan for this too. And that plan is to confer statehood on Washington D.C. and Puerto Rico. Given the political make-up of these two territories, statehood would result in additional Democratic members in both houses of Congress.

Another roadblock faced by the democrats in their quest for political dominance is the United States Supreme Court. President Trump was able to appoint three Supreme Court Justices during his administration, giving the Court a conservative majority, something it hasn't had for quite some time. The Democrats have shown a willingness to try and sidestep the Constitution, or simply ignore it, in various proposed legislation and presidential directives and have had the Supreme Court rule against them on occasion. They know that, with the Court's current conservative majority, they will never be able to achieve their radical socialist agenda. But they have an answer to that too. And that is to pack the Supreme Court with liberals, which they are threatening to do.

The Constitution does not specify the number of justices on the Supreme Court, and this number has varied over the years. Nine has been the number for many years now, and the justices seem to agree that that number is as near to optimal as they are likely to get. But Congress can adjust that number. Back during the depression in the 1930s, Democrat President Franklin Delano Roosevelt tried to pack the Supreme Court with justices favorable to his New Deal policies. Congress refused and he was unable to do so.

It is interesting that, some years back, when the question of increasing the number of Supreme Court Justices came up, which it periodically does, and Roosevelt's attempt to pack the Court was mentioned, Senator Joe Biden made the comment: "It was a dumb idea then, and it's a dumb idea now." Apparently, after Biden became president, he no longer thought it was a dumb idea.

America is more divided today than at any time since the Civil War. In some respects, the division today is even more serious than that during the years leading up to the Civil War. For the first time in our history, we have a major segment of one of our two major political parties - namely the secular progressive, socialist, radical, liberal wing of the Democratic Party, denying our historical, traditional, Christian heritage and foundation, and using Marxist strategies to drive a wedge between political conservatives and liberals. The only difference is that, whereas Karl Marx used class division and warfare to foment revolution, our home-grown revolutionaries use race division and warfare. The results of this race division and warfare over the recent past have been riots, burning of our cities, and destruction of life and property. The fact that these continue to this day is testimony to the monumental failure of leadership in the cities involved, which virtually all are under Democratic leadership.

The crisis America faces today has been stewing for some time and can be laid at the doorstep of the citizenry. In a Democratic Republic, which the Founders gave us, the citizens choose their leaders, and therefore get the leaders they deserve. Our Founding Fathers gave warning to the people to elect leaders of Christian virtue, integrity, honor, honesty, and the ethics and morals of the Ten Commandments. John Jay, one of the Founders and the first Supreme Court Chief Justice appointed by President Washington and considered by many to be our best Supreme Court Justice, gave warning of this when he advised the people that when they select their political leaders, in order to preserve the Nation, they must select devoted Christians. He said

> "Providence has given to our people the choice of their rulers, and it is the duty as well as the privilege and interest of our

Christian nation to select and prefer Christians for their rulers." Noah Webster, soldier, statesman, legislator, educator, and judge, wrote: "When you become entitled to exercise the right of voting for public officers, let it be impressed on your mind that God commands you to choose for rulers just men who will rule in the fear of God. The preservation of a republican government depends on the faithful discharge of this duty. If the citizens neglect their duty and place unprincipled men in office, the government will soon be corrupted. Laws will be made not for the public good so much as for selfish or local purposes. Corrupt or incompetent men will be appointed to execute the laws, the public revenues will be squandered, and the rights of the citizens will be violated or disregarded. If a republican government fails to secure public prosperity and happiness, it must be because the citizens neglect the divine commands and elect bad men to make and administer the law."

This statement of Webster's applies precisely and with total accuracy to our situation today and to many in our previous Democratic administration. The election of November 2020, has been shown to have had many discrepancies with reputed claims of corruption by the Democrats, involving ballot harvesting, numerous Republican ballots uncounted and found stored away, election timelines ignored, state election rules and regulations deliberately violated, and election monitors deliberately prevented from being able to visually view the counting process. Fortunately, these discrepancies were resolved by the time of the 2024 election and resulted in a resounding victory for Trump.

For the first 160 years or so of our nation's history, the Christian worldview undergird our spiritual, governmental, educational, and cultural institutions. Although this is still the case to a large extent, it has been significantly replaced by a secular worldview taught by our educational institutions for decades now. This contrast between the Founders' Christian worldview and the current secular worldview of many of our progressive liberal politicians, educators, and cultural leaders could not be greater, and affects every aspect of peoples' lives.

This conflict of world views is the major theme of this book, and without an understanding of this conflict, it will not be possible to understand the reasoning behind the conclusions stated in the book.

In view of the fact that for decades now, American History has either not been a required course in our public schools, colleges, and universities, or if taught, has been glossed over, we have millions of citizens who are fundamentally illiterate in our nation's history, tradition, and heritage, and are therefore unaware of the above conflict of world views. Therefore, I consider it necessary to devote some time and space to a review of the characteristics of these world views, and how the Founders' Christian worldview has been, and is being, replaced to an alarming degree in the radicalized Democratic Party with the secular liberal socialist worldview, so that as we continue our analysis of the corruption of the Democratic Party, I and the reader are operating from the same frame of reference.

John Jay

Noah Webster

CHAPTER 2
THE OPPOSING WORLD VIEWS

Although the Founding Fathers strongly recommended the selection of Christian leaders in government, a testament to their wisdom is that they recognized the dangers inherent in both a theocratic form of government subservient to religious authorities, and a government purely secular in nature, devoid of any religious influence. They knew the situation in England, where if you were not a member of the Church of England, you were discriminated against. But they also emphasized the vital importance of the religious influence (specifically Christian influence) on government, education, culture, and society. President George Washington, in his farewell speech to the nation on September 19, 1796 said:

> "It is impossible to govern the world without God and the Bible. Of all the dispositions and habits that lead to political prosperity, our religion and morality are the indispensable supports. Let us with caution indulge the supposition that morality can be maintained without religion. Reason and experience both forbid us to expect that our national morality can prevail in exclusion of religious principle." John Adams, our second President and Chairman of the American Bible Society, said the following in an address to military leaders: "We have no government armed with the power capable of contending with human passions, unbridled by morality and true religion. Our Constitution was made only for a moral and religious people. It is wholly inadequate to the government of any other."

Of the fifty-five signers of the Declaration of Independence, fifty-two were devout orthodox Christians and the other three also believed in the God of Scripture, the Bible as the Divine Truth, and God's personal intervention in the affairs of men.

The term "separation of church and state" is widely misunderstood today and grossly misused by those seeking to displace our Christian foundation and heritage and capitalist economy with a progressive secular liberal foundation and socialist economy. The claim that the Founders proposed a strict separation of religion and government is totally wrong, evidenced by their numerous statements and writings. The book they most often quoted was the Bible. They made it crystal clear that the Democratic Republic they were establishing could only survive and prosper through the public morality which only religion could provide. And again, when the Founders spoke of religion in general terms, they were referring to Christianity. Thomas Jefferson said:

> "The Christian religion…is a religion of all others most friendly to liberty, science, and the freest expansion of the human mind."

In denying the nation's Christian foundation and heritage, secular progressive liberals demonstrate either an appalling ignorance of the nation's founding and the Founders, or an anti-American agenda that has no respect for the truth. I suspect it is a combination of the two.

The term "separation of church and state" is not found in our Declaration of Independence or Constitution, but in a letter Thomas Jefferson wrote to the Baptists in Danbury, Connecticut assuring them of their Constitutional freedom to practice their faith in the event Connecticut declared a different state religion, which apparently they were planning to do at the time. So, what is the meaning of "separation of church and state" according to the Founders? Simply this! The Church would have no political authority over the State, and the State would have no ecclesiastical authority over the Church. It is deeply unfortunate, if not a major internal danger, that so many citizens today, including authorities in government, in education, and even in the church, are ignorant of our Founders' intentions, especially in view of the fact that numerous Supreme Court decisions in the past have affirmed the Founders' intentions. But then, perhaps those government and educational authorities are knowledgeable of the Founders' intentions but are engaged in deliberate deception in order to revise our history and further a secular progressive socialist agenda.

I offer this final comment on the controversial issue of "separation of church and state." It bears emphasis and reemphasis that our Founding Fathers and their successors would adamantly oppose and condemn all efforts to remove God from the public square, from our public institutions, and from free public and government discourse. The citizenry must be reminded that our Founders clearly understood and plainly stated that true morality stems from a higher authority than man and man's government, that the morality of the Judeo-Christian tradition contained in the Bible is absolutely essential to the welfare of a democratic society, and that without this morality, moral and ethical chaos results, followed inevitably by cultural confusion and breakdown in the societal restraints necessary for democracy to function effectively.

It is sobering to realize that the above mentioned moral and ethical chaos, cultural confusion, and societal breakdown precisely describes the situation that exists today in many of our nation's cities. The radical wing of the Democratic Party justifies the riots, burnings, looting, and destruction of life and property on the basis of racial revolt against so-called white supremacy, a term they have yet to define with any clarity. Whereas Karl Marx used class distinctions to divide his people, the secular progressive radical democratic liberals use race to divide our people and further their socialist agenda. And in doing so, they reject and cast aside the heritage and accomplishments of the Rev. Dr. Martin Luther King, whose civil rights movement had the primary objective of racial harmony.

The internal corruption we are experiencing in politics, education, and culture should not surprise us. It has been increasing gradually over the past six decades or so as we have moved farther and farther from our Judeo-Christian heritage and moral compass. We would do well to remember and adhere to Thomas Jefferson's warning when he said:

> "God who gave us life also gave us liberty. And can the liberties of a nation be thought secure when we have removed their only firm basis, conviction in the minds of the people that those

liberties are the gift of God, and that they are not to be violated but with His wrath." "Indeed, I tremble for my country when I reflect that God is just, and that His justice cannot sleep forever."

I submit that we are living in a time when all Christian citizens and patriots should be trembling for their country.

Our Founding Fathers recognized and emphasized that education was critically important to the nation they were founding. Its republican form of government and democratic society depended on an informed and educated citizenry to prevent both tyranny and anarchy. Thomas Jefferson said:

"If we are to guard against ignorance and remain free, it is the responsibility of every American to be informed."

The Founders were virtually unanimous in their insistence that religious education, specifically the Judeo-Christian morals and teachings be part of the curriculum of the public schools since such teachings were essential to the development of moral character and integrity of the individual. Joined to this religious curriculum, a proper curriculum in civics, government, philosophy, and science was essential to provide a thorough, well-rounded education. Horace Mann, one of the great advocates of public education in the mid-19th century, said:

"Our system earnestly inculcates all Christian morals. It founds its morals on the basis of religion; it welcomes the religion of the Bible."

Horace Mann would be appalled, incensed, at the state of our public school system in America today, which has banished the Bible from the classroom, forbidden prayer, and discouraged all forms of Christian expression.

Horace Mann would also be appalled and incensed at the mediocre, dismal education a vast number of our public schools are giving students in the other disciplines mentioned - civics, government, philosophy, and science, not to mention reading, writing, and math. I can speak of this on the basis of personal knowledge. After my military career, I taught high school for eleven years. I was rudely shocked at the educational level of many of my students. They were fundamentally illiterate in disciplines I had been forced to master when in the fourth grade in Christian elementary school. I remember thinking to myself: "What the (expletive) happened to our public school system? What has happened, I believe, is that the public education system has too long been under the control of the liberal Democrats and the teachers' unions, and both of these have shown time after time that the students' welfare and learning are not their top priority. As an aside, Horace Mann, the great advocate of public education, would be kicked off any public school board today because of his priorities. Today, we are witnessing a major demand from parents for school choice, who are making every effort to remove their children from public schools and enroll them in charter schools or religious schools.

Martin Luther, leader of the Protestant Reformation and instrumental in laying the basis for Western Civilization, wrote this, which parents today would be wise to consider:

> "I am much afraid that schools will prove to be the great gates of hell unless they diligently labor in explaining the Holy Scriptures, engraving them in the hearts of youth. I advise no one to place his child where the Scriptures do not reign paramount. Every institution in which men are not increasingly occupied with the Word of God must become corrupt...The Bible was written for men with a head upon their shoulders."

Immanuel Kant, renowned German philosopher whose work "Critique of Pure Reason" is considered as comparable to the works of Plato or Aristotle, said:

> "The existence of the Bible, as a book for the people, is the greatest benefit which the human race has ever experienced. Every attempt to belittle it is a crime against humanity."

Daniel Webster, famous American politician and diplomat, and considered one of the greatest orators in American history, said:

> "If we abide by the principles taught in the Bible, our country will go on prospering and to prosper. But if we and our posterity neglect its instructions and authority, no man can tell how sudden catastrophe may overwhelm us and bury all our glory in profound obscurity."

Daniel Webster would grieve to discover how far we have retreated from our Judeo-Christian heritage and Biblical standards.

Professor Gelernter, professor of computer science at Yale University, and a national fellow at the American Enterprise Institute, wrote the following in an article dated June 4, 2007:

> "For the schools to take it on themselves to contradict and correct the religious and moral instruction parents give to their children represents the height of arrogance, and exactly what they have come to expect from today's public schools… Today's radical left liberal faith despises the Bible, Judaism, and Christianity, family life, and the patriarchy. It believes in multinational government and hates patriotism on principle, just as it does Christianity, and its fundamental principle is that men and women are not just equal but interchangeable."

Progressive left liberalism has also been referred to as "soft-boiled paganism."

The Founders' unanimous insistence on the importance of religious education went hand-in-hand with the founding of schools in America. It is notable that 106 of the first 108 schools in America were founded on the Christian faith. Our main universities and colleges were denominational. Princeton University's official motto was "Under God's Power She Flourishes." Yale University's stated purpose was "To Plant, and under the Divine Blessing to propagate in this wilderness, the blessed Reformed Protestant Religion in the purity of its Order and Worship." The motto of Harvard University was "For Christ and the Church."

In the original Harvard University's student handbook, rule number 1 was that students seeking entrance must know Latin and Greek so that they could study the Scriptures, with the explanation:

> "Let every student be plainly instructed and earnestly pressed to consider well the main end of his life and studies is to know God and Jesus Christ, which is eternal life, John 17:3, and therefore to lay Jesus Christ as the only foundation of all sound knowledge and learning. And seeing the Lord only giveth wisdom, let everyone seriously set himself by prayer in secret to seek it of Him. (Proverbs 2: 3)."

For over 100 years, more than 50% of all Harvard graduates were pastors. How far these Ivy League institutions have wandered from their original mottos and charters!

It is clear from history that the Bible and the Christian faith were foundational to our educational and judicial systems. So how did we go from there to the present time where our educational institutions are 90% or more progressive liberal and the courts more and more secularist? Radical liberal educators and judges, that's how. Consider the following.

In 1947, there was a radical and disastrous change of direction for the Supreme Court. The Court ruled in a limited way to affirm a wall of separation between Church and State in the public classroom, despite the fact that, as mentioned, no such wall of separation is mentioned in the Constitution. This ruling, in effect, required the setting aside and ignoring every precedent of Supreme Court ruling for the previous 160 years, and what followed afterward were rulings in direct contradiction to our history, tradition, and heritage, and numerous previous rulings by some of our most honored and respected Supreme Court justices.

In 1962, prayer was removed from our public schools. Here is the prayer that was banished, and apparently thought to be a threat to students and unconstitutional. What do you think?

> "Almighty God, we acknowledge our dependence on Thee. We beg Thy blessings upon us and our parents and our teachers and our country. Amen."

In 1963, the Supreme Court ruled Bible reading unconstitutional in the public school system, despite the fact that the Bible was quoted 94% of the time by those who wrote the Constitution, who shaped our nation and its systems of education, government, and justice, and who adamantly insisted that the morals and ethical standards taught in the Bible were absolutely essential to a good education.

In 1965, the Court denied as unconstitutional the right of a student in the public school cafeteria to bow his head and pray audibly over his food. Imagine that! A student praying over his meal constituted a threat to his fellow students, according to the Court.

In 1980, the Supreme Court, in the case of Stone vs. Graham, outlawed the Ten Commandments in our public schools as unconstitutional. The Supreme Court said this:

> "If the posted copies of the Ten Commandments were to have any effect at all, it would be to induce school children to read them. And if they read them, meditated upon them, and perhaps venerated and obeyed them, this is not a permissible objective."

And here the Court demonstrated a level of utter stupidity that stuns the imagination. The Court essentially ruled that it was not a permissible objective to allow our children to follow the moral principles of the Ten Commandments; e.g. "do not murder," "do not steal," "do not commit adultery," "do not bear false witness against another," (that is, do not lie), "do not covet what belongs to someone else," (that is, plot to take what belongs to someone else illegally or immorally).

Our Founding Fathers would be in a rage over this removing the Ten Commandments from our public schools and other public institutions and would condemn it in the strongest possible terms. We can imagine what James Madison, the primary author of our Constitution, would say, because he stated the crucial importance he attached to the Ten Commandments. In discussing the limited powers of government in a Democratic Republic, James Madison said:

> "We have staked the whole future of our new nation, not upon the power of government; far from it. We have staked the future

of all our political institutions upon the capacity of mankind for self-government, upon the capacity of each and all of us to govern ourselves, to control ourselves, to sustain ourselves, according to the Ten Commandments of God."

Why did James Madison and the other Founders consider the moral principles of the Ten Commandments foundational to the nation they were building? Because they understood that the Ten Commandments are theology, and as theology, they are the very foundation of all true ethics because they express the highest standards for relationships commanded by God Himself, our relationship to Him and our relationship to our fellowmen. The Ten Commandments are not only foundational to America's Republican form of government and Democratic society, but foundational to Western Civilization as a whole.

Radical liberal democrats are still today trying to eradicate the Ten Commandments from the public square and public institutions where they are still displayed, including the Supreme Court. I consider, as evidence of God's sense of humor and His having the last word, the fact that the Supreme Court, which removed display of the Ten Commandments from our public schools and public institutions, has its nine justices sitting and deliberating beneath a copy of the Ten Commandments chiseled into the marble wall of their chamber.

There are no true ethics apart from theology. Ethics are also empowered by theology. Any set of ethics developed apart from theology is simply a code of behavior developed by man or a group of men. I'm a man, and who is to say their code of ethics is better than mine. I'll live my life according to my own code of ethics. You can see that if everyone felt this way, chaos and confusion would result and society would disintegrate. Citizens must be motivated to obey a code of ethics and behavior that undergirds a society. This motivation can be provided either by a tyrannical form of government, a dictatorship, based on fear and terror, or provided by a democratic, republican form of government with a code of ethics empowered by theology which acknowledges a higher authority than man, and a Truth that is absolute in its nature and essence. And that is precisely what our nation has with the Ten Commandments.

Therefore, to have removed those Ten Commandments from our public schools and public institutions was and is a crime against the American people.

Here we have another core reason for the divided nation we have today. Radical, progressive liberals, which comprise a major segment of the Democratic Party today, reject the concept of absolute truth and claim that moral relativism is the standard. According to their ideology, both truth and morality are relative to existing conditions and circumstances. This moral relativism is a major factor in the decision making process of liberals vs. conservatives. Whereas conservatives govern with compassion, they also place an emphasis on facts and evidence when making legislative decisions. Liberals place an emphasis on feelings and emotions and their ideology of relativism. This has led in the past to legislation and laws being passed that may have sounded good, felt good, and thought best for the American people, but which ignored or mutilated the truth, facts, and evidence and their passage brought utter disaster to the nation, our people, and our culture. Two prime examples of this were the removal of the Ten Commandments from our public schools and institutions, and the passage of Roe vs. Wade which legalized abortion. More on that later.

This moral relativism which undergirds progressive liberal ideology also gives liberals, in their opinion, the option to decide what is sin and what is not sin. We see the Democratic Party today doing that in matters concerning life, marriage, and family. More on that in the next section of this book. This is pure heresy, arrogance, and blasphemy. God does not give man the option or the right to determine what is sin and what is not sin, which He clearly identifies in His Word, the Bible. When man no longer considers as sin that which God clearly identifies as sin in His Word, then man is standing in direct opposition to God - not a good place to be, but where many Democrats, some Republicans, and many citizens are standing today. In effect, that person is saying to God: "I am sovereign over these aspects of my life, not You!" It is the height of stupidity to give the finger to God, and that is precisely what these people are doing.

The radical progressive liberal also fails to understand that when truth and morals are relative, the distinction between right and wrong and the distinction between good and evil become blurred, and over time, if not corrected, eventually become reversed. Good becomes evil, evil becomes good, right becomes wrong, and wrong becomes right, and the ability to wisely discern between the two grows weaker and weaker until it is finally lost. Or perhaps the radical progressive liberals do understand this and are counting on that loss of discernment between good and evil, between right and wrong, in order to pass their radical anti-American agenda.

The great danger is that over time, people can become so inundated with coarseness and immorality that they are desensitized to it and become oblivious to it. Also, continued exposure to, and tolerance of, cultural immorality can lead to a loss of will or desire to change the situation or to raise the moral bar, so to speak. A person, or a nation, can become so caught up in sin and immorality that they don't want to change. This is precisely what happened to Old Testament Israel, which I described and analyzed in my previous book entitled *Divine Love / Divine Intolerance*. Israel, as a nation, had become so corrupt that, although they continued to go through the motions of worshipping God and obeying His commands, their hearts were far from Him, and their morals, ethics, and behavior had sunk to the utter depths of depravity, including child sacrifice to pagan gods. God loved His people and didn't want to destroy them, but He knew He would have to bring judgment upon them, or they would never turn back to Him. This He did, and the judgment was terrible, but it did serve to awaken His people to what they had done and turn them back to God in confession of their terrible sins and repentance of them. God forgave them and restored them to His grace. I showed how America is following Israel's path to depravity and judgment in six areas of our national life, and unless we wake up and turn back to our Christian heritage and the God Who led our Founders to establish our Democratic Republic, we will suffer the same judgment. Again, I quote Thomas Jefferson: "When I consider that God is just, and that His justice cannot sleep forever, I tremble for my country."

Consider just one example of becoming desensitized to coarseness and immorality - the entertainment industry. If what we see and hear in movies today and other venues of so-called entertainment occurred seventy or more years ago, the general population would have been up in arms in vehement protest. Today it is just accepted as normal. Corruption of a culture, an organization, a person, does not happen all at once. It grows over time until it corrupts the whole. It is like the example of yeast that Jesus used in His teaching. You insert a little yeast in a mass of dough, and before long the yeast has permeated and leavened the whole loaf. So, it is with sin. You accommodate a little sin, and before long that sin has grown and grown until it infects the whole body. I believe it was Francis Schaeffer who said: "Accommodation leads to accommodation, leads to accommodation."

We cannot leave a discussion of our Founding Fathers' values, vision, and theology which were so crucial in the establishment of our nation and its Democratic Republican form of government without a word concerning the Judiciary. Thomas Jefferson had his qualms and concerns about this third branch of government. He feared what he called "the tyranny of the Judiciary," that is, their tendency to make law rather than strictly keeping to their Constitutional mandate to interpret the law. Does that sound familiar? That tendency exists today, perhaps even more so than in the past, especially when the Court has a liberal majority. And it is precisely what the progressive wing of the Democrat Party wants to achieve today. They know that they cannot achieve their radical agenda through legislative means because of the filibuster and lack of support of the majority of the American people. They have announced their plan to pack the Supreme Court with radical liberal justices so that they can force their radical socialist agenda on the American people.

Among other comments on this, Thomas Jefferson wrote the following concerning his wariness of the judiciary:

> "The Constitution is a mere thing of wax in the hands of the Judiciary, which they may twist and shape into any form they please." Jefferson's advice to justices on interpreting whether or not a law was constitutional was: "On every question of

construction, carry yourselves back to the time when the Constitution was adopted, recollect the spirit manifested in the debates, and instead of trying what meaning may be squeezed out of the text, or invented against it, conform to the probable one in which it was passed."

Unfortunately, too many Supreme Court Justices in the past have not complied with Jefferson's advice, and in not doing so, have brought indescribable harm to the nation. One of the most egregious examples of this is the exceptionally cruel and brutal murder of more than 62 million babies in the womb and out of the womb since 1973 when Roe vs. Wade legalized abortion on the basis of a constitutional right that is not mentioned in the Constitution but was invented by the liberal justices. Secular progressive judges do not really care what the Founders would or would not agree with. Their secular progressive liberal Democrat agenda overrules both the Founding Fathers' wisdom and the greatest Constitution ever promulgated in the history of man.

I have gone into great detail in this introductory section of the book describing the characteristics of the Democratic Party as it exists today, and the corruption that has changed the character of the party so much that it would be unrecognizable to the Democratic statesmen I mentioned at the beginning of the book. Which of the two opposing world views will win out - that of our Founding Fathers who built our Democratic Republic on the foundation of Judeo-Christianity and its divine code of morality and ethics, or the secular progressive liberal radicals who want a secular foundation, a socialist country and government, and a moral code of relativism? The answer to that question will determine the destiny of our country. Before I close this chapter, I would like to briefly review those dominant policy goals which define. The Party's character because in order to understand what has happened to the spiritual nature of the Party, it is necessary to keep in mind what has happened to the political character of the party.

I have emphasized as a dominant character trait the consuming and ongoing hatred for former and now current, President Donald Trump, a hatred that has become pathological in nature and effect. Along with this hatred is the policy goal of undoing all the positive accomplishments of his administration and basically erasing even the memory of those accomplishments from the peoples' minds. This all-consuming hatred has caused irrational, unreasonable, and even illegal responses and behaviors on the part of Democrat leadership and members, which I noted in the previous narrative. When a political party absolutely refuses to give any credit whatsoever, refuses to say anything good, refuses to give even a hint of praise to a political opponent who had the most effective administration in recent times, and did more good for the American people in four years than the previous Democratic administration did in eight years, and now at the beginning of his second administration, is dedicated to an even greater America and greater good, prosperity, and security for the American people and our allies around the world, then you know that the Democratic Party has corrupted its very nature with lies, deception, and hypocrisy to an utterly disgusting level.

Another dominant character trait of today's Democratic Party is their lust for total political power and political dominance which they have openly admitted. They have little, if any, interest in true bipartisanship which our Founders insisted was necessary for effective political leadership in a Democratic Republic. Now every political party is going to strive to increase their power but there are right ways and wrong ways to do this, honorable and dishonorable ways, ways that do not divide the people, and ways that do divide the people. Unfortunately, the Democrat Party has chosen the wrong way, the dishonorable way, the way that divides the people, to achieve that power. The Democrats have threatened to get rid of the filibuster, add States to the Union which would add democratic legislators to Congress, pack the Supreme Court with liberal justices, and pass legislation to transfer control of elections, including federal elections, from the States to the federal government - that is, Congress, who can then make changes to election regulations and procedures that would insure Democratic dominance for the foreseeable future.

The secular progressive wing of the Democratic Party has given every indication that it wishes to replace our Judeo-Christian foundation and capitalist economy with a secular progressive liberal foundation and a Marxist Socialist economy, and also replace our Judeo-Christian code of ethics, morals, and standards embodied in our Declaration of Independence, Constitution, and other founding documents, with a progressive secular moral and ethical code of relativism.

The Democratic Party has made it clear that it wants to place restrictions on the freedom of speech, freedom of religion, and the 2nd Amendment right to bear arms that the Constitution guarantees.

If the Democratic Party is able to achieve the political dominance it seeks, thereby able to dispense with bipartisanship and compromise, and also able to establish a substantial liberal majority on the Supreme Court, the people can expect legislative and legal decisions that will have disastrous consequences upon the America we have known - spiritually, politically, economically, educationally, and culturally, and what minuscule political unity remains will probably be destroyed for the foreseeable future.

Before we turn from the political corruption infecting the Democratic Party's character to the Spiritual corruption infecting the very nature and soul of the Democratic Party, I want to include a chapter on ten clear and present dangers to America in the religious, political, economic, and cultural realms, and the critical warning signs pointing to these dangers. Also, a chapter on America's condition today, discussing the extent of our turning away from our Christian foundation and heritage, and the way back. Again, I feel that an understanding of the issues discussed in these chapters will benefit the reader's perspective on subsequent chapters dealing with the spiritual corruption in the Democratic Party, since the issues of decline discussed in these chapters can primarily be laid at the doorstep of the Democratic Party.

George Washington

John Adams

Thomas Jefferson

James Madison

Martin Luther

Martin Luther King Jr.

Horace Mann

Immanuel Kant

Daniel Webster

CHAPTER 3
WARNING SIGNS OF DECLINE

My outline for this chapter is from Dr. Jim Nelson Black's book *When Nations Die*, in which he identifies ten critical warning signs of a nation and culture in crisis and decline . Dr. Black wrote this book in 1994 and I referred to it in my first book *Divine Love / Divine Intolerance* in 2009. These warning signs of Dr. Black were serious back then; today they are at crisis stage. They are applicable not only to the United States, but to all Western nations which comprise Western Civilization.

Dr. Black's warning signs are prophetic in nature, and like the Old Testament Israelites who ignored the warnings of the prophets God sent to them until disaster overcame them, I fear that the majority of leaders of the western nations, including America, are ignoring the prophetic nature of these warning signs and the disaster they portend.

I have used only the titles of these warning signs as an outline for the chapter. The narrative comments on each one, as well as the comments on the Biblical passages, are mine, and I take full responsibility for them. The ten warning signs and the Scripture passages are as follows:

1. Decay of Religious Belief: Matthew 24: 9.
2. Devaluing of Human Life: Deuteronomy 12: 31,32.
3. Gross Immorality: 2Timothy 3: 1-5.
4. Increasing Lawlessness: 2Thessalonians 2: 7 10.
5. Gross Materialism: Luke 12: 16-21.
6. Decline of Educational Excellence: Judges 2: 10-13.
7. Weakening of Cultural Foundations: Matthew 7: 24-27; Psalm 11: 3.
8. Loss of Respect for Tradition: Daniel 9: 4-6.
9. Loss of Economic Discipline: Luke 15: 13-16.

   10. Oppressive Bureaucracy: 1Samuel 8: 10-18.

Let's consider each of these warning signs. First, the *Decay of Religious Belief.* Certainly, there has been a decay in religious belief in recent decades, especially since the 1960s. This is evidenced by a radical decline in church attendance. One poll, as I recall, had this decline range from a percentage in the 70s to a percentage in the 30s. This radical decrease in church attendance has led to a corresponding increase in Biblical illiteracy. I mentioned before that the Bible was the most often quoted source of our Founding Fathers, that they emphasized their building this nation on the foundation of Judeo-Christianity, that the Bible's Ten Commandments were the greatest code of morals and ethics ever produced, that the survival and prosperity of the democratic-republic they were giving us was absolutely dependent on the leaders and the citizens adhering to the central teachings of that moral code, that is, the Ten Commandments. The Founders were very knowledgeable of the Bible's theology and believed that, without the Bible, it was impossible to govern, especially in a Democratic Republic because of the freedoms it provided to the people.

The Bible is the foundational source for the Truth that all men, male and female, are created equal, and the proof of this equality is the fact that all men, regardless of race, nationality, ethnicity, or culture, are created in the image of God. This makes every human being precious in the sight of God. God does not create second-class humans or second-class citizens. The Founders believed that, if this nation ever fell, it would not be due to outside forces but to forces within that turned away from our Christian foundation, tradition, and heritage. I firmly believe that Biblical illiteracy, if not corrected, will be at the root of that fall.

This lack of Biblical literacy has led to confusion and chaos on the part of religious, government, educational, and judicial authorities as well as the people overall. It has led to foolish and disastrous decisions by the ruling authorities mentioned and continues to do so today. In the Scripture passage referenced, Matthew 24:9 Jesus spoke of the persecution that would come upon Christians during the latter days before He returns:

"Then you will be handed over to be persecuted and put to death, and you will be hated by all nations because of Me."

Christians have always been persecuted for their faith, but the persecution today is greater than any time in the past. And what is different from the persecution in the past is the fact that, for the first time, Christians are being persecuted in the United States, and this persecution shows every sign of increasing, which gives great emphasis to Jesus' warning. To withstand and overcome that persecution will require a strong foundation of Biblical literacy and faith on the part of individuals and the Church. I will speak more of this in a later chapter.

Satan is a brilliant strategist and tactician. He knows that in order to accomplish his objective of bringing total corruption to people and nations he must first corrupt the Church. Corrupt the Church and corruption of society and its institutions of government, education, and culture will inevitably follow. Or, at the very least, make the Church irrelevant to people and the doorway is open for turning society away from God and toward the moral relativism that will enable corruption to work its way through society and culture just as, in Jesus' parable of a little yeast working its way through the whole loaf of dough, until God's standards of truth and righteousness are no longer considered binding on people or nations. Just a reminder that moral relativism which holds that there is no absolute truth and which sanctions exceptions to the moral and ethical code of the Bible, which is central to our nation's founding, is an important ideological principle of the secular progressive liberal wing of the Democratic Party.

I consider this first warning sign *Decay of Religious Belief* and its effects over the years of removing Christian materials and expression from our public schools and other public institutions and the accompanying Biblical illiteracy to be the major factor contributing to all the other warning signs, and if it continues, it will eventually result in the nation's fall from within which our Founders feared. We, as a nation, would do well to heed the words of Benjamin Franklin in a letter dated April 17, 1787. He wrote:

"Only a virtuous people are capable of freedom. As nations become corrupt and vicious, they have more need of masters."

I believe Franklin's words have more meaning for America today than when he wrote them. Consider how the decline in virtue and righteousness over the past decades, which has given birth to the increase in cultural decay, crime, and licentiousness, has in turn resulted in the people turning more and more to government leaders and institutions for solutions to the nation's problems. Yet, many of those problems have their very roots in the spiritual and moral erosion which has infected government and our institutions, as well as the church. Until this spiritual and moral erosion infecting both our institutions and society is addressed and reversed, it is hopelessly naive and irrational to expect government or other secular institutions to provide effective solutions to problems of a spiritual and moral nature. Scripture tells us that "righteousness exalts a nation," and also reminds us that there is no righteousness apart from God. And I believe it was President Ronald Reagan who said: "Government can't solve the problem; government is the problem."

The second critical warning sign is the *Devaluing of Human Life,* which I submit is a direct result of the Decay of Religious Belief. If man is not considered as having been created in the image of God, then man is nothing but another animal. And if man is simply man and nothing else, without accountability to a transcendent authority, why should I, a man, feel bound to obey any code of ethics and morality devised by other men? Who is to say that the morality and ethics devised by others are better than the morality and ethics I devise for my own? So, unless I am forced to obey the moral and ethical code established by a tyrannical and dictatorial government, I shall go my own way.

It doesn't take much imagination to realize the confusion, chaos, appalling increase in crime and degradation of society and culture when man becomes a law unto himself. And of course, the devaluing of human life both causes and perpetuates this degradation of society and culture. We see this clearly in the pure evil of abortion, which is the ultimate devaluing of human life and corruption of the sanctity of life, which I discuss specifically in later chapters. In the Bible passage referred to, Deuteronomy 12:31-32 God warns the Israelites not to depart from the true religion and worship He gave them, and not to take up the ways and practices of the heathen nations around them:

> "You must not worship the Lord your God in their way, because in worshipping their gods, they do all kinds of detestable things the Lord hates. They even burn their sons and daughters in the fire as sacrifices to their gods. See that you do all that I command you; do not add to it or take away from it."

Not much has changed except today's heathen god to whom people sacrifice their baby sons and daughters through abortion is the god of convenience.

The third critical warning sign is *Gross Immorality*. This too, I submit, is a direct result of the Decay of Religious Belief. We have mentioned this before, and need not go into greater detail here, except to say that it is extremely naive and utterly foolish to expect man to be moral, ethical, just, selfless, law-abiding, and righteous on his own, without the moral and ethical code and teachings of the Bible to guide him.

One of the fatal flaws of secular progressive liberal theology is its belief that man is basically good and will eventually always choose the good. No! No! If history teaches us anything, it is that man is not basically good. Man is sinful, has a sinful nature inherited from Adam, and has proven throughout history that he is capable of evil, great evil. However, man is also capable of good, great good, but only through the leading of the Holy Spirit and the wisdom given him in Holy Scripture, the Bible. The gross immorality we experience today in this world is but a prelude to the even greater gross immorality spoken of in our Bible passage from 2Timothy 3:1-5 which will come in the latter days before Christ' return. We are told:

> "But mark this: There will be terrible times in the last days. People will be lovers of themselves, lovers of money, boastful, proud, abusive, disobedient to their parents, ungrateful, unholy, without love, unforgiving, slanderous, without self-control,

brutal, not lovers of the good, treacherous, rash, conceited, lovers of pleasure rather than lovers of God — having a form of godliness but denying its power. Have nothing to do with them."

It is eye-opening to realize that the gross immorality described in these passages bears a striking resemblance to today.

The fourth critical warning sign is *Increasing Lawlessness*. I am writing this in the midst of a rapidly increasing wave of lawlessness that has been going on for the past few years or more. It has become common for the news to have accounts of rioting, violent protests, burning, looting, destruction of life and property. The vast majority of this lawlessness and destruction is taking place in cities and states where Democrats rule as Governors, Mayors, Chiefs of Police, etc., and they are either incapable or unwilling, or both, to deal with it in an effective manner. And we have a Democratic President and administration who are also either incapable or unwilling to deal with it as long as the protests and rioting suit their political purposes and objectives , and to hell with the destruction of life and property. The police are either forbidden by authorities to deal with it in an aggressive, effective, manner or fear to do so because of the lack of support of their democratic superiors and the very real possibility of being sued or indicted by liberal democratic courts.

At this critical point, how this is all going to turn out only God knows. The country desperately needs solid leadership, faithful to God, the Constitution, and the conservative principles of the majority of the American people. The Scripture reading from 2Thessalonians 2:7-10 speaks of the increasing lawlessness that accompanies the approach of the end times to be the work of Satan, and all who participate in this lawlessness will be condemned:

"For the secret power of lawlessness is already at work; but the one who now holds it back (the Holy Spirit) will continue to do so till he is taken out of the way. And then the lawless one will be revealed, whom the Lord Jesus will overthrow with the breath of his mouth and destroy by the splendor of his coming. The coming of the lawless one will be in accordance with the work of Satan displayed in all kinds of counterfeit miracles, signs and wonders, and in every sort of evil that deceives those who are perishing. They perish because they refused to love the truth and so be saved."

The fifth critical warning sign is *Gross Materialism.* This is clearly evident throughout society today. Ask any young person today, "What is your goal in life?" Their likely response would not be "to fulfill God's purpose for my life," or "to leave a lasting legacy for my family and fellowmen," but rather "to achieve my highest financial potential," or, in other words, " to get rich." Gross materialism has undoubtedly increased with young American adults as a result of secular progressive liberal Democratic politicians and others touting socialism and its supposed free benefits which promise a utopia that never seems to materialize. These radical Democratic socialists are apparently ignorant of the fact that socialism as an economic system has been a dismal failure everywhere it has been tried and has brought immeasurable misery to millions upon millions of people. The Bible passage referenced, Luke 12:16-21, is Jesus' parable warning about making material wealth and riches the priority in one's life. He tells of a rich fool whose main goal was to store up great wealth so he could eat, drink, and be merry for the rest of his life. His soul was required of him and he died before he could enjoy that wealth, and someone else received it:

> "And He told them this parable: The ground of a certain rich man produced a good crop. He thought to himself, 'What shall I do? I have no place to store my crops. "Then he said, 'This is what I'll do. I will tear down my barns and build bigger ones, and there I will store all my grain and my goods. And I'll say to myself, "You have plenty of good things laid up for many years. Take life easy; eat, drink, and be merry.'" "But God said to him, 'You fool! This very night your life will be demanded from you. Then who will get what you have prepared for yourself?' This is how it will be with anyone who stores up things for himself but is not rich toward God."

The lesson is: "Where your treasure is, there your heart will be," and a man's life does not consist of the abundance of his possessions.

The sixth critical warning sign is the *Decline of Educational Excellence.* Previously, I wrote of education in the early years of our nation, and how 106 of the 108 early universities and colleges, including Harvard, Princeton, and Yale, were established to the glory of God and our Savior Jesus Christ, how the early leaders of these institutions were nearly all pastors and theologians, how virtually all our Founding Fathers considered a good and valid education to consist of first, a solid religious grounding in the teachings of Christ and the moral, ethical standards contained in the Bible; second, a thorough liberal arts curriculum of history, civics, economics, social studies, etc., which alongside the religious curriculum, they considered essential to shaping the person into a wise, productive citizen; and third, a solid grounding in science and technology.

Our Founders unanimously held that, without the religious curriculum in our schools, graduates could not be considered as educated. Benjamin Rush, signer of the Declaration of Independence and Father of Public Schools, said: "The only foundation for a useful education in a republic is to be laid in Religion. Without this, there can be no virtue, and without virtue, there can be no liberty, and liberty is the object and life of all republican governments...did they (schoolmasters) often enforce the discourses of our Savior as the best rule of life, and the surest guide to happiness, how great would be the influence of our schools upon the order and prosperity of our country."

As recently as 60 or 70 years ago, the educational system of America was considered one of the best in the world. The goal of students around the world was to come to American schools. However, for some years now, an education in America no longer has the elite status it once had. The state of our public schools today is appalling and a major scandal. Parents are demanding school choice and the waiting lists of charter schools and private schools are huge. I've already mentioned the shock I experienced when I became a public high school teacher after my military career over the deterioration in the quality of education. This deterioration in the quality of education has occurred despite the astronomical amount of taxpayer's money appropriated by Congress for education in the past fifty to sixty years, an amount in the trillions. Yet, it seems that despite the huge amount of funding that continues to be devoted to education, the deterioration in the education of our children and young adults continues. Never in the history of education has so much been expended for so little a return.

I mentioned previously the disastrous effects on the public schools of court decisions when they sought to remove from the public schools any direct Christian teaching or expression, and banned the Bible and the Ten Commandments from the classroom. I could go on and on recounting the devastation that secular progressive democratic authorities in government, education, and the teacher's unions have wrought on education in America. It continues today with the controversy over Critical Race Theory, a curriculum of indoctrination rather than education which the secular progressive liberal democrats heartily support, a racist curriculum that teaches students to hate their country and each other based on race. Our Founders, other great American leaders in education, and the Revd. Dr. Martin Luther King, leader of the Civil Rights Movement, would condemn this curriculum in the strongest possible terms.

I'll close this section with a statement from Dr. William Lyon Phelps, former author, critic, and scholar of Yale University. I quote:

> "I thoroughly believe in a university education for both men and women, but I believe a knowledge of the Bible without a college course is more valuable than a college course without the Bible. Everyone who has a thorough knowledge of the Bible may truly be called educated, and no other learning or culture, no matter how extensive or elegant, can form a proper substitute."

It is an indictment against the educational hierarchy that Dr. Phelps would be fired and severely criticized for making such a statement today.

The Bible passage listed from the Book of Judges 2:10-13 refers to how the parents failed to educate their children on the miraculous works of the Lord, how He miraculously freed them from slavery in Egypt, how He miraculously cared for them during those forty years in the wilderness, and how He brought them to the land He had promised them. We're told:

> "After that whole generation had been gathered to their fathers, another generation grew up, who knew neither the Lord nor what He had done for Israel. Then the Israelites did evil in the eyes of the Lord and served the Baals. They forsook the Lord, the God of their fathers, who had brought them out of Egypt."

Due to this failure in education, the children forgot the miraculous works of the Lord and their glorious past. They forsook the Lord, adopted the evil habits, lifestyles, and the worship of false gods of the heathen nations around them, and suffered the punishment of the Lord.

The seventh critical warning sign of a nation in crisis is the *Weakening of Cultural Foundations*. The fact that our Founding Fathers built this nation on the foundation of Judeo-Christianity is irrefutable due to numerous writings and statements of the Founders, numerous Supreme Court judgments and statements, and numerous other historical documents and events substantiating the claim. Then too, despite numerous attempts by the radical secular progressive liberals to revise history and claim a secular foundation for our nation, they have failed. Unfortunately, however, they have managed to chip away little by little at that Judeo-Christian foundation over the years, causing a weakening of our cultural foundations. What are those cultural foundations being weakened? None other than the moral and ethical code of the Bible which defines right and wrong and behavioral standards set by God, the Sanctity of Life established by God, the Sanctity of Marriage established by God, and the Sanctity of Family established by God, which constitutes the core content of this book.

Our country desperately needs a return to strong conservative leadership in order to reverse this weakening of our cultural foundations. A nation that trashes its spiritual, political, and cultural history, traditions, and heritage, is a nation suffering confusion and chaos, heading for a fall, and which no longer has contemporary spiritual, political, and cultural justification for continued existence. The referenced Scriptural reading from the Book of Matthew 7:24-27 is Jesus' parable of the wise man and the foolish man. I refer to this parable in full near the end of the book, so I will briefly summarize it here. The wise man built his house on a rock, and when the storms came and pounded that rock, his house did not fall. The foolish man built his house upon the sand. And when the storms came and the seas pounded the house foundation, it fell.

Like the wise man who built his house on a rock, our Founders built our national house on the rock of Judeo-Christianity, and it has survived the storms of centuries. The secular progressive radical liberals who want to change that foundation to secular liberalism and socialism are like the fool who built his house on the sand.

The Scripture passage from Psalms 11:3 asks:

> "When the foundations are being destroyed, what can the righteous do?"

The answer, I submit is, Appeal to those who are attempting to destroy the foundation to stop. If they are the government authorities and they do not cease their attempts to weaken our Judeo-Christian foundations, we must do what the Founders advised the people to do in such a situation - Revolt, just as they did against the British tyranny.

The eighth critical warning sign of a nation in crisis is *Loss of Respect for Tradition*. This ties in closely with the previous warning sign "A Weakening of Cultural Foundations." Tradition is critically important to both individuals and nations. Tradition, over time, comes to establish the identity of a person, an organization, or a nation. Let's consider a few of the traditional characteristics of the United States, which over time have come to form the identity of the nation both at home and abroad.

1. A nation established under God whose founding document states: "All men are created equal, and endowed by their Creator with certain unalienable rights, that among these are life, liberty, and the pursuit of happiness.

2. The freest nation on earth with a Constitution that guarantees this freedom and the rights given to men by God, regardless of race, religion, nationality, or gender.

3. The top nation on earth where, with its freedoms and capitalist economy, provides the greatest opportunities for those willing to work to prosper and thrive and achieve financial stability greater than they could have imagined in their previous circumstances.

4. The most affluent, generous, benevolent nation on the face of the earth, as well as in history, always ready to help those who are in poverty, downtrodden, suffering persecution and discrimination, and loss due to war and natural disasters.

These characteristics, along with many more form the tradition of the United States communicated to its own people along with the peoples of other nations. I would like to add one more characteristic common to Americans, and that is a characteristic common to the American military person, whether soldier, sailor, airman, Marine, or Coast Guardsman. Americans are known as fierce warriors in combat. They are tough, smart, dedicated, and courageous in battle. They are also known as compassionate, sympathetic, and soft-touches for those suffering innocently, especially children.

A prime example of that is, during America's wars, who do children, fearful and suffering, gravitate to - the enemy soldier or the American soldier? The American soldier, because the child knows he or she will be safe with the American soldier and treated with kindness, and undoubtedly will receive a treat - whether food, candy, chocolate or whatever that soldier has. The kindness of the American soldier, I believe, goes back to the Judeo-Christian morals and ethics of the nation in which that soldier was reared, or became a citizen of. This kindness of the American soldier may be thought of as a little thing, but it is a thousand and more such little things, along with the big things previously mentioned that go into building the tradition and heritage of an individual and nation.

The tradition and heritage of the United States is bold, exciting, and to be admired and treasured. Have we as a nation made mistakes? Of course we have, and sometimes terrible mistakes - slavery, the Indian wars, segregation, removing our Japanese citizens to containment camps after Pearl Harbor - being a few examples. Show me an individual or nation that hasn't made terrible mistakes. But we, for the most part, have admitted those mistakes and striven to rectify them and make amends. Our tradition and heritage is a Godly one and will remain so as long as we hold fast to the principle of Sanctity of Life, and receive our leading, guidance, and direction from the wisdom of Holy Scripture, the Bible. It would be an act of the greatest danger, of the highest ignorance and utter stupidity to turn from the glorious riches of our Christian tradition and heritage to the rags of a progressive, secular, socialist tradition.

In our referenced Scripture passage from the Book of Daniel 9:4-6, we read of Daniel's prayer to God seeking God's forgiveness for his peoples' sin of rebelling against God and turning away from the foundational covenant God had made with them, their unfaithfulness and disloyalty to God in seeking a different way, a different tradition which had resulted in their being taken into captivity to Babylon. A summary of Daniel's prayer follows:

> "O Lord, the great and awesome God, who keeps his covenant of love with all who love him and obey his commands, we have sinned and done wrong. We have been wicked and have rebelled; we have turned away from your commands and laws...O Lord, we and our kings, our princes and our fathers are covered with shame because we have sinned against you...All Israel has transgressed your law and turned away, refusing to obey you. Therefore the curses and sworn judgments written in the law of Moses, the servant of God, have been poured out on us, because we have sinned against you...O Lord, in keeping with all your righteous acts, turn away your anger and your wrath ...Now, our God, hear the prayers and petitions of your servant ...We do not make requests of you because we are righteous, but because of your great mercy. O Lord, listen! O Lord, forgive! O Lord, hear and act! For your sake, O my God, do not delay!...

God answered Daniel's prayer, released His people from captivity, allowing them to return to Israel and rebuild their temple and cities. What can we learn from this passage? The vital importance of praying for our nation, its leaders and our fellow citizens, that God would forgive us for our unfaithfulness to Him and our rebelling against Him, that God would provide His counsel and leading to both the leaders and citizens of this nation, and give us the wisdom to seek His will and follow His leading so that God's purposes which He established for our nation may be fulfilled and our tradition and heritage may be a blessing for all.

The ninth critical warning sign of a nation in crisis is *Loss of Economic Discipline*. Economic discipline is something many people find extremely difficult to apply, and which Congress finds virtually impossible to apply. The last time the United States was debt free, according to an article I read, was in the 1920s when President Calvin Coolidge's administration managed to pay off the national debt.

Today, the national debt is over 30 trillion dollars and growing exponentially. This amount of money is realistically beyond the imagination, and the previous democratic administration kept wanting to throw multiple trillions of more dollars to their pet projects and special interest groups in an attempt to, in their words, save the country, or in the case of climate change, save the world. Of course, keeping the support, not to mention the votes, of those special interest groups might have something to do with their insane spending proposals.

It is totally naive and futile to hope for economic discipline and wise economic policies from a democratic administration, given the Democratic Party's historical tradition of tax and spend. Our only hope is that the previous democratic president and administration did not do irreparable damage to the nation's economy during their four year term, that the new Trump administration can repair.

Our referenced Scripture passage in Luke 15; 13-16 is Jesus' parable of the Prodigal Son which, among other critical lessons, emphasizes the foolishness and disastrous consequences of squandering wealth and spending profusely:

> "There was a man who had two sons. The younger one said to his father, 'Father, give me my share of the estate.' So, he divided his property between them. Not long after that, the younger son got together all he had, set off for a distant country, and there squandered his wealth in wild living. After he had spent

everything, there was a severe famine in that whole country, and he began to be in need."

"Squandered his wealth" is a perfect description of the economic policies of the previous radicalized Democrat administration. The yearly interest on our 30 trillion national debt is in the multiple billions. I heard from a reputable conservative news source that for the first time in history our national debt has equaled or surpassed our national annual income, and that economic experts claim that the debt to income ratio should not exceed twenty percent. That twenty percent is now one hundred percent. We have bequeathed this unthinkable debt to our succeeding generations, assuming that it is even possible to pay off such debt. As far as squandering wealth is concerned, our politicians in Washington, particularly the secular progressive liberal Democrats, make the Prodigal Son look like a rank amateur.

The tenth and final warning sign of a nation in crisis is *Oppressive Bureaucracy*. I think we all to some extent can relate to that since all of us, at one time or another, have had to deal with a government agency. There's a saying that goes something like this: "If you have a project that must be done, and you want it to take longer than the time allotted, cost more than the funds appropriated, and end up with glitches that must be corrected, requiring even more time and money, give it to the government to do." Now there are rare exceptions to this, times when government organizations have accomplished extremely complex and difficult projects in reasonable time and for reasonable costs given the fact that the science and technology had to be advanced to new levels. The Manhattan Project to develop the first atomic bomb, and the Apollo Program to put the first men on the moon and bring them home safely are two grand successes that come to mind.

Normally however, a bureaucracy is not primarily interested in efficiency and cost effectiveness, but in its own self-interest, acquiring as much power, influence, and financial resources as it can. Our Scripture passage from 1Samuel 8: 10-18 alludes to this and the danger to the citizens of giving the government too much power. The government of Israel at the time was streamlined and very effective. At the top of the hierarchy was God who was both God and King. Next in line was a God appointed Judge who was the go-between and mediator between God and the people. The Judge would communicate God's Word and instructions to the people and communicate the peoples' requests and concerns to God. Each of the twelve tribes had a tribal leader who would evaluate the peoples' requests before presenting them to the Judge to present to God. The Judge at the time of this passage was Samuel the Prophet. I say the system was streamlined and effective because communication was a two-way street between God and the Judge Samuel, with little or no chance of duplication, confusion, or misunderstanding.

However, the people weren't satisfied with this system of government. They wanted a human king like the heathen nations around them, with all the pomp and ceremony that entailed. Samuel was fit to be tied, but the Lord told him: "Give the people what they want but warn them solemnly what the king who will reign over them will do. And here is where the bureaucracy sets in. Samuel gave the people the following warning from the Lord:

> "This is what the king who will reign over you will do. He will take your sons and make them serve with his chariots and horses, and they will run in front of his chariots. Some he will assign to be commanders of thousands and commanders of fifties, and others to plow his ground and reap his harvests, and still others to make weapons of war and equipment for his chariots. He will take your daughters to be perfumers and cooks and bakers. He will take the best of your fields and vineyards and olive groves and give them to his attendants. He will take a tenth of your grain and of your vintage and give it to his officials and attendants. Your menservants and maidservants and the best of your cattle and donkeys he will take for his own use. He will take a tenth of your flocks, and you yourselves will become his slaves. When that day comes, you will cry out for relief from the king you have chosen, and the Lord will not answer you in that day."

How's that for an oppressive bureaucracy? You would think that after hearing all that, the people would say: "Forget it! We don't want a king after all." But no, the people refused to listen to Samuel. "No!" they said. "We want a human king over us. Then we will be like all the other nations." There are some important lessons for us in this passage, two of which are: 1. Be careful what you ask for! And 2. If we insist on having our way, God will let us have our way, even if it is not His will for us. He will let us suffer the consequences, but because of His love for us, He will be ready to forgive us and restore us into His favor when we return to Him in repentance.

So, there are the ten critical warning signs of a nation in crisis and decline. And each of them exists to an even greater and more alarming degree in our nation today than in 1994 when Dr. Black wrote his book, and twelve years ago when I referred to them in my first book. Their corrupting influence grows daily in our churches, in government, in our schools, and in our culture and society. Each of these warning signs is a stain on our national tapestry and poses an internal danger to the country, and the synergistic effects of all of them pose a clear and present danger to our very survival as a free nation founded on Christian teachings and values. As I mentioned before, our previous democratic President and Congress were either incapable or unwilling, or probably both, to address these dangers. Prior to the previous ineffective democratic leadership, we had four years of solid conservative leadership that was effectively attacking these dangers to the country. Thank God for the return of such leadership.

A final word before we leave this subject. Despite the fact that former President Obama and other democratic progressive liberals deny it, the United States of America is truly an exceptional nation. This has been proven time and time again from its birth and throughout its history. John Quincy Adams, sixth President of the United States, spoke of this exceptionalism on July 4, 1821 when he said:

> "The highest glory of the American Revolution was this: It connected in one indissoluble bond the principles of civil government with the principles of Christianity."

John Quincy Adams was right. America was the only nation to have done this, and that is truly exceptional.

Calvin Coolidge, our 30th President of the United States, reaffirmed this truth when he wrote:

> "The foundation of our society and our government rest so much on the teachings of the Bible that it would be difficult to support them if faith in these teachings would cease to be practically universal in our country."

Old Testament Israel was the most exceptional nation of all nations because they were God's chosen people. Yet, in their incomprehensible ignorance they were willing to trade their exceptionalism for the status of being like other nations. God save us from such ignorant disaster, from the appalling stupidity of listening to the secular progressive radical Democrats among us and trading in our exceptionalism as a nation under God, built on the foundation of Judeo-Christianity, for a mediocre, miserable, godless foundation of secular progressive liberal socialism.

Benjamin Franklin

Benjamin Rush

Dr. William Lyon Phelps

President John Quincy Adams

President Calvin Coolidge

CHAPTER 4
"ITCHING EARS"

"The time will come when men will not put up with sound doctrine. Instead, to suit their own desires, they will gather around them a great number of teachers to say what their itching ears want to hear. They will turn their ears away from the Truth and turn aside to myths."

(2Timothy 4: 3-4).

We are now living in the time described above, a time when more and more people, including many who call themselves Christian, would rather hear what their itching ears want to hear than hear the truth of God's Word. This has always been the case to some extent; however, I believe it is much more prevalent today than any other time in our history. And there is certainly no shortage of certain ones in authority - false and misleading, pastors, teachers, theologians, professors, and politicians - who are ready, willing, and anxious to actively scratch those itching ears, ready to corrupt, manipulate, and interpret God's Word and our Constitution according to their own desires, wants, ideologies, and lifestyles, and defy truth, wisdom, and common sense in order to scratch those itching ears.

And then there are others in authority who passively scratch those itching ears by simply compromising the truth or ignoring it altogether, hoping to avoid conflict or contention, not realizing that in doing so they are actually contributing to the growing corruption in our institutions, society, and culture.

We live in a time when certain progressive secular liberal beliefs, ideologies, and practices, which would have been discarded decades ago as clearly contradictory to God's Word, and utterly irrational, if not downright dangerous, are considered to be innovative, intellectually progressive, and even culturally advanced. Truth is considered as relative, depending on the circumstances, instead of absolute. In the past, when a person, a people, a nation, was going through confusion, chaos, and bewilderment, the absolute Truth of God's Word, God's promises, God's assurances, and yes, the truth of our Judeo-Christian foundation and the nation's founding documents, provided the stability, the virtue and wisdom to clear away the cobwebs of confusion and chaos, right the ship-of-state, and set her back on a true course. But if truth is relative - one thing today, and another thing tomorrow, where is that stability, virtue, and wisdom so needed at such times.

Many, many citizens today, myself included, feel that the nation under the previous democratic administration, went off the rails - spiritually, politically, and culturally. George Washington spoke of times like this. I believe it was in his farewell address when he said:

> "Much to be regretted indeed would it be, were we to neglect the means and depart from the road which Providence has pointed us to so plainly. I cannot believe it will ever come to pass. The Great Governor of the Universe has led us too long and too far…to forsake us in the midst of it…We may, now and then, get bewildered, but I hope and trust that there is good sense and virtue enough left to recover the right path."

Religious, political, and cultural traditions and practices, which have proved true and valid and of inestimable value to humanity for the past three or four thousand years are shunted aside as no longer relevant to a "sophisticated, post-modern, post-Christianity culture. The progressive secular radical wing of the Democrat Party is doing the lion's share of this shunting aside the time-tested, true and valid religious, political, and cultural traditions, while the so-called moderate Democrats in the party (that term moderate Democrat is becoming more and more of an oxymoron) are doing little to prevent the radicals from taking over the party, probably because many of them are themselves seduced by the socialist policies, insane spending, and international agenda pushed by the radicals.

The Democratic Party is one of those I mentioned earlier that is ready, willing, and anxious to scratch the itching ears of those who want to hear about socialism, who want to hear about all the free benefits they will have without having to work for them, about having all one's needs - housing, health-care, college education, etc., etc., being provided by the government.

Our Founders and succeeding generations of Americans endured considerable suffering and great sacrifice in order to build this nation, its grand tradition, heritage, culture, and way of life. Would the current generation willingly endure such suffering and sacrifice to keep it and continue to build on that grand tradition and heritage? History shows us that it is possible for a people, a nation, a civilization, to reach a point where they become no longer willing to undergo great sacrifice in order to maintain their heritage, culture, and way of life. This usually occurs when a society has become so affluent, so materialistically oriented, and so tolerant of creeping spiritual corruption that they refuse to take any action that might endanger that affluence, any action that requires significant material sacrifice, any action that requires submission of self-interest and self-desire to a higher cause, to the greater good. The question: "What is God's will and best for my country?" becomes "What is my will and best for me?" Or to paraphrase democratic President John F. Kennedy and his challenge to the people when he said: "Ask not what your country can do for you; ask what you can do for your country!" becomes "Ask not what you can do for your country; ask what your country can do for you!" And this is the progressive secular socialist drivel with which the radical wing of the Democratic Party scratches the itching ears of those whose primary interest is self-interest and whose primary desire is self-desire.

In Tom Brokaw's book, *The Greatest Generation,* he extolled that generation of Americans who went through the Great Depression of the 1930s and endured all the suffering and sacrifice that entailed. While the Great Depression was still ongoing, they then had to go through the greatest war in history - World War II - and the incomprehensible suffering and sacrifice that entailed. Yet, despite all that unimaginable suffering and sacrifice, and with courage, determination, and iron will, that generation emerged victorious and set about building this nation to its apex of power and influence and its reputation as the shining beacon of freedom and opportunity for the rest of the world to emulate and aspire to.

To top it off, that generation then set about rebuilding the countries of our two primary enemies of World War II, Germany and Japan, which lay in total ruins. And they not only rebuilt them in record time, a decade or so, but changed them from two of the most totalitarian, tyrannical, dictatorships on earth into two of the strongest democracies on earth. The accomplishments of this Greatest Generation stuns the imagination.

And so the question: "Would the present generation of Americans, having experienced the affluence and benefits available to them today, have the will, the determination, the passion, and the sheer guts, to endure such suffering and sacrifice as the Greatest Generation and emerge victorious as they did?

This is not an unreasonable question, given the fact that today, with the all-volunteer military force, only 1% of the population experiences military service. And of those seeking to join the military, 74% of them, according to the latest statistics I've read, fail to pass the entrance criteria, either physically, mentally, or morally. Consider the gigantic negative impact of this on the nation. Six or seven decades ago, 50% to 60% or more of the nation's young adults had some form of military experience, and I believe 50% to 70% of the members of Congress had previous military experience. Today, in Congress, according to recent statistics, that percentage is somewhere around 14%.

So, what is the gigantic negative impact on the nation of this disastrous decline in military experience among the population and our leaders in Congress, as well as our other institutions? First, a disastrous decline in both patriotism and the attitude that, given the freedoms, benefits, and opportunities this country offers, one is obligated to repay to some extent with a tour of military service. Second, the loss to the nation of not having a substantial percentage of its population with prior military experience available to quickly build up the force to meet immediate or near immediate threats. And third, consider the following. The average age of a person entering military service is 18 to the early 20s. What is the best time for a person to learn character traits such as discipline, responsibility, integrity, honor, accountability, leadership, perseverance, and physical and mental toughness? In the late teens and early twenties, right?

The point is this. Those character traits, absolutely essential for the security and prosperity of a Democratic Republic, engrained in the young adult during his/her military experience, stays with them when they leave the military, re-enter civilian life, and pursue a career using those character traits learned in the military, perhaps even without realizing it because they are part of his/her physical and mental being. Imagine the tremendous positive effects on our society and culture of having 60% or more of the population living their lives exhibiting these character traits engrained in them in the military. And imagine the tremendous negative effects on our society and culture of having that 60% or more reduced to 1%. Apparently businesses and employers recognize the significant value of these character traits because a job seeker will be asked if they are a veteran or not, and employers often actively advertise for veterans. Also imagine the negative impact on our government and Congress of having the percentage of military veterans in Congress reduced from 70% to 14%.

I offer this true anecdote to illustrate the value of military experience. When I joined the Marines, more years ago than I care to remember, it was a common practice for judges to give young criminals, usually gang members, a choice. Either go to jail or go into the Marine Corps. Yes, this really happened! Usually, it involved violent gang members from notorious gang centers like Hell's Kitchen and others in our major cities. And yes, I know the progressive democrat liberals would have apoplexy over this today. However, the democrats at the time, didn't seem to have much of a problem with it. Again, these were tough, hardened gang members.

The Marine Drill Instructors loved to get these guys in boot camp. As I recall, we had either two or three of them in the platoon I was in. The Drill Instructors' mode of operation at the time was to break the recruit down to nothing, rid him completely of his civilian identity, and then rebuild him into the identity of a United States Marine, with all the character traits listed above. Well, after a few days of the harsh (brutal would be a better term for it) physical and mental pressure suffered under the drill instructors, those tough, hardened former gang members were sobbing and scared out of their wits just like the rest of us.

But as that long, long, twelve weeks of boot camp continued, a gradual change of attitude and demeanor came upon those former gang members. Like the rest of us, they strove to excel in the training courses, and with the rest of us, were being welded into a unit, not a gang unit, but a military unit of precision and discipline. And after that twelve weeks of boot camp, those former gang members with the rest of us, in full dress uniform, marched in our graduation parade, and like the rest of us, were damn proud to bear the title of United States Marine. Those judges who gave those gang members the choice of jail or the Marine Corps knew what they were doing. And those Marine Drill Instructors did more to turn those gang members into productive citizens than a squad of social workers could have done.

During our nation's history, there have been periodic spiritual revivals that have served to steer the nation back to its Christian roots for a time. Surprisingly, one of those revivals occurred during our bloodiest war - the Civil War - and it swept through the officer and enlisted ranks of both Union and Confederate forces. A lesson here is that it sometimes takes a major disaster to awaken people to reality and lay the groundwork for revival. Unfortunately, with the passage of time and changes in circumstances or leadership or both, the revivals were temporary, and the nation reverted back to business as usual.

Consider our example after the September 11, 2001 terrorists attacks. After the attacks and the deaths of nearly 3,000 innocent people, our nation, its government, and its citizens came together as one and were united in our sorrow, our righteous anger, and Iron will to combat the satanic evil of terrorism and those who espouse it. But the hoped for revival did not come. Over time, complacency again set in, accompanied by a return of ideological conflict, bitter partisan politics, and an unwillingness of political parties and special interest factions, primarily democrats, to set aside their lust for power and influence and work together with singleness of purpose to meet the threat and defeat it. And so, after a period of mourning, unity and oneness of purpose, it was back to partisan politics as usual and business as usual.

I fear that it may take an even greater disaster than 9/11 to really awaken our leaders in the church, government, educational and cultural institutions, and the majority of the people, and pave the way for another national revival. Then too, given the extent to which the Democrat Party has been corrupted, both politically and spiritually, I'm not sure if it is even capable of being awakened at this point.

The other day I received in the mail a sixteen page article from Mr. James Golden, a Black American also known as "Bo Snerdley," formally the Executive Producer and Call Screener for the Rush Limbaugh show. In the following comments, I will continue to refer to him as Mr. Snerdley. Mr. Snerdley has fought for conservative values for over 30 years and has established a new political action committee entitled "New Journey." The purpose of New Journey, Mr. Snerdley says, is two-fold: 1. To correct misrepresentations about the Republican Party and Black American voters, and 2. To present a stark and inconvenient truth about the Democratic Party and Black Americans.

First, the Republican Party is often perceived as a heartless and racist villain in minority communities. The Democratic Party, in their attempt to convince people that the Republican Party hates Black people, has accomplices in the mainstream media, the entertainment industry, and American academia. The great irony of this, asserts Mr. Snerdley, Is that studies and common sense confirm that Black Americans are more likely to self-identify as conservatives, and that the majority of Black Americans largely disagree with Democratic Party talking points on abortion, taxes, immigration, climate change, transgenderism, and others. According to Mr. Snerdley, 89% of Black Americans belong to a religious faith - well above the United States average as a whole, where fewer than 60% self-identify with any mainstream faith. Black Americans favor reducing illegal immigration more than any other demographic group, Seventy-six percent of Black Americans support school choice.

Obviously, the Democratic Party is not supporting Black Americans in these preferences. Mr. Snerdly asserts that, over the past sixty years or so, the Democratic Party hasn't really done anything for Black Americans. Only during every election cycle does the Democratic leadership give them full attention and advertise the party's commitment to them. Then, when the election is over, the Democrat Party resumes ignoring them until the next election cycle.

Second, the stark and inconvenient truth about the Democratic Party and Black Americans that Mr. Snerdley reveals is that you need only look at the Democratic Party's despicable historical record to realize that they are no friend to Black Americans. He presents that history as follows:

1. The Democratic Party defended slavery.
2. The Democratic Party started the Civil War.
3. The Democratic Party opposed Reconstruction.
4. The Democratic Party founded the Ku Klux Klan.
5. The Democratic Party imposed segregation.
6. The Democratic Party perpetrated lynchings.
7. The Democratic Party fought Civil Rights Acts.

Mr. Snerdley reminds his readers that the Republican Party is the party of Abraham Lincoln and that the Republican Party was born as the abolitionist party to fight slavery. Abraham Lincoln, a Republican President, wrote the Emancipation Proclamation and freed men and women bound in the shackles of slavery. Dwight D. Eisenhower, another Republican President, ordered his administration to stand up to government segregationists, and the Civil Rights movement grew from this definitive action by a Republican President.

In 1977, Ronald Reagan, another Republican President, said:

> "The time has come for Republicans to say to Black voters: 'Look, we offer principles that Black Americans can and do

support…The Democratic Party takes the Black vote for granted. Well, it's time Black America and the new Republican Party move toward each other and create a situation in which no Black vote can be taken for granted."

Mr. Snerdly believes that, deep down, Black Americans are fed up with Democrats and their empty promises. President Trump won the day with his call to action and his ability to effect change, his policy successes, and his genuine concern for all Americans. Under Trump's tenure, the economy took off like a rocket, jobs abounded, the Black American unemployment rate became the lowest in history, massive illegal immigration was stopped, our military was rebuilt, America's international leadership and respect reestablished, our history, tradition, and heritage again honored, and religious liberties, LIFE, and FAITH championed.

Mr. Snerdly compares the decisive action of President Trump with the hollow and empty words of his predecessor, President Obama. He describes Obama's two terms as President as "sheer rhetoric." Sheer rhetoric as Black American communities became poorer and poorer, violent crime and shootings abounded, and the country became more and more divided. And if anyone dared criticize Obama's detrimental economic policies and fumbling international "resets," they were labeled "racists." On President Trump's inauguration day, January 20, 2017, America witnessed a transfer of guards and decisive action triumph over eloquent but empty words.

In short, the bigotry of the Democrats sees communities of color only as votes, not as human beings worthy of a better future, whereas President Trump, a man of action, took sheer delight in finding solutions to problems to make American life better for all Americans, regardless of political affiliation.

In Gallup's "Values and Beliefs" poll released June 4, 2007, 82% of Americans said that cultural decay and the erosion of our core beliefs and morals were getting worse. And there is no doubt that they have gotten even worse since then. Abortion, homosexuality, stem cell research, and sex between unmarried men and women were identified as "pivotal moral issues" in the peoples' response. I emphasized in previous narrative the danger of such cultural decay and erosion, but it bears repeating and repeating because, too often, "itching ears" want to hear something else and refuse to give their attention to those warning of the corruption growing within. I mentioned before that political solutions were futile without moral transformation. Our third President of the United States, Thomas Jefferson, understood this when he said:

> "When once a Republic is corrupted, there is no possibility of remedying any of the growing evils but by removing the corruption and restoring its lost principles. Every other correction is either useless or a new evil."

Our Founding Fathers clearly understood, and we as citizens must clearly understand, the fragile nature of the Democratic Republic for which they were laying the foundation. They fully realized the sinful nature of man, and thus the vulnerability of the nation and its government and institutions to chaos, confusion, corruption, and anarchy because of the very freedoms given to the people in such a Democratic Republic. Thus, the foundation they built the nation on was Judeo-Christianity, and they repeatedly emphasized Christian morality and virtues as absolutely essential traits in both leaders and citizens if the nation was to survive, grow in strength and influence, and prosper. Their statements are perhaps even more valid today than when they were spoken and written, given the rise of a godless secular progressive radical liberalism and the readiness of so many in leadership positions in government, our educational institutions, and our cultural institutions to compromise and corrupt both the Word of God and the Constitution for the sake of power, wealth, status, and personal agendas.

A fatal flaw in secular progressive liberalism is a misunderstanding of man's basic nature as good rather than sinful. Believing that man is basically good leads to blaming other things - society, culture, poverty, other people, etc., for all the bad things that happen in life. Viewing man's nature as good becomes the yardstick for evaluating morality. Therefore, what is good or moral is dependent on what man considers good and moral. This also relates to truth. Thus, man elevates himself to godlike status, and fully expects God to sanction his arrogance.

Once the restraints of absolute Truth are removed, man will devise his own truth, and this truth will often be used to support his basest impulses. Two recent modern examples of this were Naziism and Communism. Modern society's greatest failure is its failed capacity to discern, recognize, identify, and condemn evil when it plainly stares us in the face. And if we plan on recognizing evil only through human intuition without the revelation of Scripture, then we are truly the blind leading the blind. The revelation of Scripture is absolutely essential for wise discernment between right and wrong, good and evil, true and false. Truth, right and wrong are absolute realities, and it is vitally important to correctly discern between them and their opposites. This is precisely where secular progressive liberalism, moral relativism, post-modernism, and much of liberal theology, with its emphasis on a permissive tolerance, fails miserably to provide a solid foundation for the spiritual, intellectual, and physical realities of life.

Political correctness is the ideological standard for secular progressive liberals today. Political correctness replaces a value system based on religion, rationality, reason, common sense, and the Biblical moral law, with a value system based on emotions, feelings, desires, and basically allows each person to determine their own truth.

Have you ever tried to have a meaningful and somewhat intellectual discussion of issues concerning life, religion, government, education, history, or culture with a secular progressive liberal? If so, you will understand what follows. If not, let me warn you; It can be a thoroughly frustrating experience. Why? Because the progressive secular liberal conducts the discussion on the basis of those feelings, emotions, desires, and their version of the truth. Now to some extent, that is fairly normal of anyone. Where the utter frustration comes in is when the conservative member of the discussion interjects solid, incontrovertible facts, evidence, and proof that contradicts the politically correct ideological standards of the secular progressive liberal. He/She simply denies those facts, evidences, and proof, or ignores them altogether. How do you conduct a meaningful discussion with someone who denies or ignores facts, proofs, evidence staring them in the face. You can't!

And here we come to the last defense of a radical liberal when they are faced with facts they can't refute. They turn from discussing the issues to attacking their opponent. And there is no limit to the viciousness of their attack. A person who abandons the discussion and resorts to attacking the person and character of their opponent, is in fact admitting defeat in the discussion. A liberal who is supposed to be tolerant becomes vehemently intolerant. Name calling is prevalent, and they label their opponent as homophobic, racist, bigot, egoist, sexist, or any other insulting label their closed mind can come up with. Their objective, of course, is to destroy the reputation of their conservative opponent, and they will lie, cheat, deceive, mislead, or whatever else it may take to accomplish this. Basically, they are simply corrupt and thoroughly partisan in their dealings.

This was put on full public display before, during, and after President Trump's tenure, especially during Brett Kavenaugh's confirmation hearings for Supreme Court Justice, and during the two fraudulent impeachment hearings against President Trump. In all of this, the words and actions of the secular progressive radical Democrats were disgusting and demeaning to hear and see, as well as probably illegal. Their performance clearly showed how virulent hatred, in this case hatred of Trump and his candidate Kavenaugh and his pro-life stance, once it metastasizes throughout a person or organization, results in corruption of that person or organization. It also showed the alarming extent to which this corruption had infected the Democratic Party with an ungodly, un-American, and unhinged political ideology.

Political Correctness has been described as an "ideology of the mentally impaired." With political correctness as the standard, society becomes like a rudderless ship drifting this way and that way since human emotions and feelings change, and without the deep roots of a moral code established by a transcendent authority, wise discernment withers, confusion and chaos reign, and the inevitable result is a creeping degradation and deterioration in culture, precisely what we, as a nation, are experiencing today. By the way, did you know that one thing political correctness has taught us is that there are 57 (at last count) different genders that have been identified. I'll bet that came as quite a surprise to our Creator God who created only two genders - male and female - as His Word tells us in Genesis 1:27:

> "So, God created man in His own image, in the image of God He created him; male and female He created them."

Political Correctness contributes to defeatism and weakness - moral weakness, spiritual weakness, and intellectual weakness. Moral weakness is evident by the hesitancy and downright refusal by many to call sin what the Bible clearly and unambiguously defines as sin in order not to offend anyone or hurt anyone's sensibilities. I guess such people think it is better to let them die in their sin with the danger of hell, rather take the chance of hurting their feelings.

Spiritual weakness is manifested by the alarming extent of Biblical illiteracy in the land, which I mentioned earlier is greater than ever before. Again, I refer to St. Augustine who said:

> "A person speaks more or less wisely to the extent that he has become more or less proficient in the Holy Scriptures."

Wisdom, Truth, and Godly discernment is becoming more and more rare today in many churches, as well as in government, our educational institutions, and society overall, for the fundamental reason that Biblical illiteracy has become more and more widespread. Concerning our major educational institutions, which for the most part have accepted political correctness, incredible ignorance is going hand-in-hand with the false pride of so-called knowledge.

Gary Demar, author and commentator, in his book, *America's Christian History, the untold story*, on page 194, said this about Biblical Illiteracy:

> "Ignorance of the Bible and the way it has been used by our forefathers is having disastrous results. To reject the Bible as the

foundation upon which our nation rests is the rejection of America and its ideals."

Demar also quotes President Franklin Delano Roosevelt who said:

"We cannot read the history of our rise and development as a nation without reckoning with the place the Bible has occupied in shaping the advances of the Republic....Where we have been truest and most consistent in obeying its precepts, we have attained the greatest measure of contentment and prosperity."

Intellectual weakness is manifested by the extreme decline in the quality of education students have been receiving over past decades, and the fact that far too many professors in our universities are more interested in indoctrinating students rather than educating them. Professor Alan Bloom, one of the top educational leaders in the country in the 1980s, and highly respected throughout the educational hierarchy, warned of this decline in no uncertain terms in his 1987 book, *The Closing of the American Mind.* After the publication of his book, Professor Bloom was viciously attacked by the educational hierarchy who previously had given him high praise.

Political correctness not only leads to defeatism, the above described weaknesses, and loss of wise discernment, but it violates good judgment and common sense. The central doctrine of political correctness is tolerance. But tolerance, defined by secular progressive liberalism today, demands approval, and even active support of beliefs, lifestyles, and behaviors that are in direct opposition to God's Word, the source of the code of morals and ethics this nation embodies in its founding documents, including the Constitution. This is not tolerance; it is tyranny.

True tolerance is treating all people with understanding, God's grace and love, but it is not approval and support of their sin, or that matter, our sin. Tolerance, as secular progressive liberals demand, in the case of a friend whose addiction, behavior, lifestyle, etc., will certainly lead to increasing spiritual or physical decline, or both, is not an act of love, but an act of hate. Intolerance, on the other hand, out of concern for another person's spiritual, emotional, and physical well-being, is often the highest form of genuine love. In my first book, "Divine Love / Divine Intolerance," I dealt with this subject in detail. The perfect confluence of Divine Love and Divine Intolerance can clearly be seen on the cross of Christ. We see God's amazing grace and love for us sinners in Christ's sacrifice for our sins so we can be forgiven and restored to God's family for this life and life eternal, and with that love, we see God's utter and total intolerance for our sin which made that atoning sacrifice necessary.

Today, we hear politicians and other public speakers ask God to bless America. But how can He bless a nation that has departed so far from Him. We have kicked Him out of our public schools, our public institutions, and isolated Him in our church sanctuaries with a stern warning to not exit those sanctuaries and enter the public square. Not all, but many politicians today, to some extent in all political organizations, but especially in the Democratic Party, compromise or abandon religious principles and ethics (although they would deny this) for political expediency, claiming to be Christian, but their actions contradict Christian principle, doctrine, and teaching, in order to gain the political and monetary support of special interest groups, and to gain or hold onto political office and power. As the saying goes, "Politics and power, like wealth and celebrity, have a way of testing and revealing a person's true character.

Speaking of character, there are some, including politicians, that say character is not the most important issue to consider in a candidate, whereas competence is. They are dead wrong - wrong spiritually, wrong according to our Founders, wrong according to common sense, and proven wrong time and time again in our nation's past political experience. Bad character in a leader will inevitably be reflected in that leader's politics, policies, and associations, not to mention the great potential for scandal, which has soiled the careers of a number of our politicians.

For the secular progressive liberals, corruption of God's Word and corruption of the Constitution is no big deal if doing so furthers their political objectives and purposes. They need to be reminded, in no uncertain terms, that when presidents, members of congress, and judges take the oath of office, they swear to protect, defend, and uphold the Constitution, not the Constitution as they imagine it to read, not the Constitution as they would like it to read, not the Constitution as they would like to change it to read, but the Constitution as it reads. The Founders, looking ahead, included specific procedures for revising and amending the Constitution, and until these procedures and requirements are accomplished, no president, no congress, no judge has the right or authority to interpret it in a manner that does not conform both to its plain language and to a reasonable discernment of the intent of the Founding Fathers.

These criterion of plain language and reasonable discernment of intent were grossly violated on two occasions. First, in 1857 with the Supreme Court's ruling in the Dred Scott v. John F. A. Sandford decision that black people were not, and never could be, citizens of the United States. For many years, the Dred Scott decision was considered the worst decision ever rendered by the Supreme Court and the most egregious example in the court's history of wrongly imposing a judicial solution on a political problem. It was referred to by a later Chief Justice, Charles Evans Hughes, as the Court's self-inflicted wound.

The second occasion when the criterion of plain language and reasonable discernment of intent were grossly violated was in 1973 with the Roe v. Wade decision which legalized abortion. This decision can be considered even a grosser violation of the criterion since Dred Scott refused citizenship, whereas Roe v. Wade refused life itself, and opened the floodgates of brutally murdering babies in the womb. Even more than Dred Scott, Roe v. Wade is an egregious example of the court's wrongly imposing a judicial solution, in this case, to both a spiritual and a political problem beyond the court's jurisdiction, and another example of a self-inflicted wound by the court.

An important sidenote to this is the fact that the Court's imposing judicial solutions to spiritual or political matters instead of strictly legal matters which is their charter, is a primary strategy of the Democratic Party to achieve its political and policy objectives. They know that the majority of the American people would never approve their radical political, economic, and social objectives by going through the normal legislative process, so the way to circumvent the American people and their opponents in Congress is to emphasize the legal aspects of the issue and take it to court. Unfortunately, there are far too many liberal courts and liberal judges who are more than willing to go beyond their constitutional charter and make law rather than strictly interpret law.

The radical Democrats are quite willing to bastardize the Separation of Powers feature of government the Founders devised in order to prevent one branch of government gaining dominance over the others, since such dominance of power is the primary objective of the democrats. And scratching the "itching ears" of liberal courts and judges is one way of achieving that dominance.

Getting back to hypocritical political and other leaders asking God to bless America, I submit that it would be far better to ask for God's mercy, grace, and His forgiveness of our grievous sins against Him. I know that Abraham Lincoln would agree with this because he once stated:

> "Americans cannot expect the blessings and protection of God without also answering for their transgressions against Him."

The Founding Fathers, often referred to as the most brilliant group of individuals brought together by God in one period of time and for one specific purpose, left no doubt as to where they stood concerning religion, government, education, and culture. We would do well to remember and reflect on their wisdom and wise discernment in order to avoid having our "itching ears" scratched by the foolishness and ignorance of progressive liberal secularism, and foolishly and disastrously discarding the heritage and tradition the Founders gave us, and for which they put on the line their lives, their fortunes, and their sacred honor.

Most of the statements and writings of our Founding Fathers which I quote in this book, dealing with their building the nation on the foundation of Judeo-Christianity, their appeals to God during the Revolutionary War, their total dependence on God's Providence and leading during the war and the nation building that followed, the development of the most unique and brilliant Constitution in history, and the establishment of the most powerful, affluent, free, and generous nation on the face of the earth, have been either totally erased from our textbooks, or edited to the extent that they are misleading and unexceptional.

Thus, we have millions of our children and young adults, as well as not-so-young adults, who are totally unaware of our Christian history and heritage. Revisionists have rewritten history to remove the truth about our country's Christian roots. Various educational organizations are devising studies, programs, and curriculums to reeducate people who are the victims of an educational system that has gone off the tracks and equip them with the knowledge of their country's true history, tradition, and heritage which are so critical to the effective, strong, and wise citizenship and leadership that must undergird our nation. It was Winston Churchill, considered by many as the most brilliant statesman of the 20th century, who said:

"A nation that forgets its past has no future."

We have all heard various individuals, speaking on the condition of our country, refer to the passage in 2Chronicles 7:14. It seems to be a favorite passage to quote, and it reads thus:

"If my people who are called by my name, will humble themselves, and pray, and seek my face, and turn from their wicked ways, then will I hear from heaven and will forgive their sin and will heal their land."

Too often, a speaker ends his/her presentation with "May God bless America," said as almost an afterthought, with no realization of what is required for that blessing. In the Scripture passage quoted, four verbs make up that requirement for blessing: Humble themselves; pray; seek my face; and turn from their wicked ways. With these four actions on our part, God is free to bless our land and its people. It would be a good thing if every citizen would memorize that passage.

When we as a people and a nation bend our own wills to God's will and humbly acknowledge His total sovereignty over our lives, then He is free to work out the grand plan, design, and purpose He ordained for us. Our Founding Fathers clearly understood this and consistently expressed this in their speech and writing. We have allowed a godless secular progressive radical liberalism, with its feel good moral relativism, and its siren song of socialism to draw us dangerously away from God's Word and the values and vision of our forefathers. Only through the actions described in the Bible passage from 2Chronicles referred to above, and through a revival and renewal of our Judeo-Christian heritage and the Founder's vision for the nation they built, can we enjoy personal and national success, greatness, fulfillment, and our ultimate and highest good as a people and nation.

To achieve this, we are also going to need leaders who willingly and humbly bend their knees and wills and ambitions to God's will and purpose and acknowledge His sovereignty over every aspect of their lives, including their political lives. It bears repeating and remembering that our Founders emphasized that, in a free society, it was of the utmost importance for the citizenry to elect leaders of high moral character, honesty, integrity, and Christian virtue. President Thomas Jefferson, in his National Prayer for Peace on March 4, 1805, stated:

> "Endow with Thy Spirit of wisdom those to whom in Thy Name we entrust the authority of government, that there may be justice and peace at home, and that through obedience to Thy Law, we may show forth Thy praise among the nations of earth. In time of prosperity, fill our hearts with thankfulness, and in the day of trouble, suffer not our trust in Thee to fail; all of which we ask through Jesus Christ our Lord. Amen."

As shown in chapter 3, with the ten warning signs, our nation has declined significantly in the spiritual, moral, ethical, political, educational, and cultural spheres of national life during the past six or so decades. As a nation, we may not have forgotten God - although many of our fellow citizens have - but we have in many ways confined Him to the sidelines of our personal, political, and national lives. Our national condition has worsened with the previous Democrat administration, with gross complacency in matters of faith, morals, ethics, sanctity of life, sanctity of marriage, and sanctity of family. As one commentator put it:

> "The United States has either lost its conscience, or increasingly grown deaf to it."

Secular progressive liberalism, which in essence is idolatry, is the post-modern religion of many today in our religious, political, educational, and cultural institutions. Truth, even the Truth of Holy Scripture, is not accepted as such unless it conforms to the ideological precepts and agenda of secular progressive liberalism. Those who stand firm in the Truth of the Bible, calling the nation back to its Christian roots, are castigated, insulted, and called bigots, radical fundamentalists, or worse. The situation described by the prophet Isaiah in his day has much application to today. In the book of Isaiah 59:12-15, we read:

> "For our offenses are many in your sight, and our sins testify against us. Our offenses are ever with us, and we acknowledge our iniquities - rebellion and treachery against the Lord, turning our backs on our God, fomenting oppression and revolt, uttering lies our hearts have conceived .....So justice is driven back, and righteousness stands at a distance; truth has stumbled in the streets, honesty cannot enter. Truth is nowhere to be found, and whoever shuns evil becomes a prey."

Egoism, narcissism, materialism, self-indulgence, and self-satisfaction have, to a dangerous degree today, taken priority over patriotism, humanitarianism, morality, self-control, and self-sacrifice. This does not describe contemporary society as a whole, since I believe the great majority of citizens still hold to the beliefs, traditions, and Judeo-Christian principles and standards that made our nation the greatest on earth. Unfortunately, however, it does describe a large segment of society who, with their "itching ears," have fallen victim to a godless, hedonistic, and materialistic secular progressive liberal ideology. As someone once said: "Too often error makes more noise than the truth."

This attitude and ideology is not new. John Adams, our second President of the United States, wrote of the subtlety and danger of such an ideology in his diary as follows:

> "We see every day that our imaginations are so strong and our reason so weak, the charms of wealth and power are so enchanting, and the belief of future punishment so faint that men find ways to persuade themselves to believe any absurdity, to submit to any prostitution, rather than forego their wishes and desires. Their reason becomes at last an eloquent advocate on the side of their passions, and they bring themselves to believe that black is white, that vice is virtue, that folly is wisdom, and eternity a moment....I dread the consequences."

Our nation is suffering the consequences of the foolishness of not all, but much of the past six decades, and which continues today with the absurdity, folly, and intellectual idiocy of secular progressive radical liberalism, moral relativism, and political correctness. Our Founding Fathers never hesitated to invoke the name of God, or seek His blessings, forgiveness, and protection in their public statements and writings. In fact, the Bible was the source most quoted in their speeches and writings. Many of our early judges, and even more recent ones, did not hesitate to invoke Holy Scripture in their judgments and opinions. Yet today, the majority of our politicians and judges either neglect mentioning God, or they simply give Him a passing reference, and rarely do they use the Bible to give moral justification to government laws and policies or court decisions. When is the last time you heard a politician justify a law or regulation just passed by quoting the Bible? When is the last time you heard a judge justify his/her decision by quoting the Bible? You can't remember? Neither can I! Since the Bible is the source for our code of morals and ethics, you would think it extremely valuable for justifying a course of action.

Do you think that politicians and judges neglect to quote the Bible because most of the laws and regulations and decisions cannot be justified by Scripture, but only by partisan politics, special interests, and legal complexities. Or is It because they think it will violate the separation of church and state. If so, they display their ignorance of the history of that statement and what it really meant, and they should know better. Then too, perhaps our leaders rarely invoke the name of God because they are afraid of offending this or that special interest group or political faction on whom they are dependent for support. If so, they are not someone I would consider worthy of respect or honor. In any case, by not doing so, they fail in an important aspect of leadership demonstrated by their predecessors and the Founding Fathers - that being to remind the citizens of this great nation of their Christian roots and heritage.

A nation that fails to remember its roots, heritage, and traditions, whether deliberately or through increasing illiteracy, is a nation on the path to cultural decay and erosion. Czeslaw Milosz, Lithuanian poet and Nobel Prize winner, spoke of this, and his words have direct application to our society today. He said:

> "Our planet that gets smaller every year, with its fantastic proliferation of mass media, is witnessing a process that escapes definition, characterized by a refusal to remember. One senses in this a foreboding of a not too distant future when history will be reduced to what appears on television, while the truth, because it is too complicated, will be buried in the archives, if not totally annihilated."

Given the extent of current Biblical illiteracy, as well as illiteracy in other great historical events and their meaning, all due to a failed educational establishment and clearly documented in numerous reports, studies, and surveys, it is not unreasonable to say that the "not too distant future" that Milosz spoke of is here today.

Woodrow Wilson, 28th President of the United States, spoke on the dangers of failing to remember our roots. He said:

> "A nation which does not remember what it was yesterday does not know what it is today, nor what it is trying to do. We are trying to do a futile thing if we do not know where we came from or what we have been about...The Bible...is the one supreme source of revelation of the meaning of life, the nature of God,

and the spiritual nature and needs of men. It is the only guide of life which really leads the spirit in the way of peace and salvation. American was born a Christian nation. America was born to exemplify that devotion to the elements of righteousness which are derived from the revelation of Holy Scripture."

The question our nation, our leaders and we citizens must consider in all seriousness is this: "Are we still a Christian nation that exemplifies that devotion to the elements of righteousness which are derived from the revelation of Holy Scripture?"

Our Constitution, which is the soul of our nation, was written by men who used the Bible and the teachings of Jesus Christ as the spiritual and moral foundation for that Constitution and the nation itself. Radical liberalism today, far different from the genuine liberalism of the past and the liberalism of the Democratic statesmen I referred to in the beginning of the book, has weakened, and continues to weaken and chip away at that Christian foundation, resulting in a weakening of the critical spiritual and moral fabric of the nation. It is time, past time, for our leaders and all of us to confront and combat this danger whenever it raises its ugly head, to honor our Christian heritage, and work to reverse the spiritual and cultural decline and decay before it is too late.

America is at a crossroads. We have come to many crossroads in our history thus far, and by the grace of God, successfully navigated them. But this one is different. We faced previous crossroads strengthened and supported by a strong Christian foundation and heritage. We face this crossroads with that foundation and heritage weakened by a corroding secular progressive liberalism and a democratic administration that, with its political, economic, and social agenda, seems determined to weaken that foundation and heritage even further, or as the Democratic Party's radical faction wants to do, replace it altogether.

I'm not sure if this is the first time in our history when a political party, in this case the Democratic Party, has abandoned the best interests of the nation and the majority of its citizens as the overall political priority, and exchanged it for the priority of pure partisan politics and the best interests of the Democratic Party. The new top priority for the

Democrats is taking control of the election process, which has served the nation well as designed by the brilliant Founders. The Democrats want to get rid of the Electoral College, designed by the Founders to prevent the possibility that only a few of the more populated states be able to elect the President while the other states' votes are irrelevant, which testifies to the radical liberals' ignorance and pure partisanship. They want to put control of the election process under Congress and remove control from the States where the Founders wisely put it. Just as the 2020 election showed strong indication that there was widespread corruption on the democrat's part, putting the election process under congressional control would open the way for corrupting the process to such an extent that it would provide a Democratic plurality into the indefinite future.

It is obvious, and becoming more and more obvious, that our previous democratic administration has done great harm to the nation's welfare. It is becoming more apparent to the American people, including even many Democrats, that the administration was a disaster. Obviously, a change of administrations was necessary. But political change is futile without moral transformation, for only moral transformation can remove the corruption that has been allowed to infect our nation and its institutions. It appears that, with the new Trump administration, the seeds for such moral transformation are being sown, and we must pray that God will bring those seeds to fruition.

Therefore, the top priority for enabling our nation to defeat the dangers, overcome the challenges, and turn back enemies, both within and without, is to reclaim and reinforce the Judeo-Christian heritage and beliefs that bound us together for the past 249 years, and which we have foolishly and ignorantly either discarded or allowed to be weakened to a dangerous level. If we don't, it is a sure bet that God's protecting and guiding hand, which our Founders relied and depended on, will be removed from us, and we will not find the inner strength, the fortitude, the willingness to sacrifice, and the iron will necessary to confront and defeat the enemies within and those without who are battering on the nation's gates. Implacable, fanatical enemies bound on our destruction cannot be defeated with the straw and mush and touchy-feely political correctness of a godless, soulless, faithless, secular progressive liberalism, with its moral relativism, ungodly tolerance, and ever- failing socialism. Only by seeking again, through national repentance and humility, the power of that protecting and guiding hand of a merciful and gracious God will we be able to overcome the dangers and challenges facing us as a people and nation.

America is the first and exceptional example to the world of a "government of the people, by the people, and for the people." People are familiar with that phrase from Abraham Lincoln's Gettysburg Address. But did you know that that stirring phrase goes back long, long, before that. John Wycliffe was a 14th century English theologian, philosopher, church reformer, promoter of the first complete translation of the Bible into English, and one of the forerunners of the Protestant Reformation. When Wycliffe translated the Bible into English before his death in 1384, he wrote in the flyleaf of his own translation these words:

> "This Bible is translated and shall make possible a government of the people, by the people, and for the people."

I believe that Wycliffe's words were a prophecy given to him by God, for how could he know that 400 years later these words would be lifted from the page of his Bible and immortalized in the New World by our Founding Fathers, brought together by God, who would establish for the first time a government of the people, by the people, and for the people? These words were again immortalized by President Abraham Lincoln in his speech at Gettysburg, Pennsylvania where he honored the dead and commemorated a cemetery for the dead who had died in that battle during our greatest war, the Civil War. Lincoln's words were as follows:

> "..that we highly resolve that these dead shall not have died in vain - that this nation, under God, shall have a new birth of freedom - and that government of the people, by the people, for the people, shall not perish from the earth."

Our Founding Fathers firmly believed that God directs the affairs of men. Wycliffe's words must have encouraged them greatly, to know that over 400 years before, God had already planned their destiny. They followed that destiny, and giving God the glory, they built that nation and government and fulfilled Wycliffe's prophecy. It would be a tragedy of the most monumental proportions if their successors, 249 years later, and like Esau of the Bible, traded their priceless birthright and destiny for a bowl of secular progressive liberal socialist stew.

I close the chapter by again referring to the passage in 2Chronicles 7;14. for it is the only solution to the problems plaguing our land today. If we humble ourselves before Almighty God, pray, seek His face, and turn from our wicked ways, He will keep His promise to forgive us, heal our land, and continue to bless as He has blessed us so incredibly in the past, and with His continued blessing, we will continue to be the greatest, most powerful, most affluent, and most generous nation on the face of the earth.

Thus far, we have discussed the political corruption infecting the character of the Democratic Party. We have discussed the opposing world views of conservatives and secular progressive liberals. We have discussed ten major warning signs of a nation in crisis which grow worse under Democratic Party rule. We have discussed America's condition today which gives ample evidence of the crisis of decline those warning signs point to and what we must do to get back to the wisdom and common sense of our Christian roots. We now turn from the political corruption infecting the Democratic Party to a higher form of corruption that corrupts the very nature, or soul, of a person, organization, or nation - Spiritual corruption - a corruption that is clearly evident in the Democratic Party today.

The following chapters identify the policies of the Democratic Party that are the source of this corruption. Some of these policies have support of Republicans also; however, that support ranges from minimal to rare. The vast bulk of support for these corrosive and corruptive policies lie within the Democratic Party. I would advise the Democrats to remember and seriously ponder Thomas Jefferson's statement:

"When I remember that God is just and that His justice cannot be delayed indefinitely, I tremble for my country."

George Washington.

Abraham Lincoln

Dwight D. Eisenhower

Ronald Reagan

St. Augustine of Hippo

Thomas Jefferson

Franklin D. Roosevelt

John Adams

Czeslaw Milos

Woodrow Wilson

John Wycliffe

CHAPTER 5
THE SANCTITY OF LIFE

"So God created man in His own image,
In the image of God He created him,
male and female, He created them."

Genesis 1:27

The above passage is highly significant in that it makes clear two crucial facts about man and woman. First, man did not evolve from some other species; man was created by God, and not only created, but created in God's image. As such, man represents the highest divine act of creation by God. No other act of creation at the beginning matches that of man's creation. And God alone creates.

The second crucial fact about man in the verse is that man is a generic term for humanity. God created man (singular) as male and female (plural). Male and female are the terms for gender and notice the fact that there are only two genders, male and female. Together man, as male and female, bear the image of God and share the blessing God gave to man:

> "Be fruitful and increase in numbers; fill the earth and subdue it."

This divine benediction commands man to flourish, fill the earth with his kind, male and female, and exercise dominion over the other earthly creatures. Man was to share, as God's steward, in God's Kingly rule. As the Biblical note on the passage states:

> "As God's representative in the creaturely realm, man is steward of God's creation and creatures. He is to use, but not to exploit,

waste, or despoil this earth, its resources or its creatures, but care for them and use them in the service of God and man.

Man being created in God's image gives full meaning to the term *Sanctity of Life*. The Sanctity of Life, the holiness of life, applies only to the human being because of the "image of God" in which he was created. It is necessary to have a good understanding of the meaning of Sanctity of Life in order to understand and appreciate its inseparable relationship to what follows in this book.

In his book, *Christian Theology*, Baker Book House, 1985, Millard J. Erickson tells us that:

> "Of the variety of philosophical conceptions of the nature of humanity, none of them is satisfactory as a view by which to live."

They fail, Erickson says, because even though they may meet the fundamental needs of men and women (economic or physical, etc.), there is still a sense of emptiness and dissatisfaction. In other words, that question, "What is the meaning of life?" Or "Why am I here?" cannot be answered by any human philosophical or psychological theory. Why? I would say because none fits the definition of Sanctity of Life. The Christian view of the nature of man, by contrast, is an alternative view compatible with all our experience.

The Christian view of man is that man is a creature of God, created by God through a conscious, purposeful, act of God. God is a God of purpose. Therefore, there is a reason and purpose for man's existence, a reason and purpose which lies in the mind and intention of the Supreme Being. Next, the image of God is intrinsic to man. Man would not be human without it. Whatever all it is that sets man apart from the animal world and the rest of the creation, the image of God makes man alone capable, through the leading of the Holy Spirit, of having a conscious, personal relationship with the Creator, and of responding to Him.

Erickson goes on to say: "Man can know God and understand what the Creator desires of him. Man can love, worship, and obey his Maker. In these responses, man is most completely fulfilling his Maker's intention for him, and thus being most fully human, since humanity is defined in terms of the image of God." Thus, I would say, "if you do not know God as Creator, Savior, Lord, and Friend, you are not most fully human." Erickson reminds us that the image of God gives man an eternal dimension:

"Man had a finite point of beginning in time, but since he was created in the image of an eternal God, he has an eternal future. Thus, when we ask, 'what is the good for man,' we must not answer only in terms of man's temporal welfare or physical comfort. There is another, and more important, dimension to man that must be fulfilled -the eternal. Therefore, no favor is done to man if he is sheltered from thinking about the issues of eternal destiny."

I would add the following to Erickson's statement. When he says that various views and philosophies of man other than the Christian view invariably leave a sense of emptiness and dissatisfaction, he is agreeing with Saint Augustine who said:

"O Lord, our souls come from Thee, and they know no rest until they rest in Thee."

Next, I would submit that man is a creature of worship. Worship is an intrinsic need of man. Wherever you go in this world, whether to the most advanced civilized areas, or to the most undeveloped and uncivilized areas, you will find that the inhabitants worship someone or something, whether it is the God of the Bible or some other god or object of creation. Why is this? Could it be the embers of the image of God within them that was not totally marred or snuffed out by man's fall into sin?

Erickson's statement that there is a reason for man's existence, a reason which lies in the intention of the Supreme Being, is taken from the Bible in the book of Ephesians 2:10 where the Apostle Paul tells us:

"For we are God's workmanship, created in Christ Jesus to do good works, which God prepared in advance for us to do."

Let us consider this passage which is filled with meaning concerning the sanctity of life and the question, "Why am I here?"

First, we are told that we, that is all men and women, are God's workmanship. The original language of the New Testament was Greek, and the Greek for the word workmanship sometimes has the connotation of a "work of art." Since man (male and female) were God's prize creation, the term "work of art" is certainly appropriate. How about it? Do you, the reader, feel like a work of art? You should! Because you are, in the sight of God!

Second, we are told that, as God's workmanship, man (male and female) was created in Christ Jesus. This agrees with the Apostle John's introduction to his Gospel which speaks of the Word, or the "Living Word," a common Biblical reference to Christ Jesus, Son of God and Son of man. We read in John 1:1-3:

> "In the beginning was the Word, and the Word was with God, and the Word was God. He was with God in the beginning. Through Him all things were made; without Him nothing was made that has been made."

Third, we are told that man was created to do good works. Thus, man was given a purpose at his creation, and this conforms to the nature of his Creator. As stated before, God is a God of purpose. Through His attributes of omnipotence (all-powerful), omniscience (all-knowing), and omnipresence (everywhere present), there is nothing in all God's creation, as He created it, that is useless, of no value, and without purpose. Such an object would be contrary to God's nature.

Fourth, we are told that these good works assigned to each of us were prepared by God in advance for us to do. In advance of what? Certainly, in advance of our own creation, but not only that, in advance of all creation, in advance of the foundation of the world. And here we have an insight into the marvelous, glorious, majestic, and incomprehensible loving nature of our Creator God. But before we consider that insight, we must understand that God, being eternal, is not bound by time and space as we are. Time and space are part of God's creation, but He is not bound by them. In the book of 2Peter 3:8 we are told:

> "With the Lord, a day is like a thousand years, and a thousand years are like a day."

We humans, however, like all the rest of creation, are bound by time and space. So how can we humans have a relationship with God when He stands above time and space and we are captive to time and space? Simple, and yet awesome, beyond our puny intellects to fully comprehend. God chose to enter our time and space continuum in a specific way at a specific time. The reason He chose to do so is foundational to the Sanctity of Life as ordained by God and corrupted by man as discussed in subsequent chapters. For the reader unfamiliar with Christian Doctrine, I offer the following summary to aid in their understanding of why certain political policies, primary those of the Democratic Party, are at the heart of this spiritual corruption of God's Sanctity of Life.

With man's fall into sin, the image of God created in man was not lost, but it was marred to a great extent, and the fellowship of oneness man had enjoyed with God was lost. God, being omniscient (all-knowing), knew that man, both male and female, would fall into sin, and that the oneness of His fellowship with them would be broken. It is a testimony to God's incredible love that He created them anyway because of His desire for human fellowship. Further testimony to God's surpassing love for His human creation is the fact that immediately after the fall, God decided to do what was necessary to restore that fellowship. He promised Adam and Eve a Savior, a Redeemer who would redeem them from their sin and restore them into fellowship with Him. And this redemption and restoration would extend to all of Adam's and Eve's family of humanity, to all who would accept it through faith in that Redeemer.

But why a Redeemer was necessary in the first place requires some explanation. A Redeemer was necessary because sin had to be, and has to be, cleansed and punished in order for fellowship with God to be restored. God is perfectly Holy, and sin is anathema to His Holy Nature;

therefore, it has to be cleansed. It cannot simply be ignored or passed over. God is perfectly Just, and therefore sin must be punished to satisfy His Just Nature. This punishment and cleansing required a Savior, a Redeemer to suffer that punishment so God could provide forgiveness and cleansing for his human creation. And who would that Savior, Redeemer be? And here we have the absolutely unique and profound meaning and nature of the Christian faith!

The Savior Redeemer had to be a man, a human, because sin had come into the world through a man, and Adam's and Eve's sin had been inherited, passed on, to every human being, male and female, born ever since, and to all who will be born until the end of time. Redemption, cleansing from sin and death, required the blood of a perfect sacrifice, since life is in the blood, and only this blood of perfection could cleanse man from sin. Thus, the sacrifice had to be a perfect man, a man whose life was sinless. But no human male could fulfill these criteria because: "All have sinned and fall short of the glory of God." (Romans 3:23)

God alone is perfect. But God is Spirit and not human. God cannot die. Thus, the only solution to this dilemma was for God, in the Person of the Son, to take on our humanity, and while remaining fully divine as the Son of God, become also fully human as the Son of Man. Thus, we have the two natures of Jesus Christ, the Divine and the human. As Son of God, He retained all His divine powers, but used them sparingly in HIs human ministry, primarily in the healing miracles. As the Son of Man, in order to be the perfect sacrifice for our sins, He had to live the perfect life without sin. And He had to do this without using his divine powers to avoid temptation and sin. He had to face every temptation and every onslaught of the devil that man faces in His human nature as Son of Man just as we do. For Jesus the temptations and attacks by Satan were even worse than we experience because Satan knew who Jesus was and what His mission was - to defeat him, the sin he had brought into the world, and the eternal death resulting from that sin. If Jesus, in HIs human nature had sinned just once in His 33 years of ministry on earth, He would not have met the criterion for Savior and Redeemer, and we would still be dead in our sins with our destiny being eternal suffering in hell.

But Jesus did live the perfect, sinless, life for us, and then went to the cross for us as the innocent perfect sacrifice for our sins, to suffer the terrible punishment for our sins, the mocking's, being spit in the face, the beatings, the crown of thorns, the floggings until nearly dead, and finally being nailed to the cross to die the agonizing death to pay the price for our sins, to ransom us from eternal suffering to eternal joy and glory. And with His bodily resurrection from the dead and His ascension into heaven, His payment for our sins was sealed by the Father as "paid in full," and with His resurrection, the resurrection of his faithful followers after the temporal death on this earth, to eternal life in glory in heaven is assured. 1John 2:2 tells us:

> "He" (Jesus Christ) "is the atoning sacrifice for our sins, and not only for ours, but also for the sins of the whole world."

Philippians 2:6-11 gives us the whole Gospel in a nutshell where it says:

> "Christ Jesus, who being in very nature God, did not consider equality with God something to be grasped, but made Himself nothing, taking the very nature of a servant, being made in human likeness. And being found in appearance as a man, He humbled Himself and became obedient to death - even death on a cross. Therefore, God exalted Him to the highest place and gave Him the Name that is above every name, that at the Name of Jesus every knee should bow, in heaven and on earth and under the earth, and every tongue confess that Jesus Christ is Lord to the glory of God the Father."

And Hebrews 2:18 and Hebrews 4:15,16 are passages of immense comfort and assurance to us sinners (that's all of us). They read:

> "Because He Himself" (Jesus) "suffered when He was tempted, He is able to help those who are being tempted." "For we do not have a high priest" (Jesus) "Who is unable to sympathize with

our weaknesses, but we have one Who has been tempted in every way, just as we are - yet was without sin. Let us then approach the throne of grace with confidence, so that we may receive mercy and find grace to help us in our time of need."

These passages are clear and powerful testimony to the Sanctity of Life. God the Father gave His Son to be our Savior because our lives are so precious and sanctified to Him. And God the Son gave His all in all for us because our lives were, and are, so precious and sanctified to Him. And God the Holy Spirit strengthened, encouraged, and ministered to the Son throughout his ministry on earth, just as He strengthens, encourages, and ministers to us during our lives here on earth because our lives are so precious and sanctified to Him. God entered our time and space continuum in order to save us, and He continues to enter our time and space continuum every day in order to bless us with His presence, to give us His guidance and counsel, to share our sorrows and our joys, to be our rock, refuge, fortress, and deliverer in all the storms, pitfalls, and dangers of this life. In short, God humbles Himself to enter our time / space continuum in order to have a relationship and fellowship with us.

And why does He do this? Because of His deep love for His creation, and especially for His human creation, you and I and all humanity, Again, in our human weakness, frailty, and intellectual limitations, we cannot even begin to comprehend the height, depth, and breath of this divine love. We can only marvel at it. Scripture is literally filled with passages expressing God's love for us and His overwhelming desire to have a parent / child relationship with us. More on this in a later chapter. Yet, God will not force Himself on us. He did not create human robots, but humans made in His image with flesh and blood and a free-will. Our free-will, corrupted in man's fall into sin, is free to reject God's grace in Christ, and God will not override it. But God does not leave man in a hopeless situation; again, God's love for his human creation and the Sanctity of Life comes to the fore. God the Holy Spirit convicts man's spirit of sin, and prompts man, leads man, to respond to His call to repent of their sin and receive, through faith, Jesus Christ as their Lord and Savior. And those who do respond in faith, receive the forgiveness of sins, salvation, eternal life, as well as the promise of fellowship God gives for this life:

> "Yet, to all who received Him, to those who believed in HIs Name, He gave the right to become children of God." (John 1:12) "The Spirit Himself testifies with our spirit that we are God's children." (Romans 8:16) "I will be a Father to you, and you will be my sons and daughters," says the Lord Almighty, (2Corinthians 6:18) "How great is the love the Father has lavished on us, that we should be called children of God! And that is what we are! (1John 3:1).

With the preceding insight into God's love, His plan for our salvation, and His continuing presence in our lives, we return to our passage that says that God prepared for each of us in advance the good works we are to do, in advance meaning before creation. Before God, being omniscient (all-knowing), spoke the first words of creation, "Let there be light," He knew every aspect of His creation, including every person who would live and die until the end of time. He knew when and where in that time and space continuum you and I would be born. He knew all your spiritual, physical, and mental attributes. He knew your strong points, your weak points, and everything in between. And, knowing all there is to know about you, He chose the works He would ordain for you to do for Him in your lifetime that would coincide with the talents, skills, and abilities He would give you. And all that applies not only to you and I, but to every human being who has ever lived, who is living, and who will live. Consider what this means!

1. The highest intellectual goal of a person's lifetime is to discover the works God has ordained them to do.
2. The greatest accomplishment of a person's lifetime is to accomplish the works that God ordained for him/her to do.
3. The true definition of a successful life is a life in which a person discovered God's ordained works for them and accomplished them.

Now, a few qualifying words of encouragement and comfort. Keep in mind, and let the realization sink deep into your consciousness, that God does not expect you, or me, or any of His children to discover the works He ordained for them, and to accomplish them on their own. He knows the weakness of our frame, our tendency to procrastinate, and our quickness to decide that something is too hard for us. God requires only that we seek His will and the guidance, counsel, and strength to accomplish His will. He has promised that if we do this, He will most certainly answer:

> "I love those who love Me, and those who seek Me find Me." (Proverbs 8:17).

> "You will seek Me and find Me when you seek Me with all your heart." (Jeremiah 29:13).

> "Ask and it will be given to you; seek and you will find; knock and the door will be opened to you. For everyone who asks receives; he who seeks finds; and to him who knocks, the door will be opened." (Matthew 7:7-8)

God's will for us is our highest good. There is none higher! Who would not want to ask, seek, knock, in order to achieve their highest good?

All the preceding clearly and forcefully testifies to the priceless value God gives to His creation and the Godly Sanctity of Life He attaches to each of His human creations in his image, from Adam and Eve right to the last man and woman He will create before the end of the eons, the return of Christ in glory and the end of time and this world as we know it. All those who have rejected the Sanctity of Life or who have demeaned it, along with those who are doing so today through abortion and those who will do so in the future, will be forced to give an account of their violation of the Sanctity of Life to their Lord Almighty God at the Last Judgment. I wonder what they will say in their attempt to justify themselves. Will they blame the church? Will they blame government? Will they blame society and culture? Will they blame their political party? It will all be to no avail. Rejecting the Sanctity of Life is direct and arrogant opposition to God Himself. Each person has the freedom to say "Yes" or "No," and therefore the blame is theirs and theirs alone.

Human delight in creation and the Sanctity of Life has clearly and alarmingly decreased during the past six decades or so. The reasons for this may be varied, but I submit that the primary reason was the decrease in Biblical literacy accompanied by a decrease in the spirituality stemming from the timeless love of God in Christ that was a central feature of the Judeo-Christian foundation of the nation, as well as Western Civilization. This decrease in Biblical literacy and spirituality was accompanied by an increase in secular progressive liberalism and moral relativism.

Although the human delight in creation may have decreased, God's delight in His creations has not decreased, nor will it ever decrease. Only God can create, and Scripture shows that God takes great pleasure in creating. In the book of Job, chapter 38, verse 7, we're told of the heaven's response to God's creative acts:

"The morning stars sang together, and all the angels shouted for joy." As Brennan Manning said in his book, *The Signature of Jesus:*

> "Imagine the ecstasy, the cry of joy, when God makes a person in His own image! When God made you He rejoiced, and gave you as a gift, not only to your parents, but to Himself. You and I, and all our human brothers and sisters, are a response to the vast delight of God. Out of an infinite number of possibilities, God invested you, me, and all humans, with our own individual and personal existence, our own characteristics and personalities, our own DNA."

The fact that out of the billions and billions, ad infinitum, humans created, no two are exactly alike, is a testimony to God's creative power and majesty which, again, our puny human intellects cannot even begin to comprehend.

Since God, who created life, holds the Sanctity of Life so precious and high, how can we, as mere mortals, reject the Sanctity of Life, rebel against God by demeaning life, trashing life, and committing mass murder and genocide in various areas of the world, including the United States. You ask, "Where is mass murder and genocide being committed in the United States?" My response - everywhere! For mass murder and genocide is a precisely accurate description of abortion on demand.

Have we become so jaded, so degenerate, so evil, that we consider certain lives no longer of value, requiring the expenditure of resources more valuable than those lives are worth? How about the elderly who are no longer able to care for themselves? Do we simply euthanize them? How about the deformed, the disabled, who require expensive special care and resources? Do we euthanize them? How about babies in the womb who will be born with severe disabilities? Do we abort them? All of these actions have been seriously considered by authorities. The mass murder and genocide of abortion on demand, however, is no longer under consideration. It is a fact and has been for years. And it is not unreasonable to say that it is the most damnable act of all the others listed. Why? Because it is mass murder, genocide, against perfectly healthy babies in the womb for the crime of being inconvenient, inconvenient to their mother or both parents, and thus, to society as a whole.

Before we sink even deeper into the evil morass of violating the Sanctity of Life, we should seriously consider the condition of the people in the time of Noah in the Bible. They too had sunk into the morass of evil, even to the extent we're told in Genesis 6: "that every inclination of the thoughts of man's heart was only evil all the time." The earth was corrupt in God's sight and was full of violence, for all the people on earth had corrupted their ways. Again, the example of the yeast which I have used before. Just like a little yeast leavens the whole loaf, a little evil cannot be contained and restrained, but will grow until the whole product, whether an individual, group, or nation, is corrupted.

We're told, however, that Noah was a righteous man, blameless among the people of his time, and he walked with God. Noah had three sons - Shem, Ham, and Japheth. Well, we know the account of the flood that covered the earth. God instructed Noah to build an ark, with specific dimensions and characteristics large enough to hold two of every kind of species of land animals and birds, male and female, in order to continue all the species after all other life had been destroyed by the flood. The exact time for Noah and his sons to build the ark is unknown; however, estimates range from 60 years to 120 years, the latter time frame being extended to give people time to repent and turn back to God. We can imagine Noah, as an evangelist preacher, warning the people of the cataclysmic disaster to come. But they would not listen. And we can only imagine the abuse, jeers, insults, mocking, and name-calling Noah had to endure while building the ark.

Finally, the day came when God prompted two of every kind of species of land animals and birds, male and female, to come to the ark for Noah to accommodate them. God then told Noah to enter the ark with his wife, three sons and their wives, and seal it so no one else could enter. And the drenching rains came for forty days and forty nights, the floodgates of heaven were open, and all the springs of the great deep (the oceans) burst forth. Water covered the earth to its highest point, and all human and animal life, with the exception of Noah and his family and the animals in the ark, were destroyed. Efforts of secular, atheistic organizations to disprove the flood have consistently failed. The historical evidence, the ancient, literary evidence, and the wealth of scientific geological evidence overwhelmingly support the Genesis account of the flood.

The reader may wonder why I contributed much space in this chapter on the Sanctity of Life to a review of the Gospel of Salvation, followed by the account of Noah and the flood. First, the Gospel of Christ and man's salvation is the incontrovertible proof of God's divine love for His creation, and especially for His human creation. This divine love gives full meaning to the Sanctity of Life, and we mortals tamper with, demean, violate, and destroy this divine Sanctity of Life only at our terrible and terrifying peril.

Second, if this divine Sanctity of Life continues to be demeaned and violated, the corruption of the guilty persons, groups, organizations, and even nation, will grow and grow because, as emphasized, evil cannot be contained and restrained; it can only be confronted and defeated. And if the evil grows and grows, one of two conditions will be reached. First, throughout the time of growing corruption, which I would refer to as the present time, God's patience, mercy, compassion and forgiveness remain available to those who follow the Holy Spirit's leading to confess and repent of their grievous sin of violating the Sanctity of Life. But if the people, and the nation, continues to reject God's grace and refuses to repent and turn away from this ultimate violation of the Sanctity of Life, the national abomination of abortion, God will bring judgment on the land because judgment is the last resort in God's attempt to awaken the people to their corrupt condition and turn them away from their abomination. And by the way, that is precisely what God did to rid our land of the abomination of slavery. And the judgment that removed the stain of slavery from the national character was the Civil War that cost 600,000 lives.

The second condition that could result if the people refuse to repent and turn away from the abomination of abortion and its evil is allowed to grow and grow, is that eventually the peoples' hearts become so hardened that even judgment would not cure them, and they become like the people in Noah's time - that they had become so corrupt that "every inclination of the thoughts of their hearts was only evil all the time." In this condition, like the people of Noah's time, they have essentially lost the Sanctity of Life and become worthless as a people and a nation to God, to others, and to themselves, with destruction the only healing.

With abortion on demand having been legal for the past 49 years, that hardening of peoples' hearts has gradually proceeded, with more and more of the population being desensitized to a baby in the womb being decapitated and murdered. Does anyone seriously believe that God, who created life, who established the Sanctity of Life, will allow this to continue indefinitely? If so, that person has a naive, foolish, and unrealistic understanding of God's nature and is what Scripture calls a fool.

Our Founding Fathers clearly understood that of all the freedoms, liberties, rights, and blessings of Almighty God, the Sanctity of Life, or as they referred to it in the Declaration of Independence, the Right to Life, stood as the pillar of all the unalienable rights. The reason, of course, is obvious. To deny a person the Sanctity, the Right to Life, is to deny them all rights, for human rights are meaningless if you are dead.

I add, however, that the power of denying a person the right to life is given by God in HIs Word to the government authority as punishment for murder and for the purpose of maintaining justice and public safety. Also, a soldier's killing in combat during war against an aggressor is not considered murder unless the method or the circumstances are in violation of the Articles of War. The standard of justice given in Scripture as "eye for eye," "tooth for tooth," "life for life," does not refer to vengeance as some suppose, but refers to assuring that the punishment fits the crime and is not too severe or less severe.

Along with his gift of life, God stores up for each person He creates all the other manifold gifts and blessings He will distribute to that person at certain times during his/ her lifetime. Think of your own life, the multitude of gifts and blessings you have received from God - not the least of which are family and friends - and, depending on your age, the multitude of blessings to come. All swept away in an instant when the Sanctity of Life is denied a person. But that's not all. Remember the Scripture we referred to that says God ordained works for each created person to do during their lifetime, works that will honor God, honor themselves, and honor their fellowman. To deny the right to life is to deny also the opportunity to accomplish these works and rejoice in the success and fulfillment of those works. The abortionist and the people who support abortion never think about this, but the day will come when they will be forced to not only think about it, but see it and the terrible abomination, the utter horror, and the pure satanic evil of what they have done and what they supported.

To deny the Sanctity of Life is to play God, something that never works out well for us sinful human beings. We have been created in the image of God, but that does not mean that we share to some extent in His divinity. No! We carry God's image, although marred by sin, but we do not share one iota of the divine. To act as though we do is arrogant idolatry and a direct insult to Almighty God.

When the Pharisees asked Jesus, "Is it right to pay taxes to Caesar or not?" they were trying to trap Him in his words to renounce Caesar's authority so they could condemn Him to the Romans. Jesus asked them to show Him the coin used to pay the tax. They showed Him the coin and He asked them: "Whose portrait is this? And whose inscription?" "Caesar's," they replied. Then Jesus said to them: "Give to Caesar what is Caesar's, and to God what is God's."

I'm sure Jesus' words to the Democratic Party today, as well to others who support the democrat's abominable murder of the unborn, would be:

> "You must concentrate your activity on the powers and authority I have given you as a human government, and do not presume, in your arrogance and sinful pride, to trespass on any of my powers and authority I possess as Almighty God, one of which is the Sanctity of Life. Otherwise, I most assuredly will bring judgment upon you. And it will be a terrible judgment."

The following recent event depicts the extent to which the corruption of the Sanctity of Life has infected the Democratic Party. Forty-six years ago, in 1976, 107 House of Representatives Democrats voted in favor of the Hyde Amendment which prohibits using taxpayer funds to fund elective abortions. Ever since then, the Hyde Amendment has been attached to the appropriations bills that go through the House and Senate. The Democrats, for some time now, with the support of Planned Parenthood and other pro-abortionists, have been trying to abolish the Hyde Amendment. President Biden, over the years, supported the Hyde Amendment up until his candidacy for the Presidency and his inauguration. One of his promises to his constituency is to cancel the Hyde Amendment. So much for standing on principle when political expediency is at stake.

On July 29, 2021, every House Democrat who cast a vote supported an appropriations bill that did not include the Hyde Amendment. Every one of those House Democrats failed to stand up for babies in the womb on that day, and not only that, they failed to support their fellow citizens who are pro-life and honor the Sanctity of Life. They too, sacrificed principle for political expediency. Planned Parenthood, the largest abortion provider in the country and a major contributor to the Democratic Party, claimed that taxpayer funding for abortion was necessary to give poor women who cannot afford an abortion equal status with affluent women who can afford an abortion.

Archbishop Salvadore Cordileone of San Francisco had this to say about that:

> "The right to life is the most fundamental right. To use the smokescreen of abortion as an issue of health and fairness to poor women is the epitome of hypocrisy. What about the health and fairness of the baby being killed? What about giving poor women real choice, so they are supported in choosing life? This would give them fairness and equality to women of means who can afford to bring a child into the world. It is people of faith who run pro-life crisis pregnancy clinics. They are the only ones who provide poor women life-giving alternatives to having their babies killed in their wombs. They are the ones worthy to call themselves "devout Catholics!"

A majority of Americans have consistently supported the Hyde Amendment according to numerous polls. Also, in those polls, a majority of Americans strongly support restrictions to legal abortion. And a substantial number of Americans support abolishing abortion altogether.

Well, concerning that recent vote on the appropriations bill in the House that did not include the Hyde Amendment, during consideration of the appropriations resolution in the Senate, Republican Senator James Lankford of Oklahoma, saved the Hyde Amendment with his amendment that bars federal funds from being used to pay for abortions. But his amendment went further. It also blocks funding for government programs that discriminate against individual health care professionals or institutions that object to abortions.

Democratic Senator Joe Manchin of West Virginia provided the deciding vote for the measure. He joined all the Republicans who were present in the evenly divided chamber in support of Lankford's amendment. God bless Senators Lankford and Manchin.

One damning sidetone to this. Along with the Hyde Amendment which the House Democrats left out of their version of the appropriations bill, they also purposely left out the Helms Amendment, which protects American taxpayers from having to fund abortions in foreign countries. An overwhelming majority of Americans at 77% oppose having to fund such abortions. President Trump banned funding for such abortions, but President Biden promised to restore it. Apparently, funding the murdering of our own babies in the womb and wanting abortion legal right up to the moment of birth so more babies can be aborted, doesn't satisfy the Democrats. They now want us to contribute to murdering babies in foreign wombs. I cannot find the words to adequately describe my utter disgust and vehement resentment of my government using my taxes and your taxes and our fellow citizen's taxes to fund the most brutal and cruel murdering of the most innocent and helpless among us - our babies in the womb.

I thoroughly agree with Thomas Jefferson who said:

> "To compel a man to furnish funds for the propagation of ideas he disbelieves and abhors is sinful and tyrannical."

And so, to the Democrat Party's characteristics today of corruption, partisanship, dishonesty, deceitfulness, and lust for power, we can add sinful and tyrannical.

St. Augustine

Archbishop Salvadore Cordileone

Thomas Jefferson

CHAPTER 6
THE TRAVESTY OF ROE V. WADE

"Let no one be found among you who sacrifices his son or
daughter in the fire.

Deuteronomy 18:10a.

"And you took your sons and daughters whom you bore to me,
and sacrificed them as food to the idols. You slaughtered my
children and sacrificed them to the idols."

Ezekiel 16:20-21

Our two Bible passages above refer to the abominable practices of the heathen nations who were living in the land of Canaan which God had promised to Israel. Among other detestable practices, they sacrificed their children to their heathen idols. God sternly warned the Israelites that when they came into the land He promised them not to take up these heathen practices, or his judgment upon them would be severe.

As the passage from Ezekiel notes, the people, under a succession of evil kings, eventually turned from God and did adopt many of the heathen practices including sacrificing their children to idols. It was the low point in Old Testament Israel's history, and would bring God's judgment upon them.

We're told that King Manasseh, the most evil of the evil kings, shed so much innocent blood that he filled Jerusalem from end to end. And yet I wonder! Could he possibility have shed the amount of innocent blood that has been shed in our land since the passage of Roe v. Wade legalized elective abortion - the blood of over 62 million babies in the womb and counting. Just as those heathen, and then Israel, sacrificed babies to heathen idols, so today our babies are being sacrificed to an idol. And that idol's name is convenience.

I previously mentioned the two infamous Supreme Court cases that are considered by many legal authorities as the two most brazen examples of judicial activism by the high court in its history. The first was the 1857 Supreme Court's ruling in the Dred Scott v. John F. A, Sandford decision that black people were not, and never could be, citizens of the United States.

The second occasion of brazen judicial activism, when Jefferson's criterion of plain language and reasonable discernment of the Founders' intent, were grossly violated, was in 1973 with the Roe v. Wade decision. As I mentioned, Roe v. Wade was even a grosser violation of the Court's mandate to interpret law and not to make law than Dred Scott, since that decision refused freedom and citizenship, whereas Roe v. Wade refused life itself, and opened the floodgates of the most brutal, cruel, and murderous genocide of the modern ages against the most helpless and innocent of our citizens. Dred Scott was reversed and thank God Roe vs. Wade has finally been reversed after nearly fifty years and the land freed from this abominable law.

It appears obvious that the seven liberal justices who approved Roe v. Wade were determined from the outset to find some kind of justification in the Constitution upon which to base the right of legalized abortion. The justification need not be obvious, it need not be plain or clear, it just had to be sufficient to get a majority of the justices to vote for it. And so, they totally ignored Thomas Jefferson's advice on interpreting the Constitution which he wrote in a letter to Supreme Court Justice William Johnson on June 12, 1823, and which I mentioned in a previous chapter. They also ignored the advice of James Wilson, signer of both the Declaration of Independence and the Constitution and one of the original Justices on the Supreme Court.

I ask the reader's indulgence for my repetition, but I think It is worth repeating Jefferson's statement, along with giving Wilson' statement, in order to properly emphasize just how far those seven justices went in their desperate efforts to find within the Constitution something that could be used to justify legalized abortion. In his letter concerning interpretation Jefferson said:

> "On every question of construction, carry ourselves back to the time when the Constitution was adopted, recollect the spirit manifested in the debates, and instead of trying what meaning may be squeezed out of the text, or invented against it, conform to the probable one in which it was passed."

Justice James Wilson agreed with Jefferson when he said:

> "The first and governing maxim in the interpretation of a statute is to discover the meaning of those who made it."

The seven justices who declared war on the most innocent and helpless among us made it clear that convenience was a major issue. Their biased reasoning included the possibility, and I quote, that "having unwanted children may force upon the woman a distressful life and future." Well yes, that's true, but there are many things in life that may cause a person to have a distressful life and future. My not having a job and being unable to support myself and family would undoubtedly cause me to have a distressful life and future. Do I have a constitutional right not to have a distressful life and future? Does the Constitution guarantee this?

The seven justices reasoned that having unwanted children may bring "imminent psychological harm." Again, there are many stresses in life that can cause imminent psychological harm. Do I have a constitutional right not to suffer imminent psychological harm? Does the Constitution guarantee this?

The seven justices reasoned that "caring for the unwanted child may tax the mother's physical and mental health." Again, yes! Anyone who is a parent knows that raising children is one of the toughest jobs a person can have in this life. Children, especially younger ones, can be very demanding and certainly the mother's, as well as the father's, physical and mental health will be taxed at times to the point of exhaustion. But do they have a constitutional right not to be physically or mentally taxed? Can the Constitution guarantee this?

The seven justices reasoned that having the unwanted child "may cause distress for all concerned who are associated with the unwanted child." I assume they had in mind not only the parents, but the grandparents, other children, etc. Well, again, yes! It may very well cause distress to other members of the family. But again, do others associated with the unwanted child have a constitutional right not to be distressed? Can the Constitution guarantee this?

It stuns the imagination to think that such biased and ridiculous reasoning could come from seven justices of the United States Supreme Court who are supposedly some of the most brilliant legal minds in the country. Their rationale has nothing to do with the Constitution and was probably designed to stir up pro-abortion feelings and emotions rather than stick to their responsibility for strict legal adjudication and procedure.

The court rejected the argument that a fetus should be considered a person with a legal and constitutional right to life. Their rationale for rejecting this was their claim that there was still extensive disagreement over when an unborn fetus becomes a living being. They held that the court need not try to resolve the difficult question of when life begins because those trained in the disciplines of medicine, philosophy, and theology are unable to arrive at any consensus. Therefore, the Judiciary at this point in the development of man's knowledge, was not in a position to speculate as to the answer.

How is that for a copout by those distinguished justices? The question of when life begins was the central issue of the whole matter. It was, and remains, the cohesive linchpin of the case and the determining factor which should have dominated the discussion and dialogue. The court should have brought in the top experts in medicine, philosophy, and theology to testify. If a consensus could not be reached as to when life begins, then the best and the most just option would have been the legal doctrine of "Do no harm!" The decision they made was arbitrary, and arbitrary decisions are not popular in a court of law. It is interesting that Justice Blackmun, the justice that guided the discussion and wrote the final decision, admitted that he made an arbitrary decision when he divided the baby's term into trimesters, and held that there should be no restrictions on abortion during the first trimester since there was no consensus on whether the fetus at this point was or was not a person.

Of course, the seven justices were not interested in the legal doctrine of "Do no harm!" Their priority was to find something, anything, in the Constitution they could use to legalize abortion. You would think that they would have given great attention and weight to the Founding Fathers' and their legal view on abortion. The Founding Fathers stood firmly against abortion. Both the Colonial Statutory Law and the Common Law of that day were also against abortion.

Dr. Blaine Consatti, a columnist and research fellow at the Family Policy Institute of Washington, claims that during the Founding era, one of the most authoritative sources for law was William Blackstone's "Commentaries on the Laws of England." Blackstone was very popular with the Founding Fathers and was frequently cited in the American political writings of the founding era. In his commentaries, Blackstone held that an individual's right to life is an "immediate gift of God." Blackstone also considered fetuses in the mother's womb to be legally born. The law considered a fetus to be his or her own person, independent of the mother. Therefore, the right to life was legally binding as soon as an infant is able to stir in the mother's womb.

When the Founders stated that life begins with the infant's stirring in the womb, referred to as the "quickening," they were not making an arbitrary decision. They based their opinion upon a thorough and reasonable assessment of the best scientific, legal, and medical jurisprudence of the time. The quickening was the first positive evidence of pregnancy and the presence of a fetus. They did not have X-ray equipment, ultrasounds and other modern equipment of today that provides proof of pregnancy much, much, earlier than the quickening - actually just a few days after conception. Without this modern technology, it was assumed that life began with the quickening of the infant in the mother's womb, a reasonable and understandable assumption. Had the Founders had access to the discoveries of modern biology, they most certainly would have agreed that life begins at conception, and that the fetus is to be protected from conception to delivery, and that abortion is not acceptable at any time during the full term of pregnancy.

There is no doubt that the Founders recognized that unborn infants are owed the full protection of the law. They took the Blackstone position that any abortion perpetrated after the quickening of an infant in the mother's womb was a "heinous misdemeanor." Founding Father and original Supreme Court Justice James Wilson, mentioned before, taught his law students that "with consistency, beautiful and understanding, human life, from its commencement to its close, is protected by the Common Law. In the contemplation of law, life begins when the infant is first able to stir in the womb. By the law, this life is protected not only from immediate destruction, but from every degree of actual violence, and in some cases, from every degree of danger.

Henry Bracton (1216 - 1272), known as the "Father of the Common Law," categorized the abortion of a formed or quickened fetus as a "form of homicide, the slaying of man by man."

In the years following the American Revolution, medical discoveries increasingly encouraged America and England lawmakers to come to the conclusion that life began before the infant stirred in the mother's womb. The old traditional idea of quickening was questioned , and in 1803, England adopted a law that established severe penalties for aborting infants in the first trimester as well.

Physiologists came to believe that the child is a living being from the moment of conception. The state of Maine, in 1840, became the first state to ban abortion of infants, "quickened or not." Subsequent federal and state laws banning abortion altogether were a logical sequence of the Founding Fathers' absolute commitment and reverence for the "self-evident" and "unalienable" right to life.

> "We hold these truths to be self-evident, that all men are created equal, that they are endowed by their Creator with certain

unalienable rights, that among these are Life, Liberty, and the Pursuit of Happiness."

Jameson Taylor, in his "The Founding Fathers and the Right to Life," says that it was by design that the Declaration of Independence, as written by Thomas Jefferson, characterizes the right to life as the first of those three foundational rights - Life, Liberty, and the Pursuit of Happiness - for the sake of which government itself is established. In a political system where there is no guarantee of the right to life, legitimate political authority simply does not exist, and if there is no guarantee of life for both the weak and the strong, the rights to liberty and the pursuit of happiness for all are at risk. Without the right to life, all other rights are tenuous at best and subject to the will of tyranny.

A self-evident truth, by the way, is a truth that is evident to anyone who is sane. Therefore, persons who do not accept that all human beings, including the unborn babies in the womb, are endowed by their Creator with an unalienable right to life, e.g., the pro-abortionists, primarily Democrat, who insist that abortion must be legal right up to the moment of birth, are by this definition, insane.

To get back to the seven justices who passed Roe v. Wade, they were busy, busy, scouring the Constitution, searching for a constitutional right to legalize abortion. Finally, they introduced the concept of a constitutional "right to privacy." There was one problem, however. The Constitution does not contain the word "privacy," nor the phrase "right to privacy." The justices maintained, however, that this right to privacy can be found in the Fourteenth Amendment's concept of personal liberty, and restriction upon state action, or in the ninth amendment's reservation of rights to the people. Either the Fourteenth Amendment or the Ninth Amendment, they argued, were broad enough to contain a woman's right to choose whether or not to terminate a pregnancy.

The Fourteenth Amendment contains the following: "No state shall make or enforce any law which shall abridge the privileges or immunities of citizens of the United States, nor shall any state deprive any person of life, liberty, or property, without due process of law; nor deny to any person within its jurisdiction the equal protection of the laws."

Again, the justices claimed that the right to privacy can be found in this statement, and that the right to privacy gives the woman the right to kill the baby in her womb. One may ask: "Just where can it be found?" If it's in there, it is exceptionally well hidden. It is supreme irony of the most evil kind that the justices used this amendment which forbids the state to deprive any person of life and liberty without due process, nor to deny to any person within its jurisdiction the equal protection of the laws, to justify the murder of babies in the womb.

The Ninth Amendment, which the justices also cited reads as follows: "The enumeration in the Constitution of certain rights shall not be construed to deny or disparage others retained by the people." The justices held that the right to privacy was one of those rights not specifically mentioned in the Constitution that should not be denied or disparaged.

The question that should have been put to those justices, with a demand for an answer is: "How is it that these amendments which forbid the states to deprive any person of life and liberty, nor to deny equal protection of the laws, nor to deny or disparage other rights retained by the people, apply only to the pregnant woman, and not to the baby in her womb? Their answer, of course, would have been their arbitrary decision that the baby in the first trimester is not a person, and therefore is not addressed by these amendments.

With modern advances in medicine and biology, to consider the baby not a person in the first trimester stands out as an arbitrary decision by the court. It is blatantly obvious that throughout the proceedings the justices gave scant attention to babies in the womb. Guarding the nation's interest in protecting its unborn children seemed to have no priority in their deliberations. Apparently the justices did not know, or did not care, that an infant's heart begins beating at five weeks of gestation, early in the first trimester, or that at eight weeks, early in the first trimester, brain waves can be measured, and at twelve weeks, the child can and does cry and sometimes sucks his/her thumb. Again, their sole priority was finding something in the Constitution they could use to justify mothers killing their babies in the womb.

I mentioned before, and it must be emphasized, that the right to privacy upon which the justices based their case for abortion is not in the Constitution or the amendments they cited. How then did they manage to establish this right and then use it to justify their case for abortion? The answer is that the justification was based in large part on "smoke and mirrors." The justices found a Penumbra in the Constitution and emanations from that penumbra that indicated a right to privacy, and that right to privacy protected a pregnant woman's decision whether or not to abort the pregnancy. If you are unfamiliar with this, you are undoubtedly asking "What is a penumbra?"

A penumbra involves the rights guaranteed by implication in a constitution or other governing documents. The key word here to remember is "implication." The rights are not specifically spelled out but are implied by the language and circumstances referred to. The Third Amendment was used as an example for such a penumbra. The Third Amendment reads: "No soldier shall, in time of peace, be quartered in any house without the consent of the owner, nor in time of war, but in a manner to be prescribed by law."

What does quartering soldiers in civilian residences have to do with a woman choosing to abort her baby? The rationale went like this. To quarter soldiers in civilian residences was forbidden by the Constitution because it would be an invasion of the homeowner's privacy. Therefore, although not spelled out in clear language, the fact that it was forbidden implies that a penumbra of the right to privacy does exist in the Constitution.

According to Washington Post journalist Desmond S. Caulfield Bowie, Justice Douglas, one of the seven justices, when he was unable to find a generalized right to privacy in the Constitution itself, for the simple reason that neither the "right to privacy" nor the word "privacy," is in the Constitution, he went on to discover a "penumbra," taken from the Latin "paene umbra," meaning "almost a shadow." This penumbra was formed, he said, by unspecified "emanations" from the Bill of Rights. Justice Douglas then placed within this extra-constitutional, almost a shadow, penumbra a hitherto unknown "zone of privacy," which was transformed into a "right of privacy" by the court's simple substitution of the term "right" for "zone" in its later decisions.

Justice Douglas used the term penumbra when he wanted to refer to a "peripheral area," or an "indistinct boundary" of something specific. Justice Holmes, another of the seven justices, used the term penumbra to describe the "gray area where logic and principle falter."

So, there you have it! Legalized abortion was decided not on the basis of solid constitutional grounds, but on the basis of an emanation of a penumbra to the Constitution, on the basis of the gray area in a document where logic and principle falter, and where clarity and rationale can only be gained by use of a penumbra, on the basis of a peripheral area and indistinct boundary which only a penumbra to the Constitution can clarify.

After the seven justices, through their "legal" sleight of hand, introduced their newly found constitutional right to privacy, they, with virtually no further explanation of this discovered right, ruled that the U.S. Constitution's guarantee of liberty covered a right to privacy, which in turn, was broad enough to cover a woman's right to legalized abortion. How this mysterious trinity of privacy, penumbra, and emanations had eluded the top legal scholars for the then 176 years of our constitutional history, was, and is, a question left unaddressed by the court. Again, I quote journalist Desmond S. Caulfield Bowie who said:

> "The right to abortion is little more than an intellectually clumsy contrivance of the Supreme Court and an astonishing display of judicial arrogance."

Since that day in 1973, over 62 million babies have been brutally and cruelly murdered on the basis of an emanation of a penumbra to the Constitution. It is beyond human intellect to fully comprehend the extent of satanic evil involved in this, and for which our nation will be called for account unless we turn away from it through national prayer and repentance.

There were two dissenting opinions on the court by Justice Byron White and Justice William Rehnquist. These two justices refused to participate in the shenanigans, judicial activism, and judicial arrogance of the other seven justices. It is interesting to consider their dissents. Justice White believed that the legality of abortion should be left with the people and the political processes the people have devised to govern their affairs. In his dissent, Justice White said:

> "I find nothing in the language or history of the Constitution to support the court's judgment. The court simply fashions and announces a new constitutional right for pregnant women and, with scarcely any reason or authority for its action, invests that right with sufficient substance to override most existing State abortion statutes…As an exercise of raw judicial power, the court perhaps has the authority to do what it does today, but in my view, its judgment is an improvident and extravagant exercise of the power of judicial review that the Constitution extends to the court."

In Justice William Rehnquist's dissent, he said:

> "To reach its result, the court necessarily has had to find within the scope of the Fourteenth Amendment a right that was apparently completely unknown to the drafters of the amendment. As early as 1821, the first State law dealing directly with abortion was enacted by the Connecticut Legislature. By the time of the adoption of the Fourteenth Amendment in 1868, there were at least 36 laws enacted by State or Territorial Legislatures limiting abortion. While many States have amended or updated their laws, 21 of the laws on the books in 1868 remain in effect today."

Summary:

1. The right to life is unalienable because it is not of human origin, but of divine origin.
2. Children's value to God and the nation are not determined by whether or not the parents want them. Their value and rights, as well as ours, are inherent to the fact that we are human beings created in the image of God.

3. From conception to birth, throughout life unto death, each human life bears the marks of the Creator's hand. Thus, we are to uphold the sanctity of all human life, for each life gives witness to the Lord's sovereignty and handiwork.

4. A fundamental right to abortion does not exist in the writing and language of the Constitution or its amendments. It is inconceivable that the framers intended constitutional protection for abortion as a fundamental right. From their perspective, the unborn child has a fundamental right to life, a right that would be denied by abortion.

5. Laws in the American states during the founding era criminalized abortion from the beginning, which with medical science available at the time, they considered as the "quickening." If modern medical science had been available to them, there is no doubt, given their stance against abortion, that they would have considered the beginning of life to be at conception. The laws against abortion at the time were crafted by many of the same individuals who framed the Constitution.

6. It is the height of intellectual dishonesty to claim that the authors of the Constitution and its amendments intended to protect abortion, as many who are pro-abortion would like us to believe. The fact that so many courts and judges have for so long upheld a legal right to abortion, which is antagonistic to the Constitution itself, reveals the rogue nature of the modern judiciary, a situation that Thomas Jefferson feared and wrote about.

7. The Democratic Party demands that there be no restrictions to abortion and that it be legalized right up to the moment of birth. This is nothing short of infanticide. It is also in direct contradiction to the obvious intent of the Founders, as well as the weight of the Common Law which compels the Congress and the Courts to prohibit abortion, for any reason, in the second and third trimesters. Abortion at any stage of pregnancy is murder, as I show in the next two chapters, but nevertheless, abortion in the second and third trimesters is clearly murder of a

human being and cannot be justified by a penumbra to the Constitution, by the fourteenth and ninth amendments, by the mother's health, or a woman's right to choose.

8. Pro-abortionists like to cite the rights of minorities who are "vulnerable" and "powerless." Yet, the rights of that minority who is unquestionably the most vulnerable and powerless - the unborn babies in the womb - are ignored by them. This is rampant hypocrisy at its most disgusting level.

9. Abortion is legal today, not because the justices did not know when life begins, but because the justices, as well as all pro-abortionists, do not know what true liberty is. For many people, liberty is the right to do whatever one can get away with. Our Founding Fathers would have condemned such an attitude as madness. Because both life and liberty are "endowments," or "gifts," from God, true liberty is the proper exercise of liberty which requires that man adhere to the "laws of nature and nature's God in the use of his freedom and liberty. Therefore, the so-called "new freedom" heralded by liberal judges and other partisans of the "sexual revolution" and abortion, is not freedom at all, but nothing less than a new enslavement to gross sin and direct rebellion against the laws of nature and nature's God.

10. The logical development of the Declaration of Independence and the recognition that all men are created equal and endowed with the divine gifts of life, liberty, and the pursuit of happiness, signaled the eventual end of slavery. The vast majority of the Founders understood this and strongly supported it. However, the political positions of the abolitionists on one hand, and the pro-slavery coalition on the other, were so deeply entrenched that resolution of the evil of slavery was no longer possible through dialogue, reason, and bipartisanship. It would require federal intervention and the greatest and bloodiest war of our history to abolish slavery. There are some issues that are totally resistant to diplomacy and political compromise. Slavery was one of those.

I submit that abortion is another issue unsolvable through dialogue and political compromise. The positions of both pro-life and pro-abortion factions are so deeply engrained and held that I see no possibility for mutual compromise. Therefore, just as the Declaration of Independence's recognition of God's gift of liberty to all men, required federal intervention to abolish slavery, so the Declaration of Independence's recognition of the unalienable right to life given by God to all men, will most probably require federal intervention to end abortion. And the first step in this process has been taken by the Supreme Court in its repeal of Roe vs. Wade. Moreover, for those who consider themselves Christian and believe that each baby is a creation of God, created in God's image, there can be no compromise with the pro-abortion faction, for such compromise would be an attack on God, His image, and His purpose.

Dr. Harold O.J. Brown, Professor of Theology at Reformed Theological Seminary, in Charlotte, North Carolina, in his essay *A Decisive Turn to Paganism,* calls the statement by the seven judges who handed down the Roe v. Wade decision, "We do not know when human life begins," the greatest lie of the 20th century. Now, more than four decades later, we have more than 62 million fewer Americans alive today who would be between the ages of twenty to forty. It stuns the imagination to think of the amount of human intellect, human knowledge, human potential, and human skill denied the nation through abortion of those more than 62 million souls. How many potential George Washingtons, Thomas Jeffersons, James Madisons, Abigail Adams, Dolley Madisons, Abraham Lincolns, Jonathan Edwards, St. Augustines, Martin Luthers, John Bunyans, George Whitefields, Winston Churchills, William Wilberforces, Eleanor Roosevelts, and I could go on and on, were discarded through abortion and denied to us by the abortionist's knife.

That "greatest lie" of the 20th century by those seven judges, referred to by Dr. Brown, is of great comfort to the pro-abortionists among us who demand the right to terminate life in the womb up to the moment of birth in the most brutal and horrible ways at will. It is of great comfort because of the threat posed to abortion by the Supreme Court's comment that "if it is shown that life begins at conception or at the fetus stage, then life is an unalienable right of that fetus and abortion is a denial of that right. Therefore, there can be no legalized abortion. The pro-abortionists want to remove this threat by having Roe v. Wade codified - that is, having Congress pass legislation making Roe v. Wade the law of the land.

The bottom line is that Roe v. Wade was a clear repudiation of the Biblical Judeo-Christian teachings, upon which our nation is founded, and which teaches that each human being is created in the image of God. I discuss this further in the following two chapters.

The Supreme Court justices, with the exception of the two dissenting judges, did not seem to know what they had done. They had unleashed what would become the greatest holocaust, the greatest murderous genocide in modern history. It would be greater than the mass genocides of the three top mass murderers of the 20th century - Adolph Hitler, Joseph Stalin, and Mao Tse tung. Hitler, Stalin, and Mao murdered their millions and millions, but their combined total falls short of the more than 62 million murdered after the seven judges' passage of Roe v. Wade.

Then too, the mass genocide of Roe v. Wade can be considered worse than Hitler's, Stalin's, and Mao's, not only because of the numbers, but because the mass genocides of Hitler, Stalin, and Mao were conducted against victims of all ages, whereas the mass genocide of Roe v. Wade has been, and continues to be, solely conducted against the most innocent and helpless among us, our babies in the womb, and even, in some cases, outside the womb. I can only imagine the utter horror of those seven justices when God showed them the results of their playing fast and loose with the Word of God and the Constitution of the United States.

We are utter fools if we think we can continue this genocide of abortion against our babies in the womb and not come under the judgment of God. God is loving, God is patient, God is merciful, and God calls us to stop murdering our babies, who are His babies, and return to Him so He can forgive us for the sake of his Son, cleanse us of innocent blood through the Blood of his Son, and be reconciled and restored to Him. But if we refuse his call and continue on with this genocide of abortion against our most helpless and innocent, Scripture is clear that we. just like Old Testament Israel, will suffer God's judgment. And that judgment will be more terrible than we can imagine, for only such terrible judgment can remove the deep stain of the blood of more than 62 million babies' whose lives were, and continue to be, snuffed out through abortion. We have the example of Old Testament Israel who sacrificed their children as a warning of God's judgment. Their cities were destroyed, their land polluted, their capital Jerusalem totally destroyed, their Temple, an architectural wonder, totally destroyed with not one stone remaining on another, and the people taken to Babylon into captivity for seventy years.

Only when we, as a nation, return to our faith in the Creator Who gives us life and liberty through his Son, and seek his forgiveness and cleansing, can we be freed from our enslavement to the gross sin of abortion and our direct rebellion against our God and Savior. And with that return, we will be truly free.

And only when the Democratic Party retreats from its demands for abortion right up to the moment of birth, only when the Democratic Party removes abortion as the flagship of the Party, only when the Democratic Party removes legalized abortion as one of the main planks of its Democratic Party's National Platform, only when the Democratic Party turns from its policies that primarily serve special interests, and emphasizes policies that serve the common interests and welfare of the American people, only then can they claim some modicum of respect as a political party.

Until then, the politically corrupt and spiritually corrupt Democratic Party of today remains a clear and present danger to the Judeo-Christian foundation of our nation, to our political system established by our Founding Fathers, and to our Constitution. Until then, the politically and spiritually corrupt Democratic Party remains an ungodly, un-American, unhinged organization.

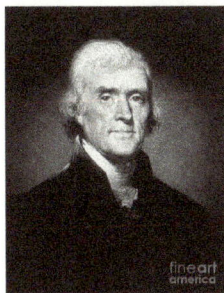

Thomas Jefferson

Justice James Wilson

Sir William Blackstone

Henry Bracton

Dr. Harold O. J. Brown

Justice Blackmun

Justice Burger

Justice Douglas

Justice Brennan

Justice Steware   *Justice Marshall*   *Justice Powell*

The seven Justices who declared war on the unborn.

Justice White   *Justice Rehnquist*

The two Justices who defended the unborn.

CHAPTER 7
ABORTION: THE ULTIMATE EVIL

"Before I formed you in the womb, I knew you;
before you were born, I set you apart,
I appointed you as a prophet to the nations"

Jeremiah 1:5

"For you created my inmost being;
You knit me together in my mother's womb.
I praise you because I am fearfully and wonderfully made;
Your works are wonderful, I know that full well."

Psalm 139:13,14

The two greatest and most controversial social issues the United States has faced since its founding are slavery and abortion. Both issues are spiritual, social, and political in their context. Both issues constitute stains on the national fabric, and both Issues involve direct rebellion against God Who, as our Declaration of Independence reminds us, creates all men equal and endows them with Life, Liberty, and the Pursuit of Happiness.

Delegates to the Constitutional Convention of 1787 hotly debated the issue of slavery. George Mason of Virginia argued eloquently against slavery, warning his fellow delegates:

> "Every master of slaves is born a petty tyrant. They bring the judgment of heaven on a country. As nations cannot be rewarded or punished in the next world, they must be in this. By an

inevitable chain of causes and effects, Providence punishes national sins by national calamities."

John Mason was right. Judgment would come to the United States for the national sin of slavery. Seventy three years after the Constitutional Convention, judgment came with the national calamity of the Civil War, our bloodiest war in which we lost more men than in all our previous and subsequent wars. It took a terrible price, but the stain of slavery was removed from the national tapestry.

The current stain on our national tapestry is abortion, and as I discussed in the previous chapter, judgment will surely come unless we, as a nation, turn to God, repent of this horrific sin of abortion, and seek his forgiveness and reconciliation.

We would do well to heed the example of Old Testament Israel who reached the depths of sin and decadence when they resorted to child sacrifice. God brought terrible judgment upon them because He knew that only such judgment would awaken them to their evil and turn them back to Him. We would also do well to heed the Psalmist's warning given in Psalm 94:21-23:

> "Can a corrupt throne (government) be allied with you - one that brings on misery by its decrees? They band together against the righteous and *condemn the innocent to death... (emphasis mine)*. He will repay them for their sins and destroy them for their wickedness; the Lord our God will destroy them."

Like Old Testament Israel, our nation has resorted to child sacrifice, for that is precisely what abortion is. Again, I ask, "Are we so foolish, ignorant, and arrogant, to think we can continue indefinitely murdering our's and God's babies without his response of judgment. God will do what He has to do to cleanse us of this abominable sin and turn our hearts back to Him.

In the previous chapter "The Sanctity of Life," God's delight in creating you, me, and every human being in his image was emphasized. Just as God told Jeremiah in the passage quoted at this chapter's beginning: "Before I formed you in the womb, I knew you..." makes it clear that God, in his all-knowing omniscience, knew you, me, and every human being He would create even before He created the heavens, the earth, the seas, and all they contain. And not only did He know you, me, and every human being He would create until the end of time, He knew everything about us, our DNA, our members, what capabilities, talents, skills He would bless us with. And knowing all this, and being a God of purpose, He ordained individual works for each of us to do that would glorify Him, fulfill his will and purpose for us, and bring us to our highest good in Him.

Psalm 127: 3-5 expresses God's delight in blessing his people with children. Solomon, writing under the inspiration of the Holy Spirit, tells us:

> "Sons are a heritage from the Lord, children a reward from Him. Like arrows in the hands of a warrior are sons born in one's youth. Blessed is the man whose quiver is full of them."

Abortion murders that creation of God in HIs own image. Abortion is rebellion against God's plan for that individual, the works He ordained for that individual, His will and purpose for that individual, and the individual's highest good through his Creator. Abortion is therefore an abasement of both the person's soul and the soul of the nation that promotes abortion. Our nation has been greatly abased by the evil of abortion. The United States is one of only four nations where abortions occur throughout all nine months of pregnancy. The United States is one of only seven countries that allows abortion of a child that can hear the mother's heartbeat.

God has revealed Himself to man primarily through Christ and His Word, but also through his creative genius, which is clearly seen in each human being He forms. We truly are "fearfully and wonderfully made," which the other passage at the beginning of this chapter says. For example, God created in each of us a three pound hard drive (our brain) that can store 15 trillion pieces of information. He also crafted for us an engine (our heart) that beats over 2 billion times by age 70, and seldom needs repairs. Abortion stills that brain before it can even get a good start storing that 15 trillion pieces of information. Abortion shuts down that engine, the heart, with no or only relatively few beats of that potential two billion beats or more.

The effects of abortion on our nation were briefly addressed in the previous chapter. Additional statistics are presented here because it is vitally important that every citizen understand just how truly and unimaginably devastating those effects have been. The statistics come from the National Right to Life Educational Foundation, and from Lutherans for Life.

There have been over 62 million abortions in the United States since Roe v. Wade was passed in 1973. There were over 800,000 abortions in 2017. That is nearly 2,400 abortions per day, 98 per hour, one every 34 seconds. Of all pregnancies that resulted in either live birth or abortion in 2017, 18.4% resulted in abortion.

To try and wrap one's mind around that statistic of more than 62 million abortions, consider the following. Total American casualties from every war we have fought since 1775 (249 years) are around 1.5 million. That is more than 60.5 million casualties less than the casualties from abortion alone since only 1973. Or consider this: The population of California is 39.51 million. The population of Florida is 21.48 million. The combined population of both states is 60.99 million. That is over one million less than the 62 million abortions since 1973. Try to imagine this: If you emptied both California and Florida of every man, woman, and child inhabitants, you would still be short of the total number of abortions performed since 1973. In God's Name, what have we as a nation done? The full satanic evil of this is hard to grasp with our limited human intellect. In the following narrative, I have included information from the National Committee for Faith and Family to supplement my own discussion.

Abortion is the place where religion and politics get entangled. Some say that abortion is a political matter only and that "separation of church and state," that misinterpreted, misunderstood, and misused phrase that is not in the Constitution, should prevent religion from getting involved. This is utter foolishness, and either blatant ignorance of the Constitution or a desperate attempt to avoid discussion of what abortion really entails.

Abortion is the taking of life, and since when is life not a vital part of religion, or the creation of life a central doctrine of religious faith. Either God forbids the taking of innocent human life or He does not. It is impossible to put up a mythical wall of separation around the issue. Protecting human life is a critical reason why governments even exist in the first place.

In an article entitled *African-American women are Exploited by Abortion,* Mrs. Akua Furlow writes:

> "Women are being exploited by abortion, especially African-American women. They have been duped into identifying the pro-choice movement with the fight for civil rights, whereas medical abortion is the induced death of a developing human baby - the destruction of a child's fundamental rights, as well as the child's civil rights."

Pre-born children are the only people group discriminated against based solely on where they live - in a womb. Is such discrimination increased if it is a black woman's womb? Consider these facts: From. 1882 to 1968, 3,446 blacks were lynched. From 1973 to 1998, 12 million black babies were aborted. Blacks total 11% of the U.S. population, yet they comprise 33% of abortions. Black women are more than three times as likely as white women to have an abortion.

A 1990 study of maternal deaths from legal abortion from 1972 to 1985, found that minority women were three times more likely to die after a legal abortion than a white woman. A 1994 "Post Abortion Research Study of African-American women" showed that of 126 women who responded to a questionnaire, 81% indicated one or more psychological complaints. Of the complaints identified, 60% felt feelings of guilt, 40% reported that they had feelings of regret and remorse, 55% reported crying and depression, and 35% stated an inability to forgive themselves for having an abortion.

For every three black babies born, two are aborted. Every month, of more than 133,000 babies aborted, more than 41,000 are Black Americans. It is no accident that 78% of abortion facilities are located in or near predominantly minority neighborhoods. The history of

America's number one abortion provider, "Planned Parenthood," reeks with the stench of racism and bigotry that adds another level to the insidious attack that has been waged on African-American women throughout the United States. Through programs such as the Negro Project of 1929, Planned Parenthood began to spin a web of deception by baiting the African-American community with the pretense of "family planning" and other "health services." It would be time well-spent if African-Americans, especially those Planned Parenthood uses for its "public service" campaigns, would spend an afternoon doing firsthand research on this organization that has caused the astronomical decline in the African-American birth rate.

It bears repeating that abortion discriminates against babies in the womb. Abortion denies them equality and their fundamental and unalienable right to life and their unalienable civil rights to liberty and the pursuit of happiness. Abortion does not just kill something, abortion kills someone. Abortion kills someone created by the hands of God in the image of God. Abortion kills someone redeemed by the Son of God through his suffering and death on the cross and his resurrection from the dead. Abortion kills someone who will never be the person - black or white, red or brown or yellow - that God intended for him/her to be. Abortion kills someone and wounds that someone's mother, and often times that someone's father and other family members.

The good news is that there is hope and help for those experiencing an unplanned pregnancy. There is hope and healing for those who have fallen prey to the lies of Planned Parenthood and the pro-abortionists and have made an abortion decision.

Although Roe v. Wade has been repealed, and the abortion issue relegated to the States, abortions are still occurring in large numbers, with the radical Democrats and only a few others, demanding no restrictions on abortions.

The good news is found in the strength, and love, and forgiveness of God through the cross of his Son Jesus Christ. The good news is that Crisis Pregnancy Centers exist throughout the country to offer support to women with unwanted pregnancies so they can carry the child to birth and then decide whether to keep the child or give the child up to adoption. Either way, the child lives, praise God.

During the busy daily details of our lives, it is easy to sometimes forget the things that matter most - in other words, the "first things." Also, when something, even something as evil as abortion, becomes commonplace, it is easy to become desensitized to it and just take it for granted. This is precisely what Satan and the pro-abortionists hope we will do. We sometimes need to set aside time and devote the energy to remember anew what is important. This is certainly true of the value of human life. We each, as citizens, have a responsibility in the civic realm to work for the protection of the lives of our unborn.

Our Founding Fathers established this nation on the foundation of Judeo-Christianity with liberty and justice for all. Yet, where is the liberty for the aborted baby in the womb, the liberty to live free, grow, prosper, raise a family, and enjoy the life given by God. Where is the justice for the aborted baby in the womb, the most helpless and innocent among us, the justice of fair treatment and equity, the justice of care and protection, the justice of being treated equally with that baby's live counterparts outside the womb.

Since we humans are made in God's image, it logically follows that how we treat other people is how we treat God. It is rank hypocrisy to say that you love God, and yet hate your fellow human being. As the Apostle John tells us in 1John 4:20b:

> "If anyone says, 'I love God,' yet hates his brother, he is a liar. For anyone who does not love his brother, whom he has seen, cannot love God whom he has not seen."

This has direct application to the issue of abortion. There are many pro-abortionists, including celebrities and government officials, who claim to be devout Christians and love God, yet they adamantly support abortion which is an act of pure hate toward the most innocent and helpless. They would strongly deny this hatred, but what else is it? There is certainly no love involved in decapitating a fellow human being in the womb. As the Apostle John says: "Such a person is a liar and is deluding and deceiving himself.

Each baby is created in the image of God. Therefore, as individuals and as a society, the way we treat babies in the womb is the way we feel about God. If we have contempt for that life in the womb, then we have contempt for the one who creates that life. The Gospel tells us that the Son of God rescued us when we were helpless:

> "At just the right time, when we were still powerless, Christ died for the ungodly". (Romans 5:6).

If Jesus rescues us when we are at our most powerless, should we not be willing to follow his example in the case of those who are most powerless of all - the babies in the womb who are legally unprotected from death.

Unborn babies are too often perceived as useless and inconvenient, and for this reason, they are considered as expendable. Abortion is viewed as a rational economic choice instead of the abominable sin and evil it actually is. As every parent knows, or should know, we must not only care for babies because their lives are precious to God, but also because they are a great blessing to us. Raising children, as God directs in his Word, is not only the most difficult job in this life, but the most important and rewarding one. God gives babies to parents, not to drain their finances and resources, but to make a positive contribution to their lives and the lives of others.

Children are the legacy and heritage of their parents. It has been said that "a good life is one that makes a difference, one that leaves a lasting legacy, and one that finishes well." Through our children, we make a difference, for they carry on the values and virtues of the parents. Through our children, we leave a lasting legacy, for they build on the family's tradition and heritage. And when the time comes to depart this life, to die surrounded by one's children is to finish well. As the Psalmist says:

> "Children are a great gift from God."

When Jesus was asked by one of the lawyers: "Of all the commandments, which is the most important?" Jesus answered him: "The most important one is this: 'Hear O Israel, the Lord our God, the

Lord is one. Love the Lord your God with all your heart and with all your soul and with all your mind and with all your strength.' The second is this: 'Love your neighbor as yourself.' There is no commandment greater than these.

If one is not to love anything more than God, one is to love God with all one's resources so nothing is left over to compete with God. And if we are never to do any harm to our neighbor, then we are to care for him and love him as we do for ourselves. Thus, the opposite to devaluing life is to protect life and, according to the Bible, showing love to those around us - especially to those most vulnerable - is not optional, but mandatory. It is bound up in whether or not we truly love God.

In many societies, children are assigned to a marginal place, In Greek and Roman civilizations, newborn infants could simply be left out to die, thrown away as garbage the parents did not want. The Church, during the Roman Empire, would take these children in and adopt them. The Israelites also knew better than many societies the value of children and gave children legal protection. It is interesting, however, that Jesus' disciples assumed that the value of children was marginal as far as Jesus' time was concerned.

We are told in Mark 10:13-14:

> "People were bringing little children to Jesus to have Him touch them, but the disciples rebuked them. When Jesus saw this, He was indignant. He said to them: 'Let the little children come to Me, and do not hinder them, for the Kingdom of God belongs to such as these. I tell you the truth, anyone who will not receive the Kingdom of God like a little child will never enter it!' And He took the children in his arms, put his hands on them, and blessed them."

The disciples thought they were doing Jesus a favor by keeping the children from distracting Him. Luke's account of the event makes it clear that these children included little infants. Jesus didn't just disagree with his disciples and the way they tried to help Him with his time, He actually got indignant with them. Far from being peripheral to society, Jesus told his disciples that children were central to his Kingdom. Rather than measuring children by adult standards, Jesus told his disciples, and us, that we had to measure ourselves according to the standard of child-like faith. Children, as weak and dependent as they are, have no choice but to trust others for their provision, protection, and care. Like children, we adults are to trust God completely for our provision, protection, and care.

God is faithful to those who trust Him, and children are precious to Him, including each one of the more than 62 million murdered through abortion. We, as individuals and a society, should reflect Jesus' attitude by protecting the most vulnerable children of all, the unborn, rather than making them vulnerable to abortion through our indifference.

The Bible emphasizes the importance of just judges and government leaders. God does not want people exposed to the perils of arbitrary power. He wants there to be justice for all on earth. Most people, throughout history, have had no say in who ruled them or how they were ruled, just or not. But we in America have power to affect who is selected for our judges and government leaders, God wants us to select judges and leaders who will rule justly, and provide justice for all, including the unborn. This standard was grossly violated by the seven Supreme Court justices in 1973 who passed Roe v. Wade. Their apathy and total disregard for justice for the unborn consigned millions upon millions of our unborn to the abortionist's knife.

Apathy, unconcern, about justice is sin according to the Bible. In Deuteronomy 16:20 we are told:

> "Follow justice and justice alone, so that you may live and possess the land the Lord your God is giving you."

And in Isaiah 5;7 we read:

> "And He (the Lord) looked for justice, but saw bloodshed; for righteousness, but heard cries of distress."

The pro-abortionists who sanction abortion and call it good should take Isaiah 5:20-21 to heart which says:

"Woe to those who call evil good and good evil, who put darkness for light and light for darkness, who put bitter for sweet and sweet for bitter. Woe to those who are wise in their own eyes and clever in their own sight."

If we are apathetic about justice, we are showing no concern for those who are being victimized. We are obligated to God Almighty to provide justice to the oppressed, to the poor, to those being persecuted, and to those undergoing the greatest injustice and oppression of all, that of being murdered in the womb. As the last line to our Pledge of Allegiance says: "With liberty and justice for all."

Unborn babies are treated as if they have no significance. Up until birth, the unborn baby is regarded as something that has no purpose. This is especially true of the fetus during the first trimester. Yet, as was said before, God, who is all-knowing, knows each human He creates intimately and from all eternity, and ordains them with certain works they are to do during their lifespan to fulfill his will and purpose for their creation. So yes, the unborn child does have a purpose, and that purpose is established by God and part of the image of God which the child bears from the moment of conception.

It is also the parent's responsibility to give their unborn child that purpose by bringing their child to term and birth. Since God established his purpose for each individual born into this world, man has no right to thwart God's call on that individual by condemning that child to an early death through abortion. To do so is to stand in direct opposition to God's will and in direct rebellion against God's purpose, not a good place to be.

Thanks to modern technology, parents can now see what our forebears could not see and could only imagine - the development and growth of their unborn baby in the womb through the blessing of the sonogram, a wonderful gift from God. It is also a powerful argument against abortion. Many mothers -to-be who had decided upon abortion changed their minds after seeing a sonogram of the unborn child growing in their wombs.

The pro-abortionists, true to form, opposed and continue to oppose, allowing expectant mothers considering abortion to be informed about the stage of their unborn baby's development through a sonogram. This is a direct and flagrant violation of the expectant mother's rights. Ultrasound technology allows us to get a glimpse of what God sees in the case of every single baby in the womb, including the ones that never get born due to abortion on demand. God sees every one of them and knows them intimately. When we think of God as an expectant parent or grandparent in the case of every single pregnancy, we get some idea of his grief when his workmanship as Creator is willingly destroyed.

As mentioned before, the temptation to sacrifice children goes back to ancient times. That is why God warned us so long ago in his Word to never do such a thing. Even though most parents react to the idea of sacrificing children in horror, our sinful nature makes us all too prone to find justification for such sacrifice - financial, social, career, personal, convenience justifications. The alternative to the child-sacrifice of abortion is self-sacrifice, following in the footsteps of Jesus and the Psalmist David by loving our children, including those in the womb, and being thankful for them as gifts from God. We show the value of life by living for the sake of our children and others.

In the Bible, we read about Jesus and his habit of eating and drinking with people whom others found unworthy of associating with. The story of Zacchaeus in Luke 19:1-10 is a perfect example of this. In doing this, Jesus, being one with the heavenly Father, was imitating his Father. Scripture reveals that the God of Israel had appointed regular memorial feasts to be held in his house, the Tabernacle, and later on the Temple which Solomon built. God made it clear to the priests that everyone from every station of life were to be invited to come and eat and drink and celebrate the feast. The Creator of the Universe made a point of commanding that the marginalized be included in these feasts - children, women without husbands, widows, children without fathers, orphans, were of concern to God. They were his invited guests just as much, or perhaps even more, than anyone else.

God wants societies to follow his example and welcome the marginalized, no matter their status, race, ethnicity, or parentage, and that includes the unborn children in the womb. Aborting them is not an option acceptable to God, no matter what the human justification is. He commands us to help and support unwed mothers and others whose pregnancy entails hardship, so they are not pressured by the abortion industry to abort the child.

Sometimes things are forbidden in the Bible that are so repulsive it is difficult to understand why God bothers mentioning them. After all, who would even want to do that is the attitude. Read the section in the book of Leviticus categorizing things forbidden to the Israelites by God for a listing of such repulsive things. God knows better than we do what human beings are capable of doing. There are those who say that man is essentially good. They are wrong! Man is capable of great good, but only through the leading of the Holy Spirit, and not through the exercise of his own free-will. Man's nature is not good; man's nature is sinful.

Our free-will was totally corrupted during the fall into sin. Therefore, the only thing our free-will enables us to do is sin. But through the death and resurrection of God's Son Jesus Christ, our sins, past, present, and future have been atoned for. The Holy Spirit leads us to faith in Christ as our Lord and Savior, and when we follow the Holy Spirit's leading and receive Christ as our Lord and Savior through faith, the Holy Spirit takes up residence in us and dwell in us. But we still have our sinful nature which we, and every human being, inherited from our forebears Adam and Eve, and which we retain as long as our life on earth. Therefore, as the Apostle Paul says in Romans 8:

> ..."there is constant tension between the Holy Spirit and our sinful nature...So I find this law at work within me. When I want to do good, evil is right there with me. For in my inner being I delight in God's law, but I see another law at work in the members of my body...the law of sin. So then, I myself in my mind am a slave to God's law, but in the sinful nature, a slave to

the law of sin. Who will rescue me from this body of death? Thanks be to God, through Jesus Christ our Lord! For through his death and resurrection, He has conquered the law of sin and death for me, and through the power of His Spirit Who dwells within me, strengthens me against the law of sin and death and empowers me to do the good that He would have me do."

And when we grieve the Holy Spirit and give in to the temptation of the law of sin and death, our sinful nature, the Holy Spirit is right there to lead us to confess and repent of that sin for the sake of our Savior Jesus Who atoned for that sin and all our sins with his Body and Blood on the cross, so we can be forgiven and, as the Psalmist says: "have our sins removed from us as far as the east is from the west," and be restored into God's favor.

There are those who refuse to accept the Biblical teaching that man's nature is basically sinful and his free-will totally corrupted by the fall, and insist that, although man sins, his nature is essentially good. This leads to blaming other persons or other things for all the bad things one experiences in life. The rationale is that, since man's nature, including mine, is essentially good, the bad things happening to me are not my fault, but the fault of society, culture, poverty, discrimination, other people, etc. Also, viewing man's nature as good, becomes the yardstick for evaluating morality. What is good or moral is not decided by a transcendent authority (God in his Word), but what man decides to be good and moral. This also relates to truth. Secular progressive liberals deny such a thing as absolute Truth and that God's Word is absolute Truth. They maintain that truth, like morals and ethics, is relative to circumstances and conditions. This is a disastrous ideology. History has clearly shown that once the restraints of absolute Truth are replaced by relative truth, man in his sinful nature will devise his own truth, and this truth will often be used to support his basest impulses. This was clearly shown to be true of the three mass murderers of the 20th century - Hitler, Stalin, and Mao Tse tung. Thus, man elevates himself to godlike status, and fully expects God to sanction his arrogance.

Modern society's greatest failure is the failed capacity to discern, recognize, identify, and condemn evil when it plainly stares us in the face. This is clear evidence of man's sinful nature and truly the case with abortion. So how do we recognize evil? By using the criterion given us by God in his Word. If we depend only on human intuition and intellect, then we are truly the blind leading the blind. The source of despair is to be found in an understanding of our sinful human nature. The source of hope, assurance, and comfort is to be found in the mercy and grace of God.

Why have practices like human sacrifice , abortion, infanticide, become so common? Because of that law of sin and death, our sinful nature within us, which tempts us to sin and which is in constant tension with the Holy Spirit within. There is a constant battle going on in every Christian, between good and evil, which will continue until the Lord takes us out of this life. There are those who say that abortion is a personal matter and should be left as such. But personal sin can grow in a people and become great national sin and disaster. This is certainly true of abortion. At one time, in the not too distant past, the idea of sacrificing a child to protect one's lifestyle, reputation, career, convenience, was unthinkable. But now it is all too widely accepted in the form of abortion. We must check our own hearts to see what sins lurk inside us which could lead to disaster and cause us to do something we never thought ourselves capable of doing and pray that God would protect us from ourselves.

God counts every child born or in the womb as his child. He has every right to do so since He is the one who created that life, and He is the one who redeemed that life. And that child is his from the moment of conception. As I mentioned in the previous chapter, the claim that during the first trimester the fetus is not a human being is wrong, dead wrong. With today's medical and biological technology, including the understanding of DNA, the evidence strongly supports life beginning at conception. Then too, when God creates, He doesn't create partially, He doesn't create life that is not yet life. He doesn't create a human being who is not yet human.

Because God counts every child in the womb as his child, whenever a child is killed God grieves as a father whose child has been taken away from Him. The reason God hates abortion is because He loves children as his own. Children occupy a special place in God's heart as was shown in the passage where Jesus rebuked his disciples for keeping the little children from Him, and He received them in his arms and blessed them. He wants every child to live and fulfill his special plan and purpose for each of them. God condemns abortion because it sheds innocent blood, ends the child's life in a brutal, cruel, and horrible manner, and rebels against God's special plan and purpose for the child. God's message to the pro-abortionists can be taken from Isaiah 1: 15-17a as follows:

> "When you spread out your hands in prayer, I will hide my eyes from you; even if you offer many prayers, I will not listen. Your hands are full of blood; wash and make yourselves clean. Take your evil deeds out of my sight. Stop doing wrong, learn to do right! Seek justice...."

God warns us that cooperation with bloodshed, which certainly includes abortion, can result in God refusing to hear us or pay attention to our worship and prayers. Although many aspects of legalized abortion may be beyond our control, we can still speak out against it, support crisis pregnancy centers, and vote for and support political candidates who will provide justice and protection for the unborn.

To close our eyes to the injustice of abortion is to invite God to close his ears to our prayers. God sees abortion going on everywhere in the United States every day. He wants our prayers and worship, but He also wants our activities and actions to be consistent with his Word, so that we can come before Him in prayer and worship Him with a pure heart and a clean conscience. How can we pray to God to save us and our loved ones from harm when we don't help save the most innocent and helpless among us from the greatest harm - death.

In Jeremiah 22:1-3, God sends the prophet Jeremiah to the king, his officials, and the people with this message:

> "This is what the Lord says: Do what is just and right. Rescue from the hand of his oppressor the one who has been robbed. Do no wrong or violence to the alien, the fatherless, or the widow. And do not shed innocent blood in this place."

Justice and righteousness are the supreme virtues of government commanded by God's Word. God warns the leaders, the judges, and the people to maintain justice and righteousness and not shed any innocent blood. It has been mentioned more than once before, but bears repeating again and again, how the leaders and the people ignored God's warning and descended deeper and deeper into sin and depravity, including shedding innocent blood through child sacrifice, until God's patience came to an end and He brought judgment upon them. The Babylonian Army came and destroyed their cities and towns, destroyed Jerusalem, the Temple, the wall, and took the people into captivity to Babylon for seventy years.

This is incredibly important to our nation and its people today, and again bears repeating and repeating. The shedding of innocent blood was the last full measure of evil that exhausted the Lord's patience. If we, as a people and nation, continue the shedding of innocent blood through abortion, God's patience will eventually come to an end, and we will face judgment just as the Israelites did. And that judgment, in order to reestablish justice and righteousness, will be fearsome and terrible indeed.

In Micah 6:8, the prophet tells us:

> "He has showed you, O man, what is good. And what does the Lord require of you? To act justly, and to love mercy, and to walk humbly with your God."

How important is it that Christians and the Church publicly stand for life? Extremely important! We are told time and time again in Scripture that God wants a people who are devoted to justice and mercy, in addition to being devoted to worship and prayer. Our worship and prayer must reflect our devotion to justice, righteousness, and mercy, including justice, righteousness, and mercy for the unborn. We love others, which Jesus said is the second greatest commandment, by acting on their behalf to help and defend them.

For the Christian, publicly standing for life is not optional. It is what the Lord requires of us. Christians are to regularly pray for all people, especially for those in authority over us, who are responsible to God to govern with justice and righteousness. In 1 Timothy 2;1-4, the Apostle Paul tells us:

> "I urge then, first of all, that requests, prayers, intercession, and thanksgiving be made for everyone—for kings and all those in authority, that we may live peaceful and quiet lives in all godliness and holiness. This is good and pleases God our Savior who wants all men to be saved and to come to a knowledge of the truth."

God is pleased with such prayers because He wants the Gospel of Salvation to be taken to every part of this earth, and promoting justice among the nations is critical to opening the pathway for that salvation to be taken to all nations as Jesus commanded in the Great Commission He gave to his disciples before ascending into heaven. God's desire, expressed above, that "all men be saved and come to a knowledge of the truth" is expressed in this Great Commission which we read in Matthew 28:18-20 as follows: "Then Jesus came to them and said:

> 'All authority in heaven and on earth has been given to me. Therefore, go and make disciples of all nations, baptizing them in the name of the Father and of the Son and of the Holy Spirit, and teaching them to obey everything I have commanded you. And surely I am with you always, to the very end of the age.'"

Of course, as we know from Scripture, not all men will be saved. There are those who will reject the leading of the Holy Spirit to receive Jesus Christ as their Lord and Savior right up to end when they close their eyes in death and experience what the rich man experienced in the parable Jesus told in Luke 16:19-26:

"There was a rich man who was dressed in purple and fine linen and lived in luxury every day. At his gate was laid a beggar named Lazarus, covered with sores and longing to eat what fell from the rich man's table. Even the dogs came and licked his sores. The time came when the beggar died, and the angels carried him to Abraham's side. The rich man also died and was buried. In hell, where he was in torment, he looked up and saw Abraham far away, with Lazarus by his side. So, he called to him, 'Father Abraham have pity on me and send Lazarus to dip the tip of his finger in water and cool my tongue, because I am in agony in this fire.' But Abraham replied, 'Son, remember that in your lifetime you received your good things, while Lazarus received bad things, but now he is comforted here, and you are in agony. And besides all this, between us and you a great chasm has been fixed, so that those who want to go from here to you cannot, nor can anyone cross over from there to us....'"

Praying for justice for the oppressed, for healing for the sick and diseased, for fairness to those who are being treated unfairly, for acceptance of the outcast, is essential to living according to the Gospel message that Jesus is Lord, because if Jesus is Lord of our life, our faith involves striving to follow his example. And what does this mean? It means backing our prayers up with action - speaking out for the oppressed, ministering to the sick and diseased, encouraging those being treated unfairly, and reaching out to the outcast. In 1Peter 2:20b-21, the Apostle tells us:

"But if you suffer for doing good and you endure it, this is commendable before God. To this you were called, because Christ suffered for you, leaving you an example, that you should follow in his steps."

Following the example of Jesus, and as a faithful follower in his steps, is why the horror and abomination of abortion can never be regarded as an optional issue for Christians. We must pray for political and religious leaders and judges who will protect the unborn, ask ourselves "What would Jesus do?" and then act accordingly.

What happens when a woman suddenly realizes what a great sin abortion really is, and she has supported this sin and even been involved in it by having an abortion herself, or working in an abortion clinic? When a person suddenly realizes their guilt, it can be a devastating experience. But God does not leave people overcome with their own sin. His forgiveness, cleansing, restoration, and reconciliation are always available to the person, and we Christians must always be ready to respond to the Holy Spirit's call to minister to such people, assuring them that, like all sin, abortion is forgivable, and the Blood of Jesus Christ which He shed on the cross to atone for our sins washes one clean of the sin of abortion just as it does all other sin. Our sin is great and real, but God's grace and mercy in Christ is greater, stronger, and more powerful than any sin.

We Christians are called to be ambassadors for Christ, and a part of that is to make sure that those who have done wrong in the past concerning abortion do not allow guilt over those deeds and their remorse to keep them from boldly standing up against the evil of abortion and working to save the unborn. We are commanded by God to trust in his grace for ourselves, and to represent his grace to others. I have found that representing his grace to others can lead to some very interesting confrontations, relationships, and experiences.

Scripture tells us that we are to love our neighbors as ourselves, and that Includes loving our enemies. In Matthew 5: 43-45, 48, Jesus tells us:

> "You have heard that it was said, 'Love your neighbor and hate your enemy.' But I tell you, 'Love your enemies and pray for those who persecute you, that you may be sons of your Father in heaven. He causes his sun to rise on the evil and the good and sends rain on the righteous and the unrighteous….. Be perfect therefore, as your Heavenly Father is perfect.'"

Let's take this a step or two further. If we must love our enemies who have wronged us, how much more are we to love those who haven't wronged us, and especially those who haven't wronged anyone - the unborn children in the womb. People tend to assume that unborn children have no relationship to God. They couldn't be more wrong. Numerous Scripture passages disprove this, Psalm 22: 9-10 being only one:

> "Yet you brought me out of the womb; You made me trust in you even at my mother's breast. From birth I was cast upon you; from my mother's womb you have been my God."

God is the God of those in the womb. We have spoken before of God being omniscient (all-knowing) and omnipresent (present everywhere) and of his not being confined by time or space. Psalm 90:4 refers to this:

> "For a thousand years in your sight are like a day that has just gone by, or like a watch in the night."

Therefore, God knows every human being He has created, and every human being He will create until the end of time, and He knows them before the foundation of the world. That is, before God ever initiated creation of the world with the words, "Let there be light," He knew when He would create you and me in the womb. God, not being confined by time or space, you and I, and every human being created existed in the mind and presence of God from all eternity. Although we would not be conceived in the womb for hundreds or thousands of years, we were still real to God, He knew us by name; he had a relationship with us, and we had a relationship with him.

This knowledge is too wonderful for us. That God knew us personally and had a relationship with us before the world even existed is too profound for us to comprehend. But it should impress upon us just how precious the life of every child, born and unborn, is in the sight of God. For man to snuff out that life through abortion is the very height of arrogance and rebellion against God, and the very depths of evil.

When does the baby in the womb become a person? This question was central to the whole issue of abortion which, as I mentioned in the previous chapter, the justices who passed Roe v. Wade decided not to address. Modern technology is making it more and more clear that life begins at conception.

In Luke 1:39-45, we're told that when Mary, who was pregnant with Jesus, went to visit her Aunt Elizabeth, who was pregnant with John the Baptist, Elizabeth told Mary that as soon as the sound of her greeting reached her ears, the baby in her womb, John the Baptist, leaped for joy. This response of John the Baptist in the womb of Elizabeth to the presence of Jesus, Son of God and Son of man in the womb of Mary, reveals what is true of all unborn children - that they are truly persons. John the Baptist did not leap for joy over a bit of tissue and cells in the womb of Mary, but over a person who was his Savior and Lord. The account of John the Baptist and Jesus, Son of God and Son of man, while still in the wombs of their mothers has profound implications for the lives of all babies in the womb.

The pro-abortionist's rejection of life at conception leads to many opinions as to when personhood begins, some of which are downright laughable. For example, take the comment of one of our female Senators in Congress who opined that the baby becomes a person when the parents take the baby home and carry the child across the threshold. Presto - a Person! It's a bit scary to realize that someone who would make such a foolish and ridiculous statement is a lawmaker in our government.

The pro-abortionists have the saying: "Every child a wanted child," which seeks to justify an unwanted child being aborted. Yet, because God is love (1John 4:8), with Him there is no such thing as an unwanted child, and neither should there be with us. God wants us to want every child , just as He wants us and our children.

In 1Corinthians 13:7 we are told:

> "Love always protects, always trusts, always hopes, always perseveres."

In this passage, the Apostle Paul tells us first that "love always protects." A parent shows love to the children by assuring them of his/her care and protection. The children's welfare comes before the parents' desires. Next Paul says, "Love always trusts." When an unexpected child presents problems of time, finances, schedule disruptions, career progression, and inconvenience, God wants the parents to trust Him to work it all out for both the baby's and the parents' highest good. God has promised to do this for those who trust and obey. Next Paul says, "Love always hopes." Scripture tells us that God has given us the "living hope" in Christ. This living hope extends to every aspect of one's life, including having an unexpected pregnancy.

> "But as for me, I watch in hope for the Lord. I wait for God my Savior; my God will hear me!" (Micah 7:7).

Next Paul says, "Love always perseveres." God's love for us is unconditional. Such love led Him to send his Son to atone for our sins. The love of this world is conditional, depending on feelings and emotions and circumstances, and therefore changes. Being unconditional, God's love for us is never changing, and therefore perseveres. God calls us to love the children He gives us with such unconditional and persevering love. Standing against abortion isn't about legalism or prohibitions; It is all about love.

Upholding traditional moral standards, the moral standards of the Bible, is often considered by society, the media, and academia as an attempt to enslave others and deny them their freedoms. Individuals calling for these moral standards are often accused of racism, bigotry, homophobia, prejudice, and discrimination. Yet, witnessing to a person in a non-accusatory manner that their lifestyle, behavior, beliefs, attitude, etc., are contrary to the Word of God is an act of love, for it shows that the one doing the witnessing is primarily concerned with the person's spiritual well-being and salvation, and there is no higher concern for another person than his/her salvation. This has direct application to those engaged in and supporting abortion. If we have a friend or acquaintance in such a situation, we are doing them no favor by not witnessing to them out of concern that we might hurt their feelings, or they might resent it and sever their relationship with us.

Of course, some people do have a hard time believing this, and do resent being restrained from freedoms they think they are entitled to. But the Bible is clear about this. It is all about love, and genuine love is sometimes telling a person something they don't want to hear. Hopefully they will understand this and respond like the psalmist in Psalm 141:5:

> "Let a righteous man strike me - it is a kindness; let him rebuke me - it is oil on my head. My head will not refuse it,"

or like the man described in Proverbs 15:31:

> "He who listens to a life-giving rebuke will be at home among the wise."

God wants us, out of love, to help one another. And this entails not only the telling, but the doing. For example, not just telling a pregnant woman considering abortion that abortion is murder but organizing the provision of the pregnant woman's needs so she can carry the baby to term, give birth, and then either keep the baby or give the child up for adoption. This is genuine love, to walk the walk and not just talk the talk.

People who oppose abortion are often accused of not wanting the person pregnant with an unwanted child to be happy. But happiness has nothing to do with it. Happiness is an emotion, and emotions easily change depending on events and circumstances. Joy, on the other hand, is an attitude, the attitude God has for us, and the attitude we are to have towards God. As the song goes, "The joy of the Lord is my strength." As previously stated, many, many, times it has been documented that a pregnant woman, being rid of the child through abortion, will suffer deep depression and terrible guilt over having her child aborted. At such a time, she needs a friend to comfort and assure her that Jesus paid the full price for her sin on the cross, assure her of God's forgiveness and reconciliation, assure her of God's joy over her, and encourage her to be joyful in the Lord which will take away her depression and guilt.

If we love our neighbors as ourselves, have respect for our fellowman and want the best for them, we cannot accept or condone abortion. We must not forget that abortion is an abasement of both the individual's soul and the nation that provides abortion. Abortion is a clear and present danger to society and culture because, after a time, it dulls peoples' sensitivity towards the evil of it, and undermines respect for human life and human rights, and will eventually bring God's judgment on the nation.

We need to take to heart the words of Moses to the children of Israel before they crossed the Jordan River to take possession of the land God had promised their forefathers and them. Moses' words are as applicable to us today as they were to the Israelites when he spoke them. Moses warned them:

> "See, I set before you today life and prosperity, death and destruction. For I command you today to love the Lord your God, to walk in his ways, and to keep his commands, decrees, and laws; then you will live and increase, and the Lord your God will bless you in the land you are entering to possess. But if your heart turns away and you are not obedient, and if you are drawn away to bow down to other gods and worship them, I declare to you this day that you will certainly be destroyed. You will not live long in the land you are crossing the Jordan to enter and possess. This day I call heaven and earth as witnesses against you, that I have set before you life and death, blessings and curses. Now choose life, so that you and your children may live and that you may love the Lord your God, listen to his voice, and hold fast to Him. For the Lord is your life, and He will give you many years in the land He swore to give to your fathers, Abraham, Isaac, and Jacob."

Of course, we know from previous discussion that the people soon forgot Moses' warning, took up the practices of the heathen nations around them, including child sacrifice, and suffered the judgment Moses had predicted.

There are those who say that one should not use a single issue to decide on a candidate for political office. In a previous chapter, I mentioned that our Founding Fathers would disagree with that. They urged the citizenry (that's us) to be very careful in their voting, to consider not only the candidate's professional qualities, but even more importantly, the candidate's character , virtues, values, and faith. Our Founders urged the citizenry to vote for candidates of Christian character. Their rationale for this was that, with the freedoms given to the people through our founding documents, it was essential that our leaders and the people submit themselves to the control of a transcendent power - God. Otherwise, anarchy would prevail, and the Democratic Republic established by the Founders would fail.

Therefore, although voting for a candidate based on a single issue may not normally be wise, there are times when the critical importance of that issue requires it. What that means to me is that if there is a candidate whose political, economic, foreign policy, etc., correspond completely to my wishes, and yet he/she is pro-abortion, I will not vote for him/her. To do so would be a betrayal of my Lord and Savior, as well as the Founders of my country.

Again, I say, we must pray for and elect politicians and judges who will protect the unborn.

We are all familiar with the statement, "Don't mix religion and politics." The statement is foolish and unrealistic because God's sovereignty is total and covers all secular aspects of our lives in addition to spiritual. Thus, every decision, every act, has a spiritual, ethical dimension to it. George Washington said: "Without religion, morality has no roots." The moral, ethical, nature of something cannot be properly evaluated apart from its theological aspects, for the two are inseparable. This perhaps is why the seers of old, the wise men of the past, considered theology the queen of the sciences.

As both Creator and Redeemer, God is Lord, Sovereign over both the spiritual and the secular. What does this mean insofar as our consideration of such controversial issues as abortion, homosexual marriage, and family breakdown are concerned? We will address this in the remainder of this chapter and in subsequent chapters.

Separation of science and secular from the theological and moral /ethical — in other words secular progressive liberal humanism — is at the heart of the great spiritual, political, and social controversies mentioned above. Secular progressive humanism, as mentioned in earlier chapters, has also tended to move us away from the foundation of Judeo-Christian morals and ethics our Founders insisted they had built our nation on. The Founders charged the citizens of this great nation with the solemn duty and responsibility to hold our elected officials accountable for any laws, regulations or policies that contradicted that Judeo-Christian foundation which included the three Sanctities, the Sanctity of Life, the Sanctity of Marriage, and the Sanctity of Family, which are the cornerstones of civilization itself. For the government to deny God's sovereignty over the nation, in the Founder's opinion, justified revolt, just as the British king's announcement that he was solely sovereign over the American colonies justified their revolt against the British crown. The Founders would have fully agreed with the Apostles Peter and John who, when they were ordered by the governing authorities (the Sanhedrin) to stop preaching in the name of Jesus, answered: "We must obey God rather than man" (Acts 4).

Jeffrey T. Kuhner, a Washington Times columnist, identifies abortion as the seminal issue of our time. He is right. No other domestic issue - the economy, taxes, health care, the environment - come close to rivaling it in importance. Mr. Kuhner describes legal abortion as "state-sanctioned infanticide, the murder of innocent, defenseless human life." Again, Mr. Kuhner is right. Then too, abortion is an assault on the very foundation of constitutional democracy. The most fundamental human right, the right that underpins our constitutional democratic republic system of government, is the right to life. Without it, all other rights to liberty, property, freedom of expression, are impossible and meaningless.

Mr. Kuhner maintains that abortion is today's equivalent of slavery. It is a cancer eating away at the spiritual, moral, and political fabric of America. Just like slavery, Roe v. Wade invested into law the pernicious principle that an entire class of people is not fully human, and therefore not entitled to basic, fundamental, human rights. In the 19th century, Southern Blacks were treated as property, things to be used and then discarded according to their master's wishes. Today it is unborn children who are murdered in the womb and then discarded as chattel. They are the slaves of our time, and the forgotten victims of the sexual revolution.

Abortion is now considered as a civil right. This belittles the historical civil rights movement of the sixties which was a courageous and noble chapter of our history. It is supreme irony that the radical democrats who fought tooth and nail against civil rights for the blacks back then, now insist that mothers have a civil right to have their babies in the womb murdered.

Consider the utter stupidity and ignorance of calling abortion a civil right. In order for a person to exercise abortion as their so-called civil right, they have to deny the baby in the womb their most basic, fundamental, and foundational civil right of all - the right to life. And in denying that right to life, the person is denying the baby in the womb the full range of civil rights.

The greatest argument against abortion, the open and shut case which clearly condemns abortion as an abomination in God's eyes, is the Old Testament description of our birth given in Psalm 139, which I give commentary on in the next chapter. As I will show, the Psalmist sees himself, as each of us should see ourselves, and as all babies in the womb should be seen, not as accidents, but as ones known, brought into being, given an allotted time, and encompassed by the everlasting God.

How is it that man can acknowledge God as Creator, the One who formed him/ her in the womb, and yet support abortion, the horrible genocide against the most innocent and helpless among us? I can think of three reasons. First, with abortion legalized for 49 years and with over 62 million babies aborted since then, many people have become desensitized to the horror of what abortion really is and what it does. Second, many have been taken in by, or chosen to believe, the pro-abortion propaganda that what is in the womb isn't really a baby, but a mass of tissue and cells, and not life. Really? Is that what God formed in the womb, just a mass of tissue? Is that what contains the image of God, just a mass of tissue and cells? Do they want to tell God that? Third, many people don't want to know the details of abortion, thinking that if they don't know, they don't have to feel guilty about ignoring it.

They don't have to feel guilty about sanctioning, through ignorance and silence, a procedure in which babies are chopped to pieces in the womb, the pieces extracted from the woman's body, and pieced together on the table to make sure all the parts are there, like putting a jigsaw puzzle together. Only these parts are the bloody pieces of a baby's remains - two arms, two legs, the little torso, the small head, etc. And they also don't have to consider that the baby, early in his/her development, can feel pain.

A few years ago in Los Angeles over 17 thousand aborted babies were found in a dumpster. As I recall, 15,000 of those aborted babies were black babies. The largest abortion provider in the country is Planned Parenthood, and the dirty secret they don't want you to know is that it was founded around 100 years ago by Margaret Sanger, whose primary purpose was eugenics, controlling the black population by aborting black babies.

Did you know that to this day, Congress allocates in the yearly budget over half a billion dollars to Planned Parenthood? That's your tax money and mine which enables them to butcher more babies. Did you know that, at a Planned Parenthood event, our former president and our first black president, President Barak Obama, in a speech asked God to bless Planned Parenthood? Imagine that - our first black president, who also claims to be Christian, asking God to bless an organization drenched in the innocent blood of black babies, as well as others. Did you know that, in the last presidential election campaign of 2020, all eighteen, or whatever the number of the Democratic presidential candidates was, strongly supported abortion throughout the nine months of gestation right up to the moment of birth? Did you know that many strong pro-abortionists claim to be devout Christians? How deluded that is!

It is vitally important that people understand clearly what abortion is, and the devastation - spiritual, physical, and emotional - it causes. The sooner the majority of citizens become knowledgeable of the horror and pure evil of abortion, the sooner irresistible pressure can be put on our elected officials and judges to remove from our national social fabric the disgusting, abominable, and filthy stain of abortion.

Pro-life David Daleiden, of the Center for Medical Progress, recently exposed an abortion procedure now in use where "in vivo" fetal tissue is used in medical research. "In vivo" means "in the living." What this means is that babies are being purposely aborted live in order to harvest their organs.

When you think that abortion can't get any worse than it is, what happens? It get worse! This "in vivo" procedure raises the insanity and evil of abortion to a level not thought possible. Medical students are being taught how to induce late term abortions, deliver the babies, and harvest the bodies for whatever organs are needed for research purposes. The rationale is that it was an abortion; the baby was to die anyway.

Late term living babies carry the purest form of human tissue. Free of the chemicals used to kill the baby in the womb, these babies enter our world with a wealth of living human tissue that medical researchers pay substantially to collect. Late term "in vivo" abortions has become commonplace nationwide and funded with millions in research grants from our nation's National Institute of Health. This is evil at its worst, and evil can only be defeated by shining the light of truth upon it.

I have mentioned the following disastrous results of abortion throughout the narrative, but before ending the chapter I want to summarize them because of the critical need for all of us to understand what abortion really is.

1. Abortion is the ultimate civil rights discrimination and abuse against the most innocent and helpless among us - our babies in the womb.

2. Abortion brutally murders someone created by God in his own image.

3. Abortion brutally murders someone redeemed by their Savior Jesus Christ who was brutally murdered for them on the cross.

4. Abortion brutally murders someone who will never be the person - black, white, red, brown, yellow - that God intended for them to be.

5. Abortion brutally murders someone who will never accomplish the works, deeds, goals, that God ordained for them to accomplish in his plan for the person before their conception, and even before the foundation of the world.

6. Abortion brutally murders someone and deprives them of the multiple blessings - spiritual and material - which God planned to pour out for them during their lifespan.

7. Abortion not only brutally murders someone, but often cruelly wounds that someone's mother with sorrow, guilt, depression, and regret, as well as that someone's father, and that someone's family.

I want to emphasize the good news that there is hope and help for those experiencing an unplanned pregnancy. Organizations like Crisis Pregnancy Centers are there to help and support the person to carry the child to birth, and then, if the mother wishes, help place the child up for adoption. The good news for those suffering from depression and guilt over having had an abortion is that, although abortion is sin, like all sin it can be confessed, repented of, and the sinner forgiven, cleansed of it with the Blood of Christ, freed of the guilt and depression once and for all. Most churches, worthy of the name, are ready to help and support such a person through the grief process. We Christians must extend our love and support to our sisters who are suffering so with agape love, the sacrificial love Jesus demonstrated during his ministry and finally at the cross, the love of intelligence and purpose, the love of action and not just words which the Apostle Paul speaks of in Romans 12.

Also, and this is extremely difficult and can only be done with the Holy Spirit's strengthening and leading, our Christian love must extend also to the abortionist and those who support abortion, that their eyes be opened to the horror and evil of it, that they go to the cross of Christ in confession and repentance and receive God's mercy and pardon.

The Psalmist says: "When I awake, I am still with you." Awake from what? From death! The Psalmist assures us that God was with us and we with God before we came into being; that God is with us and we with God during our lifespan on this earth; that God is with us and we with God when we close our eyes in death and leave this life; that God is with us and we with God when we enter the new life in heavenly glory, there to be eternally in incomprehensible joy and wonder in the presence of God and the company of our loved ones who preceded us. The Psalmist emphasizes the inescapability of God which is of immense comfort to all who are his children through faith in Christ.

And that includes every child who was aborted in the past, who is being aborted in the present, and who will be aborted in the future. We don't know their form, shape, or current state, but their Creator has taken care of that. We do know that they are in his Presence and will be with Him at the Resurrection on the last day. Our Creator does not waste his precious creations; only man does that.

Finally, we must not become complacent and forget that, although God is loving, patient, merciful, compassionate, and forgiving, He is also just, and his justice will not be delayed indefinitely. As a people and a nation, we are on weak ground and the foundation is getting weaker. There are still many, I believe the majority, who consider the United States a Christian nation and honor that tradition and heritage. Yet, there are many, and the number is growing, who deny that tradition and heritage and Christian foundation, who demand secularism and have adopted the secular progressive liberal ideology, and who arrogantly and flagrantly sanction, support, and promote cultural policies and lifestyles that are in direct opposition to God's Word. This is rank heresy and apostasy. If we, as individuals and a nation, do not repent of our sin and wickedness, including the abominable evil of abortion, Scripture shows us clearly that the time will surely come when God will say, "Enough!" "These people have so hardened their hearts that only judgment will turn them back to me. Therefore, it is time for judgment to cleanse my people and restore justice, including justice for the murdered unborn."

I again refer to Thomas Jefferson, who clearly understood from the Bible God's dealings with his people Israel, and who said: "When I consider that God is just, and that his justice cannot be delayed indefinitely, I tremble for my country."

We should all be trembling for our country!

shutterstock.com · 252134077

George Mason

Margaret Sanger

CHAPTER 8

PSALM 139: THE TOUCH OF THE CREATOR

"Did you not …clothe me with skin and flesh,
and knit me together with bones and sinews.
You gave me life and showed me kindness
and in your providence watched over my spirit."

Job 10: 11-12

"My frame was not hidden from you
when I was made in the secret place,
when I was woven together in the depths
of the earth."

Psalm 139: 15

Psalm 139 is a profound and deeply intimate portrait of our Creator who was with us before the foundation of the world, who was with us in the womb, who is with us every moment of our lives here on earth, who is with us when we close our eyes in death, and who is with us eternally in the new life in heavenly glory.

I am writing this chapter specifically for those who claim that one can be simultaneously a devout Christian and a supporter of abortion. Psalm 139 strongly disproves that concept as totally contrary to the Creator's character and the Creator's purpose. Abortion is anathema to God the Creator of life. There is no compatibility between the Christian faith and abortion.

The Psalmist David begins Psalm139 by praising the character of God, more traditionally known as the attributes or perfections of God, especially the omniscience (the all-knowing perfection) of God, and the omnipresence (God's perfection in being present everywhere) and with emphasis on the certainty of God's presence everywhere we are. David expresses the assurance that God, in his omniscience, perfectly knows him, and each of us, and all our ways, far beyond our knowledge of ourselves (verses 1-4). God knows our every deed before we do it, our every undertaking and the manner in which we pursue it before we even act on it. Even our thoughts are perceived by God before we think them, and our words known by Him before we speak them. He that formed us in the womb knows all there is to know about us; He knows us totally.

Knowing that God knows us completely can be both discomforting and comforting. Discomforting in the fact that I have done many things of which I am ashamed and would rather have God not know about them. I'm sure you can say the same. Nevertheless, God is omniscient - that is, all-knowing. There is nothing hidden from Him. On the other hand, God's all-knowing is comforting to me. Comforting in the fact that when I go to God seeking His forgiveness for Jesus' sake, that forgiveness extends to not only the sins I know, but the sins I do not know or have forgotten about. God's forgiveness is complete. In Psalm 19:12-13, David speaks about hidden sins and willful sins. He prays:

> "Who can discern his errors? Forgive my hidden faults! Keep your servant also from willful sins; may they not rule over me."

David goes on to assure us that God, in his omnipresence, is with us always and will never leave us or forsake us. (Psalm 139:5-12). David says that God hems him in - behind and before. This also includes above and below, to the right and to the left. In other words, we are surrounded by the presence of God, and all efforts to flee from his presence are futile as Scripture clearly shows us. No flight can remove us from God's presence. David says that if he goes to the heavens, God is there; if he goes to the depths, God is there; if he settles on the far side of the sea, God's right hand will guide him and hold him fast; if he tries to hide in thick darkness and light becomes darkness around him, even the darkness will not be dark to God, the night will shine like the day for the darkness is as light to God.

It is the inescapability of God that one encounters and which the Psalmist emphasizes. Whatever our experience or fate, our condition, our circumstance, we are not cut off from the presence of God in this life. Whatever we do, wherever we go, we cannot get away from God. The whole creation offers no hiding place from God. To the suffering one who cries out to God during the dark times and storms of life they are passing through, this is good news indeed. David says that such knowledge is too wonderful for him.

Nevertheless, this too can be both discomforting and comforting. There are places I have been where I would rather not have God with me to see my sin and shame. I'm sure you can say the same. But the comfort is amazing, despite that, in knowing that we are never alone, that in every situation and circumstance of life, God's presence is with us. This includes the woman having an abortion. God will not forsake her, and the Holy Spirit, in mercy and compassion, will minister to her and lead her to confess and repent of her sin for Jesus' sake so God can forgive her and cleanse her of the sin of murder and be reconciled to her.

I have spoken in recent chapters of the human creation being created in the image of God and briefly described some aspects of that image. I would like to expand on that description because, although that image was corrupted by man's fall into sin, the relic, or remnant of that image, remains in every human being which enables us to retain our humanity. Although we cannot fully understand the image of God within us, it is necessary to understand what we can of it in order to better understand the intimacy of the Creator with his creation, both in the womb and outside the womb. Let us again consider the first passages that speak of this image. In Genesis 1:26-27 we read:

> "Then God said, 'Let us make man in our image, in our likeness.....' So, God created man in his own image, in the image of God He created him; male and female He created them."

And in Genesis 5:1-2 we are told:

> "When God created man, He made him in the likeness of God.
> He created them male and female and blessed them. And when
> they were created, He called them *man*

In both passages, the statement that man was made in the image of
God is coupled with the words, "male and female He created them."
"Man" is the overall term for God's human creation, and male and
female the two genders of which man is composed. Therefore, the image
of God in man is found in man's being created male and female, with
both genders possessing the image of God. Notice also the fact that in
God's creation, which encompasses all things, there are only two genders
- male and female.

There are three general ways of viewing the nature of the image of
God — the "substantive" view, the "relational" view, and the
"functional" view. The substantive view refers to some definite
characteristics or qualities within the human nature of the human
creation. Most notable among these characteristics are man's ability to
reason, man's ability to think systematically, man's ability to discern good
from evil, right from wrong, and man's ability to exercise his will.

The relational view of the image of God consists of man being
capable of relationship both with God and his fellowman. Karl Barth,
probably the most influential Protestant theologian of the twentieth
century, maintained that the image of God consisted not only in the
vertical relationship between man and God, but also in the horizontal
relationship between man and man. Barth maintained that, since man is
capable of relationship with both God and man, he is a repetition or
duplication of the Divine Being. This in no way infers that man is to any
degree divine, but only that his capability for relationship duplicates the
relationship within the Godhead itself between Father, Son, and Holy
Spirit, three Persons within the Godhead, yet only one God. Man
therefore reflects this aspect of God's nature on two levels — man
experiences relationship with God and with man. Thus, the similarity
between God and man, as part of the image of God in man, is that both
experience an "I and Thou" relationship — God within the Trinity itself,

and man in his being created male and female. Whether positive or negative, there is always within the human creation man the "I and Thou" relationship as male and female.

The third view of the image of God in man is the functional view. This portion of the image consists of something man does, a function which man performs, the most frequently mentioned being the exercise of dominion over the rest of God's creation. In Genesis 1:26 God assigns this function:

> "Let us make man in our image, in our likeness, and let them rule over the fish of the sea and the birds of the air, over the livestock, over all the earth, and over all the creatures that move along the ground."

The exercise of dominion is considered to be part of the image of God within man. As God is Lord over all creation, man reflects the image of God by exercising dominion over God's creation. The godlikeness of man in Psalm 8 consists above all in the power and sovereignty over all other things given him by God. David the Psalmist, under the inspiration of the Holy Spirit, writes:

> "When I consider your heavens, the work of your fingers, the moon and the stars, which you have set in place, what is man that you are mindful of him, the son of man that you care for him? You made him a little lower than the heavenly beings and crowned him with glory and honor. You made him ruler over the works of your hands; you put everything under his feet: all flocks and herds, and the beasts of the field, the birds of the air, and the fish of the sea, all that swim the paths of the seas. O Lord our God, how majestic is your Name in all the earth."

The idea of dominion stands out as a feature of the image of God; however, there is no direct statement in Scripture that fully and specifically describes the image of God that man possesses. Furthermore, there is no direct statement correlating the image with the development of relationships or making it dependent upon the exercise of dominion. Experiencing relationships and exercising dominion, although very closely linked to the image of God, are not themselves that image. Nevertheless, man is most fully man as he was created when he is active in these relationships and performing his function of dominion, for he is then fulfilling God's purpose for him. All these characteristics given here are simply reasonable inferences from what little the Bible has to say about the image. In summary, however, we do know the following:

1. The image of God is universal within the human race, possessed by both male and female.

2. The image of God is a quality or capacity resident in man's nature. Although it is God who confers the image upon man, it resides in man whether or not man recognizes God's existence or his work.

3. Even in turning away from God, man cannot negate the fact that he is related to God in a way that no other creature is or can be.

4. The image of God is not something external to human nature. It is something inseparably connected with humanity. Therefore, the image of God, although corrupted greatly by the fall of man into sin, has not been entirely lost.

5. Man was intended to know, love, and obey God, to live in harmony with his fellowman, and to exercise dominion over the rest of creation. These are the applications of the image of God in man. The image itself is that set of characteristics and qualities required for these relationships and functions to take place, so that the will and purpose of God for man can be accomplished, and man can fulfill his destiny of completing the works God ordained for him to do before the foundation of the world.

6. The image of God is something in the very nature of man, in the way in which he was made. It refers to something man is rather than something he has or does. Simply by virtue of his being man, he is in the image of God. There are no statements limiting the image to certain conditions or activities, or situations.

7. The image of God and humanity are best understood not through a study of human nature, but through a study of the Person of Jesus Christ, Son of God, who through his incarnation

became also Son of Man, fully divine and fully human, except without sin. We obtain our understanding of the image of God from the divine revelation given us by Jesus Christ through his ministry on earth leading up to his death on the cross, his resurrection, and ascension into heaven.

8. Jesus, as the sinless Son of Man and the pure sacrifice for our sin, is the perfect example of what human nature is intended to be. We should strive to conform ourselves to the likeness of Jesus, who in his humanity, is the complete revelation of what the image of God is, the full image. In its purest sense, the image of God is the forming of the likeness of Christ in us. No one is fully human unless they are a redeemed disciple of God in Christ. It is only when we have a living faith in Jesus Christ as Lord and Savior that we reflect the image of God within us, and through that faith, can truly understand our own nature.

9. Everyone, through the Holy Spirit, has the potential for fellowship with God, and will be incomplete unless it is realized. To repeat Saint Augustine's comment:

> "Our soul was created by and exists for God and is therefore never quiet until it rests in God."

Finally, what makes man unique, what sets him apart from the rest of creation, is that he is made in the image and likeness of God. The question then arises: "When does God's human creation receive this image and likeness of God? The Psalmist David, writing under the inspiration of the Holy Spirit, gives us the answer as we continue our commentary on Psalm 139.

In verse 13 we read:

> "For you created my inmost being; you knit me together in my mother's womb."

The Psalmist eloquently describes the work of God his Creator in bringing him, as well as all human life, into being with the words "you knit me together." These words describe the Creator's direct activity in the creation and growth of the fetus. In verses 15 and 16 we read:

"My frame was not hidden from you when I was made in the secret place. When I was woven together in the depths of the earth, your eyes saw my unformed body. All the days ordained for me were written in your book before one of them came to be."

The "secret place" and the "depths of the earth" refer to the womb. It is called the secret place because it conceals, and depths of the earth because it is associated with darkness and separation from the visible realm of life. The womb is the concealed and depth like place where life is formed.

The Psalmist sees himself, as well as all human creation, not as an accident, but as one known, formed, and brought into being by the Creator, given an allotted time on this earth, and encompassed by the everlasting God. The fact that God knew us before we were born, before the foundation of the world, has been discussed previously. In Jeremiah 1:5, God told the prophet:

"Before I formed you in the womb, I knew you, before you were born, I set you apart; I appointed you as a prophet to the nations."

Throughout the eons, we existed in God's mind, not objectively or remotely, but intimately and in totality. And in our Creator's perfect time, He brought us forth into this world. Nothing was left to chance. Of the 200,000,000 sperm trying to fertilize the mother's egg cell, God directs the one sperm that succeeds. And at that moment, the moment of conception, a new and unique individual life begins. All the inherited features of this new person are set - the DNA is complete - its gender, its features, its personality. All the instructions are present for all that this new person will become, with his/her capabilities, potential, and skills. And at that moment of conception, the image of God is bestowed on that new creation.

All that remains, as the Psalmist David tells us, is for this new person to be knit together in the womb, and, as Job, servant of God, tells us in Job 10:11-12, which I also quoted at the beginning of this chapter, to be clothed in flesh:

"Did you not…clothe me with skin and flesh and knit me together with bones and sinews? You gave me life and showed me kindness, and in your providence watched over my spirit."

Being clothed with skin and flesh and knit together with bones and sinews is what verses 15 and 16 of our Psalm is referring to. God saw our frame, our unformed body, and wove us together from an unshaped embryo to the person He designed us to be. As the mind of God saw us then, so his hand wrought us to be.

In verse 14, the Psalmist, in awe of his creation, gives praise to his Creator:

"I praise you because I am fearfully and wonderfully made; Your works are wonderful, I know that full well."

We too can praise God and say: "You know me as my Creator who formed me, but I cannot begin to comprehend this creature you have fashioned. Such knowledge is too wonderful for me, too lofty for me to attain. I can only look upon your creation with awe and wonder, and praise you, the Divine Maker."

The Psalmist gives the glory of his creation, and that of all humans to God, entirely to Him. He is the Author of our being. Our parents were only the instruments of it. As the Author of our being, our Creator shaped our complex individuality and directed it toward our future, which is also God's future for us. The Psalmist speaks of our future being God's future for us in verse 16 where he says:

"All the days ordained for me were written in your book before one of them came to be."

The span of each human life is sovereignly determined by God, and that span of life, in order to conform our future with God's future for us, must include the accomplishment of the works God ordained for each person before that person was born. We have spoken of these works before, and their fulfillment as the mark of a successful life in which God's will and purpose for the individual was accomplished and in which the person reached their highest good in God. "Your book" in the passage refers to the heavenly royal register of God's decisions. All our members were fashioned according to as they were written in the book of God's wise counsel.

In verse 18, the Psalmist says: "When I awake, I am still with you." Awake from what? From death! Here is the Psalmist's faith affirming that, in his awakening from death, he is still with his Creator. We can affirm the same because Jesus' promise to one of the criminals crucified with Him is his promise to us also. When the criminal asked Him: "Jesus, remember me when you come into your kingdom," which was the criminal's confession of faith in Jesus as Lord and Savior, Jesus answered him: "I tell you the truth, today you will be with me in Paradise" (Luke 23:42-43). Our Creator God is with us in his mind and heart not only before we are born, but with us in the womb as He knits us together, with us through all the days ordained for us in this life, with us at our death, and for those who are his through faith in Jesus Christ as Lord and Savior, with us for eternity in the Paradise that awaits us.

The Psalmist ends his Psalm by expressing his hatred for those who hate the Lord and counting those who rise up against the Lord as his enemies. How do we reconcile his hatred for the Lord's and his enemies with our Lord's command to love our enemies and pray for them in Matthew 5:43-48:

> "You have heard that it was said, 'Love your neighbor and hate your enemy.' But I tell you: Love your enemies and pray for those who persecute you, that you may be sons of your Father in heaven. He causes his sun to rise on the evil and the good and sends rain on the righteous and the unrighteous. If you love those who love you, what reward will you get? Are not even the tax collectors doing that? And if you greet only your brothers, what are you doing more than others? Do not even pagans do that? Be perfect, therefore, as your heavenly Father is perfect."

To reconcile that appearance of disparity, consider that a very important feature of the Psalmist's expression of hatred is that it is directed toward those who hate the Lord, and that the enemies whose defeat and destruction he calls for are the enemies of God, and therefore his enemies. In fact, the only reason they are his enemies is because they are the enemies of God. It is on that ground that the Psalmist calls for divine action. The Psalmist is aligning himself with the purpose and direction of God, and in opposition to those who hate the Lord, who speak of the Lord with evil intent, and who misuse the Lord's name. Therefore, his anger can be considered as a righteous anger, and his hatred as a righteous hatred.

In God's creation, there is a moral order referred to as the *order of creation*, which is not to be ignored or violated. This order of creation reflects God's divine character and his love and purpose for his creation. Abortion is a violation of this order of creation. Homosexual marriage is a violation of this order of creation. Divorce and the break-up of the family is a violation of this order of creation.

Earlier in our discussion of the image of God, the question was asked: "When does God's human creation receive the image of God?" I referred previously to the moment of conception as the time. It is the only answer that makes sense since the image of God is not something external to man's human nature, given to him at some stage of development, but rather something inseparably connected to man's humanity. The image of God in man, male and female, is what makes him/her a human being and sets him/her apart as the highest of God's creative acts. At the moment of conception, all that is necessary for the creation of a human being is given, and certainly the image of God is integral to this since it is that image that gives that creation its humanity.

The Psalmist makes it clear that it is God Himself as Creator who conducts and controls the process of creation in verses 13 and 15:

> "For you created my inmost being; You knit me together in my mother's womb. My frame was not hidden from you when I was made in the secret place."

Since it is God who creates, it necessarily follows that his image is stamped on his human creation through every stage of its development, from conception to birth. This means that the fertilized egg is stamped with the image of God. The embryo is stamped with the image of God.

The fetus is stamped with the image of God. The baby in the womb is stamped with the image of God.

What does this mean as far as abortion is concerned? It means that the popular concept of abortion during the first trimester of development does not involve the killing of a person, since what is being created is not yet a person but simply a mass of tissue and cells, is wrong, dead wrong. God does not create non-persons and stamp them with the image of God. Therefore personhood, just as the image of God, is bestowed on God's human creation from conception onwards. And this means that abortion, at whatever stage of the child's development it is conducted, is the murder of an innocent and helpless person.

Abortion, at any stage, is an attack on the image of God. And an attack on one bearing the image of God is an attack on God Himself. Jesus made it very clear that whatever is done or not done to one who belongs to Him, is done or not done to Himself. We are told this in his parable of the sheep and the goats in Matthew 25:31-46 where He says:

> "When the Son of Man comes in his glory, and all the angels with Him, He will sit on his throne in heavenly glory. All the nations will be gathered before Him, and He will separate the people one from another as a shepherd separates the sheep from the goats. He will put the sheep on his right, and the goats on his left. Then the King will say to those on his right: 'Come, you who are blessed by my Father, take your inheritance, the Kingdom prepared for you since the creation of the world. For I was hungry, and you gave me something to eat, I was thirsty, and you gave me something to drink, I was a stranger, and you invited me in, I needed clothes, and you clothed me, I was sick, and you looked after me, I was in prison, and you came to visit me.' "The righteous will answer: 'Lord, when did we see you hungry and feed you, or thirsty and give you something to drink? When did we see you a stranger and invite you in, or needing clothes and clothe you? When did we see you sick or in prison and go to visit you?' The King will reply: 'I tell you the truth, whatever you did for one of the least of these brothers of mine, you did for me.'

"Then He will say to those on the left: 'Depart from Me, you who are cursed, into the eternal fire prepared for the devil and his angels. For I was hungry, and you gave Me nothing to eat, I was thirsty, and you gave Me nothing to drink, I was a stranger, and you did not invite Me in, I needed clothes, and you did not clothe Me, I was sick and in prison and you did not look after Me.' "They also will answer: 'Lord, when did we see you hungry or thirsty or a stranger or needing clothes or sick or in prison and did not help you?' He will reply: 'I tell you the truth, whatever you did not do for one of the least of these, you did not do for Me.' Then they will go away to eternal punishment, but the righteous to eternal life."

In Scripture Jesus is referred to as the Word, the Living Word of God, and it was through this Word that God created the heavens and the earth and all they contain. The Apostle John in his Gospel, written under the inspiration of the Holy Spirit, makes this clear in the opening verses of his Gospel (John 1:1-4) as follows:

"In the beginning was the Word, and the Word was with God, and the Word was God. He was with God in the beginning. Through Him all things were made; without Him nothing was made that has been made. In Him was life, and that life was the light of men."

It is clear from this passage that God the Father created all things through Jesus Christ, the Son of God. It is clear from our passages in Psalm 139 that our Creator created our inmost being and knit us together in our mother's womb, that God the Son saw our frame as He made us In the secret place, as He wove us together in the depths of the earth, as He ordained all our days for us and wrote them in the Book of Life. It is clear that Jesus Christ, Son of God, took on our human flesh to become also Son of Man, the GodMan, fully divine and fully human, except without sin, in order to suffer and die to redeem us from sin, death, the power of the devil and hell, and ransom us as his own through the forgiveness of sins and salvation. It is clear that Jesus Christ, as Son of

God, is our God, and Jesus Christ, as Son of Man, is our human brother. And it is clear from the parable we just read that Jesus said: "Whatever you did, or did not do, to the least of these brothers (and sisters) of mine you did or did not do to me." The least of these brothers (and sisters) of mine is a perfect description of babies in the womb.

Knowing all this, it necessarily follows as previously stated that, at any stage of the pregnancy from conception to birth, an attack on the baby in the womb who bears the image of God, is an attack on Jesus Christ the Creator of Life, the God of all creation including that little miracle in the womb, and the human brother of the least of those little brothers and sisters of the Lord in the womb.

Abortion is the direct refusal to accept the Christ as Sovereign Lord of Life. It is, in effect, telling Him: "Lord, I accept you as Sovereign Lord over every aspect of my life except this one - I reserve the right to decide whether your creation in the womb lives or dies." How in God's Name can anyone with such an attitude claim to be a Christian, much less a devout Christian?

Jesus made it very clear that to be a disciple of his and receive the salvation He purchased through his suffering, death on the cross, and his resurrection, one must accept Him totally as Sovereign Lord over every aspect of one's life. A person cannot accept Christ as Sovereign Lord over 99% of their life, and reserve 1% for themselves, or for that matter, 99.9% of their life, and reserve .1% for themselves, and call themselves a Christian. Such people delude and deceive themselves. Being a disciple of Christ and turning over 100% of our life to his sovereignty and control is not easy. In fact, with our sinful human nature, it is impossible to do in and of ourselves. Only through the Holy Spirit's power, guidance, leading and sanctification can we succeed in doing so.

The Holy Spirit brings us to saving faith in Jesus Christ as Lord and Savior, sustains and sanctifies us in that faith, and strengthens and counsels us to become full disciples of our God and Savior.

I refer the reader back to the account of when one of the Pharisees, an expert in the law, tested Jesus with the question: "Teacher, which is the greatest commandment in the law?" Jesus replied: "Love the Lord your God with all your heart and with all your soul and with all your mind. This is the first and greatest commandment. And the second is like it: Love your neighbor as yourself. All the Law and the Prophets hang on these two commandments."

The question then is: "How can one claim to love the Lord as that greatest commandment describes - totally - and yet deny Him sovereignty over one aspect of life, that of abortion? How can one claim to obey that second greatest commandment to love our neighbor as ourselves, and at the same time, sanction abortion of that baby in the womb who is our innocent and helpless neighbor?"

As mentioned, God knows every one of those more than 62 million babies aborted since Roe v. Wade, and those who will be aborted throughout the future until the pure evil of abortion is abolished throughout the land. And He knows them intimately! Their frame was not hidden from Him; He saw their unformed bodies as He knit them together in the womb and ordained their lifespan and the works He would have them do. Abortion is the rejection of God's will and purpose for each child. It is placing human will over God's will. To say, as some pro-abortionists say, that abortion is within the will of God, is extreme foolishness and appalling ignorance. It is gross heresy and apostasy. Abortion is an act of total defiance towards God and an act of contempt for God.

In Luke 17:2, concerning those who cause his little ones to sin, Jesus said: "It would be better for him to be thrown into the sea with a millstone tied around his neck." If such punishment is reserved for one who causes one of Jesus' little ones to sin, what punishment is reserved for those who cause Jesus' little ones to be brutally and cruelly murdered in the womb through abortion? Only through confession and repentance can they be spared such punishment.

Abortion is a central feature of modern secular progressive liberal ideology which seeks a society based on sex without consequences. According to the secular progressives, the conception of a child cannot be allowed to disrupt one's lifestyle, professional career, educational opportunities, and convenience with an unwanted pregnancy. Hence the progressive liberal democratic party's fierce and relentless defense of legalized abortion right up to the moment of birth. As I mentioned before, this is nothing less than genocide.

Jeffrey T. Kuhner, columnist at the Washington Times, and whom I referred to before, maintains that the Democratic Party has become hostage to special interest groups, labor unions, trial lawyers, the homosexual lobby, and feminists. Pro-abortion organizations, such as Planned Parenthood and NARAL, drive the party's agenda. Mr. Kuhner is right. He is also right in his insistence that legalized abortion is State sanctioned infanticide since it is the murder of innocent, defenseless, human life. Additionally, abortion is an assault on the very foundation of constitutional democracy upon which our nation is built. It is the human rights issue of our time, the most fundamental of human rights that undergirds our democratic republic and system of government - that is, the right to life. Without this fundamental right to life, all other human rights are both impossible and meaningless.

Finally, Mr. Kuhner maintains that abortion is today's equivalent of slavery, a cancer eating away at the spiritual, moral, and political fabric of America. And just like slavery, the democratic secular progressives want Roe v. Wade, which legalized abortion, codified into law by the United States Congress, thereby reversing its repeal, and giving the stature of law to Roe v. Wade's underlying pure evil and damnable principle that an entire class of people, babies in the womb, are not fully human and therefore undeserving of basic human rights, primarily the right to life. In the 19th century under slavery, blacks were treated as property, less than human, to be used and discarded as their masters chose. Today, it is unborn babies in the womb who are murdered and discarded, treated like chattel to be disposed of. The fact that there are multitudes of people, primarily those of democratic persuasion, who are not thoroughly sickened and disgusted over the pure evil of abortion, is clear evidence of how far the desensitizing process has advanced in our nation.

Again, Mr. Kuhner is right on with his analysis of abortion as the most important human rights issue of today, with its devastating effects on the country, and its dividing of society into two implacable groups - pro-life and pro-abortion - like no other issue in the past with the exception of slavery. This column of his could very well be the most important of his commentaries as a syndicated columnist, as well as one of the most important of our time, and he is to be commended for speaking the truth which many choose not to speak, and which many others do not want to hear.

Psalm 12:8 tells us: "The wicked freely strut about when what is vile is honored among men." What could be more vile than the slaughter of babies in the womb, and what could be more arrogant, and contemptuous of God than the pro-abortionists, primarily the radical democrats and the Democratic Party, strutting about celebrating the slaughter and demanding that no conditions or restrictions be placed on abortions so that the slaughter can continue and even increase.

Two of the many Divine attributes of God are justice and mercy. God is a just God and He demands that his people be a just people and uphold justice. Deuteronomy 16:18-20 is only one of many passages in Scripture in which God demands justice. It reads:

> "Appoint judges and officials for each of your tribes in every town the Lord your God is giving you, and they shall judge the people fairly. Do not pervert justice or show partiality. Do not accept a bribe, for a bribe blinds the eyes of the wise and twists the words of the righteous. Follow justice and justice alone, so that you may live and possess the land the Lord your God is giving you."

God is a merciful God, and He demands that his people be merciful and show mercy to their fellowman. In Hosea 6:6, God tells his people through the prophet:

> "For I desire mercy, not sacrifice," and in Micah 6:8: "He has showed you, O man, what is good. And what does the Lord require of you? To act justly and to love mercy and to walk humbly with your God," and in Luke 6:36 Jesus says: "Be merciful, just as your Father is merciful."

God relates to his human creation, to peoples and nations, in a manner that is consistent with his Divine character and purpose. Therefore, whatever is inimical to God's way of justice and mercy, is the enemy of God, and divine judgment is inevitable. Abortion is the ultimate injustice to our babies in the womb. Abortion is the ultimate denial of mercy to our babies in the womb. Again, it must be emphasized that abortion, the people who sanction and approve of it, and the nations in which abortion is public policy, will most assuredly, in God's timing, come under divine judgment in order to remove the abominable stain of abortion and reestablish justice and mercy for our babies in the womb. The only way to avoid this terrible judgment, as I mentioned before, is individual and national confession and repentance, and turning away from the evil of abortion before God's timing runs out and He says: "Enough! It is time for judgment to cleanse this people and nation."

The Catholic Bishops have recommended that Catholic politicians and other officials who support abortion should not be given Holy Communion, the Eucharist, and also risk excommunication from the Church. When asked about this, the previous Pontiff, Pope Benedict responded that such action is not arbitrary, but is allowed by Canon Law which says that the killing of an innocent child is incompatible with receiving communion.

Thus, the Bishops are not recommending anything that is new, radical, or arbitrary, but simply announcing publicly what is contained in the law of the Church - that is, anyone who knowingly and consistently, without confession or repentance, commits or allows a grave sin, such as abortion, inflicts "automatic excommunication" upon themselves. The Pope went on to say: "Selfishness and fear are at the root of pro-abortion legislation," and that "We in the Church have a great struggle to defend life....Life is a gift, not a threat."

Frank Pastore, a radio talk show host in Los Angeles, who is not a Catholic, wrote in an article about abortion that Pope Benedict drew a line in the sand on abortion. He says that he would like to hear some "Protestant Benedicts" speak out with such clarity. He asks: "Where are those men who fear God more than men, who with conviction and principle are eager to take politically incorrect stands? Where are the pastors who care more about their faithfulness to the Biblical text than they do about filling their pews or their social and cultural standing? Where are the Bible colleges and the Theological Seminaries who are faithful in their teaching and instruction of the Bible as the inspired Word of God, and the final authority for faith and life? Which are the denominations who stand fast in God's Truth and adamantly refuse to compromise that Truth in any way in order to be more acceptable to the social and cultural standards of the day? What radio and television ministries have Christ crucified and risen as their central Gospel and the source from which all other teaching emanates?" Unfortunately, Mr. Pastore concludes that all of those mentioned above are relatively few.

I agree with James C. Dobson, Founder and Chairman of *Focus on the Family*, who described America's two primary political parties' differing philosophies of governing as follows: When Republicans assume power, many of them tend to say: "Well, golly, we're in charge now. Let's see if we can stay in office and not do anything too radical or controversial to get ourselves voted out." The Democrats, in stark contrast, Dobson says, "take charge and go straight for the jugular. They begin passing numerous radical bills and legislation and do everything in their power to stifle the opposition. The result is a left-wing revolution that turns society and culture on its ear. Democrats work as quickly and quietly as possible to consolidate power and to silence those who would call attention to their agenda."

Dobson wrote that in 2007, and the irony is that it is as if he wrote it today, because it precisely describes what the Democrats did during the past four years of the Biden administration. While we sleep, the secular progressive democrat radicals are advancing a radical agenda that will, if successful, weaken or even destroy the moral, constitutional underpinnings of this great nation. The moderate Democrats, if there are any left, are intimidated by the radicals and afraid that, if they oppose or offend them, they might lose their power and status. We need to pray that God will open the eyes of our clergy, our political leaders, our educational leaders, and the American people to what is happening throughout our culture, and give them the courage and fortitude to resist and overcome the political and spiritual degradation that is chipping away our Judeo-Christian foundation, with the first step being to outlaw the pure evil of abortion. But thank God that the reelection of President Trump appears to be opening the eyes of the American people.

In summary, the key to man's identity (both male and female) is the fact that "God created man in his own image, in the image of God He created him." This image was made integral to each human creation, past, present, and future, at the moment of conception. Each person comes into existence as a result of God's unique creative power and his intention and plan for each of his created beings. Each person's identity is inseparably connected to that divine plan, and the person's lifespan determined to enable the accomplishment of that divine plan.

Man has not only received his life from God but continues to experience and enjoy life because of divine provision. His very life and each breath he continues to take is from God. The Psalmist assures us that God knows all there is to know about each of his creations, and that God is always with us, ever present where we are present. He will never leave us or forsake us, and all our efforts to flee from Him are futile.

All of our life is rightfully his by virtue of his creating us, and by virtue of his redeeming us through the Son of God as Son of Man whose sacrifice of Body and Blood on the cross paid the full and terrible price for our sin and ransomed us from the condemning power of sin, death, and the devil. God's ownership of us is complete.

In Psalm 139, the Psalmist personally and intimately expresses the creative power and love of the Creator for his creation. God surrounds his creation, and his protective hand is always near as He forms the inward parts of his creation that bears his image and knits his creation's frame together with bone and sinew. Man's value is derived from, and conferred upon him, by God and not by other men. The essential question in evaluating anything is not whether it contributes to man's pleasure and comfort, but whether it contributes to God's glory and the fulfillment of his plan. Man's creation as man and woman fulfills both these requirements - they reflect and testify to God's power and glory, and they are ordained with works to accomplish the fulfillment of God's plan.

Man, in his arrogance, pride, and rebellion, defies God will, God's purpose, and God's blessings for that creation to accomplish God's perfect plan in the lifespan ordained for it, and demands that instead of God's will, the human will prevail for that creation, which includes a brutal and horrible death through the abomination of abortion. This insistence of the human will is stark evidence of sinful man's utter contempt for God, and man's complete worthiness to suffer God's judgment.

In conclusion, every single human being is equally created in the image of God, and that requires that human dignity be extended to that creation from the moment of conception until the moment of natural death. Abortion is never right for any reason. Abortion is the greatest immoral issue we confront in this country. Abortion is direct opposition to God and contempt for God's will and purpose for his creation.

Thus, the secular progressive radical liberal Democrat Party, with its approval of, support of, and demand for full abortion rights without conditions or limitations up to the moment of birth, fully expresses its opposition to, and contempt for, God's will and purpose, and therefore is truly a party in deep crisis and out of favor with the majority of the American people.

The Psalmist King David

Theologian Karl Barth

Job, the suffering servant of God

CHAPTER 9
THE SANCTITY OF MARRIAGE

*"The Lord God said, 'It is not good for the
man to be alone. I will make a helper
suitable for him...' Then the Lord made a
woman from the rib He had taken out
of the man, and He brought her to the man."*

Genesis 2: 18,22.

*"The man said, 'This is now bone of my
bones and flesh of my flesh; she shall
be called woman for she was taken out
of man."*

Genesis 2: 23.

The corruption of the first of the three sanctities, the Biblical Sanctity of
Life, by seven secular progressive justices of the Supreme Court, was
followed by the corruption of the Biblical Sanctity of Marriage by five
justices of the Supreme Court who fell in line with the secular
progressive ideology of the Democratic Party and legalized homosexual
marriage in the fifty states. In doing so, they too elevated themselves
above God, and in effect, declared themselves wiser than the One who
in the beginning instituted and blessed marriage as the holy union of man
and woman for the primary purpose of procreation and establishment
of the family structure - husband, wife, children - as the bedrock of
society. They declared themselves not only wiser than God, but wiser

than all the seers, wise men and women of millennia past, who affirmed marriage of man and woman foundational to civilized society.

What marriage instituted by God Himself truly is, the nature of its corruption, and what that corruption entails, is the content of this chapter.

From the above passages, we're told that God Himself was the officiant at the first marriage ceremony in history, and also the first father of the bride since He gave her to her husband. Why was it not good for man to be alone? For two reasons! First, because without his female helpmeet, man is incomplete. The Hebrew word for wife -ishshah- has the connotation of completer. God created us to be incomplete on our own. Only the two - male and female - together as one, make a complete man. The word man is not a gender term but includes both male and female. Hence the term "mankind." The one flesh unity between husband and wife that Adam spoke of in our passage above is stronger than any other kinship that exists. Jesus made that clear in Matthew 19:6 when in speaking of marriage He said:

"What therefore God has joined together, let man not separate."

The second reason it was not good for man to be alone was that, without female companionship and a partner in reproduction, the man could not fully realize his humanity. God blessed the man and the woman and said to them:

"Be fruitful and increase in number; fill the earth and subdue it."

Not only is this an account of the first marriage in history, but also the establishment of the first family in history. For as soon as the man receives the woman, we are told:

"For this reason, a man will leave his father and mother and be united to his wife, and they will become one flesh."

In the future, instead of remaining under the protective custody of his parents, a man leaves them and, being united with his wife as one flesh, establishes a new family unit. The divine intention for husband and wife in the beginning was monogamy. Together they were to form an inseparable union of which "one flesh" is both a sign and an expression of this unique, divinely instituted union. At this point, a word on celibacy is appropriate. Celibacy is a gift of God given to particular persons ordained by God for a specific purpose or calling in which celibacy would serve that purpose. It is a rare gift. In Scripture, not all priests were unmarried; not all pastors were unmarried, not all prophets were unmarried. In fact, most of them were married. Again, celibacy in Scripture was rare and given by God to a person whom He ordained for a specific purpose. The universal human condition instituted by God was marriage.

I once preached a sermon entitled *Leave, Cleave, and Weave*, the theme being that a man and a woman are to leave their parents, cleave to each other as one flesh, and weave the tapestry of a new family, with all that entails concerning history, traditions, heritage, and legacy. Here we see emphasis on the Sanctity of Marriage. To whom can we be more family bound than to the father who beget us and to the mother who bore us? Yet the son must leave them and be joined and cleave to his wife, and the daughter must leave them and be joined and cleave to her husband.

There is a saying that "marriages are made in heaven." This one between Adam and Eve certainly was, for the man, the woman, and the match were all God's work. He, by his power, created them both, and now by his ordinance, made them one. It was the first, and only, marriage made in perfect innocence, for every marriage since then has been tarnished by the fall into sin.

Marriage is often referred to as a contract between husband and wife. This is wrong. Contracts can be easily broken or dissolved, which unfortunately is the case today with a majority of marriages. A contract specifically states the actions required of each party to keep the contract in force. If one party fails in this, the contract is broken or dissolved. In this sense, marriage can be thought of as a contract since each partner promises to love, honor, etc., in sickness or in health, till death do us part; however, marriage is a holy estate that goes beyond contract. Marriage is a covenant between husband and wife with those promises to love, honor, etc., in sickness or in health, in poverty or riches, till death do us part. Covenants, as opposed to contracts, are binding relationships and agreements never to be broken. God never breaks a covenant. Only man breaks covenant. In the case of marriage, the bond of the marriage covenant is not to be broken or cut off by divorce for any cause except for adultery or desertion by one of the partners. Again, the words of Jesus: "What God has joined together, let not man separate!"

The importance of covenants can be seen in the fact that the Bible, the inspired Word of God, is divided into two Covenants, the Old Covenant or Old Testament, which is the Covenant of Law, and the New Covenant or New Testament, which is the Covenant of Grace and Salvation. Testament is another name for covenant. God struck covenants with individuals in Scripture. He made a covenant with Adam and Eve to send a Savior who would defeat Satan who had tempted them and pay the price for their sin and the sins of all their successors. He made a covenant with Noah that He would never destroy creation again with a flood; He made a covenant with Abraham that his progeny would outnumber the stars and through him all nations of the world would be blessed; He made a covenant with David that of his line a King would come who would rule forever. He made other covenants, the point being that He keeps them all, and He expects us to do the same.

The concept of covenant gives the highest emphasis to how firm and strong the bond of marriage is, not to be divided and weakened by the ordinances of man. What covenant means should induce a person contemplating marriage to employ much prudence and prayer in the choice of partner with whom he/she wants to enter this estate and be one flesh, realizing that it is a lifetime condition.

Like the Sanctity of Life, the ordinances of man have tarnished and weakened the Sanctity of Marriage. The application of "no-fault divorce" in the courts has been nothing short of disastrous to the status of marriage in our land today, where it is estimated that more than half of marriages end up in divorce. It has not been that long ago (six or seven decades) when marriage was considered not only as a holy institution, but as the critical component to family, society, and culture. Divorce had a certain stigma attached to it, not a condemning or ostracizing stigma, but more of a stigma of shame in failing at the second most important relationship of life, the first being one's relationship with God, and the second being one's relationship with their spouse.

Discussion of the Sanctity of Marriage necessarily includes discussion of human sexuality, which is integral to both human creation and marriage. The following narrative includes, in addition to my own comments, information taken from the "New Dictionary of Theology," edited by Sinclair B. Ferguson, David F. Wright, and J. I. Packer, Inter Varsity Press, 1988.

"Human sexuality which is integral to marriage is a much larger concept than simply sexual behavior. It defines more of what people are than on what they do. The creation of man and woman as sexual beings is specifically linked with their creation in God's image. Therefore Biblically, sexuality is integral to human personhood." The phrase "bone of my bones and flesh of my flesh" with which Adam described Eve when God brought her to him, evokes not only their union as one, but also the special intimacy including sexual intimacy that they share as one flesh.

Scripture is overwhelmingly positive in its treatment of sexuality, and strongly affirms the goodness of sex. Read the book "Song of Songs" in the Bible, which is also a celebration of married sex, and downright erotic in some portions in a beautiful and poetic genre. Scripture contradicts the human heresy that asceticism and celibacy constitute a higher spiritual standard than the one flesh of husband and wife.

"The history of the Church, however, reveals a far less positive attitude to sexuality than the Bible's. In its earliest days, the Church was confronted by a powerful philosophical dualism, a central feature of an overall heresy called Gnosticism, which taught (among other things), the superiority of the mind and spirit over the body. It stressed salvation through "gnosis," a Greek term for knowledge, and the opposition between the spiritual world and the evil, material and physical world. Theologically, this was condemned as heresy and vigorously resisted. However, its central belief that the spirit and mind were good, and the physical, including the body, was evil, had an insidious influence on thinking about sexuality, namely that one could do anything with the body since it was material and evil. This included sexual immorality. The Church fought this vigorously: however, due to the popularity of Gnosticism among the public, and the Church's resistance against it, it was not long before ascetic idealism and celibacy gained a strong grip on Christian behavior.

With few exceptions, patristic and medieval writers condemned the sensual pleasure of intercourse as sinful. Imagine that! The act itself wasn't sinful. How could it be? After all, God Himself instituted it. But if you enjoyed it, then it was sinful. Go figure that rationale. Their attitude concerning marriage was at best ambivalent. They certainly regarded celibacy as preferable, and mandatory for clergy." The attitude of these writers in condemning sex as sinful and regarding celibacy as more spiritual than sexual union between husband and wife is incredible given the fact, as mentioned, that God Himself blessed the sexual union between Adam and Eve, and through them, that blessing applies to all married couples as man (husband) and woman (wife).

With the negative attitude towards marriage and sex, attitudes toward women at this time also reveal a similarly negative approach. There was a strong tendency to blame Eve for man's fall into sin, and this blame eventually extended to all women.

Celibacy, in some ways, became the criterion for purity. I already mentioned that celibacy was one of the gifts of the Holy Spirit, given by God to specific individuals for specific purposes, and not en masse as to the whole clergy as the Catholic Church later established. A few examples of celibates from Scripture are the prophet Jeremiah, John the Baptist, the Apostle Paul. As far as Paul is concerned, he may have been a widower when Jesus called him, since he had been a Pharisee, and it was mandatory for a Pharisee to be married.

The Catholic Papacy, in making celibacy mandatory for all its clergy, created a tremendous problem for the Church which still exists today with the sexual scandals of priests and other church authorities. Martin Luther, the Reformer, referred to this when he said:

"When celibacy is forced upon a person who has not been given the gift of celibacy, it opens the door to sin."

And that it certainly did in the Church. It is interesting to read about the various ways priests tried to obey this rule. One bishop sent his wife to a convent where she stayed. They remained the closet of friends, but never lived together again as husband and wife. Priests went to extremes trying to deaden the sexual desire including submerging oneself in ice water up to the neck, crawling through a thicket of thorns with multiple cuts to oneself, whipping oneself until the back was covered with blood. It is said that St. Augustine, who in his pre-Christian days was quite a partier with a mistress and a child, after his dramatic conversion and wanting to become a priest, but hesitating because of the celibacy requirement, once prayed: "O Lord, grant me the gift of celibacy, but not yet!"

Was Jesus a celibate? Yes, but Jesus, in his humanity, did not have the gift of celibacy. In order to be the perfect human sacrifice for our sins, Jesus had to experience every temptation to sin that you and I and everyone else experiences, and that certainly includes sexual sin. And He had to experience it all without sinning. If He had committed one sin, whether in thought, word or deed, He would have no longer been the perfect sacrifice and our salvation would not have been ransomed. Moreover, Jesus had to resist all sin in his human nature, just like you and me and everyone else, not calling on his all-powerful divine nature. Yes, Jesus had a sexual nature, and felt sexual desire, because in addition to being fully divine, He was fully human just like you and me and every other human being, except He was celibate and sinless. Thank you Jesus, for resisting all sin, for being celibate and sinless so you could be the perfect sacrifice for my sin.

The heresy of asceticism, with its arrogance of superiority and it's looking down on sexuality and the body as inferior or even evil, was reaching and being discussed in many of the young churches that the Apostle Paul had been active in planting and to which his letters, epistles, were addressed. According to our source, the "New Dictionary of Theology," "Paul, in particular, is lucidly blunt in his strong criticism of those who despised marriage and in his affirmation of the physical body life with a positive attitude towards sex, which has no room for either abuse or withdrawal."

The Bible is clear in its veto on extra-marital sexual intercourse. The doctrine of creation was widely understood in New Testament times as limiting the legitimacy of sexual intercourse to permanent, exclusive, heterosexual relationships. Hence, the specific Biblical ban on prostitution, pre-marital intercourse, adultery, and homosexual behavior. In 1Corinthians 6: 15, 18-20 we are told:

> "Do you not know that your bodies are members of Christ Himself? Shall I then take the members of Christ and unite them with a prostitute? Never!...Flee from sexual immorality...Do you not know that your body is a temple of the Holy Spirit, who is in you, whom you have received from God? You are not your own, you were bought at a price. Therefore, honor God with your body."

In Exodus 20:14, the Seventh Commandment of the Law tells us:

> "You shall not commit adultery!"

And in 1Corinthians 6: 9-11, we're told:

> "Do you not know that the wicked will not inherit the Kingdom of God? Do not be deceived: Neither the sexually immoral nor idolaters, nor adulterers, nor male prostitutes, nor homosexual offenders, nor thieves, nor the greedy, nor drunkards, nor slanderers, nor swindlers, will inherit the Kingdom of God. And that is what some of you were. But you were washed (in the Blood of Christ), you were sanctified, you were justified in the Name of the Lord Jesus Christ and by the Spirit of our God."

God's Word makes it clear that He does save and sanctify people like those described above who repent of their sins, seek his forgiveness for the sake of their Lord and Savior Jesus Christ, and strive to be faithful in the new life God gives them, realizing that if and when they fail, God's grace and forgiveness is still theirs when they confess, repent, and seek it for Jesus' sake. As God's Word assures us:

"The Blood of Jesus Christ just keeps cleansing us of our sin."

The Reformers did much to redress the balance between the extreme asceticism and celibacy of the Gnostics and the specific asceticism and celibacy contained in God's Word which fulfills God's plan and purpose for the individual. "With their Bibles open, they emphasized true ascetic humility before God, condemned compulsory celibacy for the clergy, and upheld marriage as a gift of God, confirmed by his Word and safeguarded by the authority of his Law. In their writings, there is also a recall to the Biblical emphasis on the relational aspect of marriage and family life.

Contemporary scholars are virtually unanimous in their praise of the relational values of sexuality. Nevertheless, they present a broad spectrum of theological opinions on sexual behavior, and their conclusions often differ sharply. On the one hand, you have conservatives, who while strongly affirming the relational aspects of sex in marriage, equally strongly maintain the Biblical veto on all extramarital intercourse. On the other hand, you have the liberal situationists who see no need to be tied to Biblical or traditional standards. In their view, the demands of love-in-relationships always override rules and regulations, whether they are enshrined in the Bible or some other book.

These conflicting theological opinions are clearly evident in debate and discussions concerning sexuality. As an example, on the question of divorce and remarriage, there are those who assert that marriage, from the Biblical standpoint, is indissoluble and divorce is contrary to God's will and therefore sin. And then there are those who believe that, in the case of a marriage that is irretrievably broken, Christ Himself would recommend divorce.

Both sides of this discussion claim Biblical support for their position. Let's consider what the Bible says about divorce. First, those who maintain that divorce is contrary to God's will, can quote Malachi 2:16 which says:

"I hate divorce," says the Lord God of Israel.

Second, those who support divorce can claim that God allowed divorce. The question of how God can allow divorce when He clearly states that He hates divorce is cleared up by Jesus in Matthew 19: 3-18, where we are told:

> "Some Pharisees came to Jesus to test Him. They asked, 'Is it lawful for a man to divorce his wife for any and every reason.' 'Haven't you read,' Jesus replied, 'that at the beginning the Creator made them male and female and said, for this reason, a man will leave his father and mother and be united to his wife, and the two will become one flesh. So, they are no longer two, but one. Therefore, what God has joined together, let man not separate.'" "Why then," they asked, "did Moses command that a man give his wife a certificate of divorce and send her away?" Jesus replied, "Moses permitted you to divorce your wives because your hearts were hard. But it was not this way from the beginning. I tell you that anyone who divorces his wife, except for marital unfaithfulness, and marries another woman commits adultery."

We have an important lesson in Jesus' reply that God, through Moses, permitted divorce because of the hardness of their hearts. That lesson is simply this: If we keep on insisting to have our own way instead of God's way, God will at times allow us to have our own way. Why? In order to teach us a lesson and help us grow in the knowledge of God's will for our lives. What lesson? That to substitute our will for God's will in any area of our life will never work out for our good, because our will is tainted and corrupted by sin, while God's will is perfect and always seeks our highest good.

After Jesus told them that God permitted divorce because of the hardness of their hearts, He referred them back to the beginning to remind them of what marriage truly is as instituted and blessed by God Himself with Adam and Eve. And He emphasized again the point that divorce did not exist at the beginning with his comment that whoever divorces and remarries another commits adultery.

It is interesting to note that after Moses approved divorce, two schools of thought arose among the Rabbis which were in dispute over the interpretation of Deuteronomy 24:1-4 which reads:

> "If a man marries a woman who becomes displeasing to him because he finds something indecent about her, and he writes her a certificate of divorce, gives it to her and sends her from his house….."

The dispute between the schools of Rabbi Shammai and Rabbi Hillel concerned the statements "becomes displeasing" and "something indecent." The school of Rabbi Shammai held that the statements, particularly "something indecent," meant marital unfaithfulness - the only allowable cause for divorce which Jesus referred to. On the other hand, the school of Rabbi Hillel held that the statements, particularly "becomes displeasing to him," would allow a man to divorce his wife if she did anything he disliked - even if she burned his food while cooking it.

Jesus clearly took the side of Rabbi Shammai, but only after first pointing back to God's original design for marriage. It is fascinating to consider how, after a few thousand years, the current modern positions on divorce correspond to those of Rabbi Shammai and Rabbi Hillel - divorce justified for unfaithfulness only, and divorce justified for just about any reason. Today, Rabbi Hillel's position would be presented to the court as "irreconcilable differences," the legal jargon for divorce for any reason.

"Irreconcilable differences" is meaningless, simply a catchphrase used to justify divorce. The couples are not required to describe what those irreconcilable differences are. The term also totally disregards the fact that man and woman are created in the image of God with the intellectual ability to reason, analyze, quantify, and discern right from wrong, good from bad, true from false, and best from worse. Given these God-given capabilities, I would say that there are few conditions in this life that are irreconcilable, and divorce is not one of them. What apparently is irreconcilable is the husband's and wife's lack of desire and will to reconcile.

Then too, if children are involved, there is the old tired catchphrase: "We're doing what's best for the children, removing them from an adversarial, hostile, environment." That's rubbish, meant to relieve the consciences of the divided parents and comfort them with the thought that they are doing good for the children. Someone needs to tell them: "No! No! This is not what's best for the children. What's best for the children is that you - man (husband), and you -woman (wife) use your God-given capabilities, intellect, and common sense, to systematically, with honesty and discipline, work through the situation, identify the problems, agree to work together to resolve those problems, and strive together to be loving husband and wife, loving parents to your children, and the Godly role models that your children desperately need and deserve in order for them to become loving husband and wife to their spouses, loving parents and Godly role models to their children. And realize this: Your happiness is no longer the priority. Your children are! And your greatest responsibility is to be that loving husband and loving father, that loving wife and loving mother. And if you strive to be so, I believe the happiness will follow and you will one day thank God you didn't go through with the divorce.

Don't get me wrong! I am not condemning those who have divorced. Yes, divorce is sin, but like all sin, it can be forgiven through the sacrifice of Christ's Body and Blood for all sin, including divorce. It all depends on the attitude of the divorced party. If that attitude is one of deep sorrow and regret, followed by confession and repentance of sin, the divorced party can be sure of God's forgiveness, healing, and renewal.

As I mentioned before, no-fault divorce was another of those seemingly bright judicial ideas, which has had utterly disastrous effects on family, society, culture, and the nation overall. One can only shake one's head in wonderment at the appallingly stupid decisions made by some people who are supposed to have some semblance of intellect - politicians and judges who make law and who decide the constitutionality of law. If you legalize abortion, you're going to have open season on unborn babies. If you make divorce no-fault, the divorce rate is going to skyrocket, having a disastrous effect on family and children. This isn't rocket science. It is plain common sense, a commodity that seems to be in short supply today.

The number of children being raised by a single parent, usually the mother, ranges in the millions. These children are missing the unique qualities of a father's love, care, masculine guidance, direction, sacrifice, and yes, loving discipline (emphasis on loving) that only the male husband and father can provide. In the situation where the single parent is the father, the children are missing the unique qualities of a mother's care, unconditional love, understanding, comfort, heightened sensitivity to the child's needs, and the willingness to sacrifice to meet those needs that only the female wife and mother can provide. A man cannot ideally fulfill the mother's special role, and a woman cannot ideally fulfill the father's special role, roles which the order of creation established by God designed.

In the past five or six decades, the secular progressive liberals' and the feminists' emphasis on women's equality in the marketplace, equal opportunity, careerism outside the home, and the deemphasis on motherhood and homemaker, even to the point of insulting the mother and homemaker as being inferior to her feminist sister who is CEO of a business or corporation, has been commonplace. The truth is that, in the eyes of God and children, that mother and homemaker being home when her children return from school, that mother and homemaker being able to accompany her children to school events and other events important to them, that mom and homemaker raising her children in the nurture and admonition of the Lord each and every day, that mom and homemaker teaching her children each and every day to be moral and righteousness citizens of this country, is engaged in an exceedingly greater career than CEO of a company, and in the final analysis, one that is of critical importance to the nation. When careerism takes precedence over motherhood and homemaking, it is usually the children who suffer most.

It is indeed unfortunate that the feminist organizations chose to belittle those whose priority is motherhood and homemaking. In doing so, they emphasized their bias, came across as foolish, and lost their credibility with many. Why? Check the end of the paragraph above and notice that my comment that when careerism takes precedence, it is usually the children who suffer, I used the word "usually." It is not always so. There are many, many women out there who are successful in the marketplace, who are CEOs of large corporations or small business owners who are highly respected for their leadership and managerial expertise, and who at the same time, manage to lovingly fulfill their motherhood and homemaker roles, God bless them. The feminist organizations don't usually honor these women because they prefer to keep the career and homemaking roles as adversarial roles and not as cooperative roles. Thus, as I say, their bias has become glaringly obvious.

To conclude the discussion on divorce, I again emphasize that yes, divorce is sin. But God, who loves the sinner, stands ready to receive, forgive, heal, and renew the divorced person's life. Seek that forgiveness, healing, and renewal for your Savior's sake.

Having discussed the subject of sexuality in marriage, we now turn to the subject of love in marriage. There was once a song that went:

> "Love and marriage, love and marriage, go together like a horse and carriage, this I tell you brother, you can't have one without the other."

The song would be somewhat irrelevant today since, with the divorce rate over 50%, it is common for the love to become unhitched from the carriage of marriage. Also, from the huge number of unmarried partners today, the attitude is common that the love of marriage can be enjoyed without the blessing of marriage.

The reader may be thinking, "We all know that marriage is built on the foundation of love, so what more is there to say?" The answer is that there is a lot to say about the character of this love. In the English language, we have one word for love - love. And this word has wide connotation. "I love chocolate!" "I love to go skiing!" "I love my car!" "I love my wife!" That one word covers it all. However, in the Greek language, the original language of the New Testament of the Bible, several words are used to describe different kinds of love, and these words, especially one of them, has great application to the subject of marriage.

The Greek word "Eros" refers to the attraction of desire, especially sexual desire and sexual love. It's where the English word erotic comes from. The Greek word "Philia" refers to brotherly love, the love and affection for friends and relatives. The Greek word "Agape," however, refers to a Godlike love, a sacrificial love, the love of the Father in giving his Son to save us from our sins, the love of the Son, Jesus, in going to the cross for us with all the horrendous suffering that entailed for our salvation. Agape love is clearly distinguished from the others. Agape love is also both the pattern and the motivating power of the Christian life.

Eros love and Philia love are natural even in fallen man, whereas the godly Agape love is not. All are essentially God-given, and all were drastically affected by the fall of mankind into sin which distorted the image of God created in man. For example, eros became so badly debased into lust in the Graeco-Roman world that the writers of the New Testament, inspired by the Holy Spirit, avoided the use of the word altogether. The agape love is renewed in a person when they come to faith in Jesus Christ as their Lord and Savior, and the Holy Spirit, through the process of sanctification and regeneration, renews the person progressively in God's image.

Agape love in men and women images divine grace, and therefore needs to permeate, inform, direct, and control the other forms of love, as well as all Christian relationships with others, whether believers or not. The Bible does not teach that agape love supplants erotic love or philia love. But it does teach very clearly that the erotic love and the philia love find their fulfillment only in the context of agape love. This has tremendous application to marriage which will be discussed in the following.

According to the Apostle Paul, the test of love in marriage is the agape love between husband and wife which images the agape love relationship between Christ and the Church. Agape, the Godlike love of intelligence, purpose, wisdom, and sacrifice, stands in total contrast to all pagan ideas of love in a fallen world. These so-called loves are manipulative, largely self-centered, and primarily directed towards self-interest, self-gratification, and self-protection, whereas agape love is completely unselfish, not afraid to make itself vulnerable, does not seek to get its own way, and proceeds from a heart of love and is directed to bless the other person and seek that persons' highest good.

1Corinthians 13:4-7 gives us the ultimate description of agape love. It would behoove every married person and those planning marriage, and especially those contemplating divorce, to read these passages and ask themselves: "How does my love in marriage compare to the love in these passages? We are told:

> "Love is patient, love is kind. It does not envy, it does not boast, it is not proud. It is not rude, it is not seeking, it is not easily angered, it keeps no record of wrongs. Love does not delight in evil but rejoices with the truth. It always protects, always trusts, always hopes, always perseveres."

Also, as we read in 1John 4:7-11, agape love's source is God, and its pattern and inspiration are Jesus Christ. We are told:

> "Dear friends, let us love one another, for love comes from God. Everyone who loves has been born of God and knows God. Whoever does not love does not know God, because God is love. This is how God showed his love among us: He sent his one and only Son into the world that we might live through Him. This is love: not that we loved God, but that He loved us and sent his Son as an atoning sacrifice for our sins. Dear friends, since God so loved us, we also ought to love one another."

Agape love is not merely emotion, but commitment and practical action measured by self-giving and sacrifice. Such love is the most essential and abiding quality of human life. As the Apostle Paul tells us, such love is to control all relationships, especially in marriage, family, and church. In Ephesians 5:22-33, Paul describes how this agape love works in marriage. As I comment on Paul's instructions, I ask women readers not to close the book because they are offended by the word submission. Read on to see what the husband is charged with. In this passage which I will discuss in sections, we have the Christian marriage in a nutshell, and the marital relations of both wife and husband. This description of Christian marriage is found in other Epistles, including those of Peter and John. We begin with Ephesians 5:22-24:

> "Wives, submit to your husbands as to the Lord. For the husband is the head of the wife as Christ is the head of the Church, his Body, of which He is the Savior. Now as the Church submits to Christ, so also wives should submit to their husbands in everything."

Paul is beginning to describe the special relationship and a special self-submission involved in the agape love of a Christian marriage. It is something entirely different from the worldly understanding of the word "submission." Paul is not speaking of all women submitting to all men - a wrong idea - but all wives to their own husbands. Also, this is definitely not a text claiming that women are inferior to men. It is a text on the Christian marriage relationship and that is all. It is an aspect, however, of the mutual submission of all Christians to one another, taught by Paul in the preceding verse 21 where he said: "Submit to one another out of reverence for Christ."

To submit means to yield one's own rights in favor of another's. It does not connote obedience. In fact, the word obey does not appear in Scripture with respect to wives as it does with children and slaves. Also, the submission discussed here is a voluntary self-submission, not in any way a subjugation. It is a Christian self-submission, evidenced by the words "as to the Lord." "As to the Lord" does not put a woman's husband in the place of the Lord but shows rather that a woman submits to her husband as an act of submission to the Lord, who arranged the marriage relationship at creation, as a part of the order of creation.

"For the husband is head of the wife as Christ is head of the Church" refers to Christian marriage as Christ intends for it to be. The analogy between the relationship of Christ to the Church and that of the husband to the wife is basic to the entire passage as we shall see. Every Christian wife and husband will want, or should want, their marriage to be like that of Christ and his Church. Paul here lifts Christian marriage to a remarkably high position. He compares it to the marriage of Christ and his Church. All the blessedness of Christian marriage is brought forth by this comparison.

"Now as the Church submits to Christ, so also wives should submit to their husbands in everything." The married couple is a unity, one body. As one body, they can only have one head, even as the Bride, the Church, the Body of Christ, can have but one head - Christ. The Church submits herself to Christ. Wives submit themselves to their husbands. Again, the key is that the submission is voluntary, with no compulsion or force. It is an act of blessedness.

There are many women who will take offense at the words "the husband is the head," and "wives submit to your husbands." They are thinking of those words "head" and "submission" in a worldly way and not in the Biblical or spiritual way. They relate "head" to being superior and "submission" to being inferior, which is totally wrong. Being the "head" has nothing to do with being the boss. Instead, it has everything to do with servanthood, which is a primary characteristic of true leadership. Jesus showed this at the last supper before his crucifixion. After supper, He took off his robe, took a towel and basin, and washed his disciples' feet to give them an example of the servanthood of real leadership. After He finished, He said to them:

> "Do you understand what I have done for you? You call me Teacher and Lord, and rightly so, for that is what I am. Now that I, your Lord and Teacher, have washed your feet, you also should wash one another's feet. I have set you an example that you should do as I have done for you." John 13: 12-15.

What was the lesson, the example? Simply this: If you aspire to be a leader, you must first learn how to serve. As a former military officer, I can say that the sooner one learns this lesson, the more effective he/she will be as a leader. There is always something to serve - the mission, your people, the unit, the country, and don't forget, your family. Jesus' washing of his disciples' feet was symbolic of such servanthood, and it should be presented as the greatest example of servant leadership to all students undergoing leadership training, either military or civilian.

We now consider what the Holy Spirit inspired Paul to say concerning the husband's responsibility to his wife. In Ephesians 5: 25, we read :

> "Husbands, love your wives just as Christ loved the Church and gave Himself up for her....."

Paul now shows that this is not a one-sided submission, but a reciprocal relationship. The love Paul speaks of here is higher that eros or philia, sexual love or affection for another, which is about all that most non-Christian people consider as the ideal conjugal love of marriage as God intended. Paul is speaking of the highest form of love, agape love, which I repeat is the love of intelligence, wisdom, purpose, and sacrifice, with the emphasis on sacrifice, the love which wisely comprehends what God intends for marriage to be, and which is therefore filled with the husband's purpose to carry out God's intention even to the point of sacrificing his own life.

This agape love of the husband for the wife should make it a delight for the wife to submit herself to a loving husband whose love for her mirrors Christ's love for his Church. No wife can cultivate the willing, joyful submission intended by the Lord without this wise, purposeful, and sacrificial agape love on the part of her husband.

In Paul's charge to husbands to "love your wives just as Christ loved the Church," those words "just as" denotes likeness of manner. First of all, remember that the Church is the Body of Christ, and we are that Body - you, me, and every Christian who confesses Jesus Christ as Lord and Savior. Christ's love for the Church, his Body, is to be the husband's example for loving his wife, his body in oneness of the flesh. So, how did Christ love the Church? We're told that He "gave Himself up for her!" What does this mean? He went to the cross for her! He sacrificed his Body and his Blood for her! He gave his all for her!

Wait a minute! Are you telling me that the husband is to sacrifice his own life for his wife's good if the situation requires it? Yes! Yes! That's precisely what the passage is telling us. The words "gave Himself up for her" not only expresses our Lord's love for his Church, but also describes how the husband ought to devote himself to his wife's good. To give oneself up to death for the beloved is a more extreme expression of devotion than the wife is called on to make with her submission.

Once again, because it bears repeating, the sacrificial love of Christ for his Body, the Church, is the supreme illustration for the way in which Christian husbands are to love their wives, with whom they are one body, one flesh.

In verses 26 and 27, we are told that Christ sacrificed Himself to make his Church holy, cleansing her through water and the Word, making her radiant, holy, and blameless. The Lord Jesus died, not only to bring forgiveness to us, but also to effect a new life of holiness in the Church, which is us, his "bride." The mention of water and the Word probably refers to baptism, by which one is brought into the family of God and the new life in Christ.

In verses 28-30, we are told that just as Christ loves his Body, the Church, husbands ought to love their wives as their own bodies, and he who loves his wife, loves himself. And in verse 29 we're told that:

> "After all, no one ever hated his own body, but he feeds and cares for it, just as Christ does the Church - for we are members of his Body."

The basis for these expressions and the teaching in these verses is the quotation from Genesis 2: 23-24, which is Adam's response when God brought the woman to him. Adam said:

> "This is now bone of my bones and flesh of my flesh; she shall be called woman for she was taken out of man."... "For this reason, a man will leave his father and mother and be united to his wife, and they will become one flesh."

If the husband and wife become one flesh, then for the man to love his wife is to love one who has become part of himself. Since in the original marriage, instituted and performed by God Himself, the husband and wife became one flesh, so it is with every marriage since, and each person, by loving their spouse, loves himself/herself. Where the agape love, the love of sacrifice, is present in the Christian husband, he constantly feeds and cares for his wife as his very own body. Also, and this is critical, the Christian husband and wife are members of Christ's Body, the Church, and are so loved by Christ who redeemed them with his Body and his Blood on the cross. And Christ continues to feed them, and all their brothers and sisters in Christ who comprise Christ's Body, with the living Word and the living Water every time they attend worship services, Bible studies, prayer groups - every time they gather together in Christ's Name. This love of Christ for each Christian husband and wife is their constant Inspiration and help to enable the wife's loving submission and the husband's loving self-sacrifice in their marriage.

I will call the reader's attention to the fact that three verses of the passage are devoted to the wife's obligations to her husband in marriage, and nine verses devoted to the husband's obligations to his wife in marriage. The Apostle Paul knew what he was doing when the Holy Spirit inspired him to expound on the husband's obligations, especially that of sacrifice. To appreciate this, one must consider the state of marriage at the time. As far as the Jew's regard for marriage, it was mentioned previously that any husband could divorce his wife for the most trivial of causes, or for no cause at all, and she had no recourse. As for the pagan world, it was even worse. Romans would joke about the frequent exchange of wives, asking whose wife was so and so this week? And remember, the churches were composed of converts from both Jewish and Gentile groups. Instruction on God's plan, intent, and design for marriage was definitely called for, and Paul's teaching on marriage in Ephesians and other books of the Bible must have come as a shock to those converts.

God made marriage so ideal, perfect, and blessed. However, sin entered, and just as it corrupted everything, so it corrupted this relationship. Eve fell first, Adam followed, and God's order of creation was subverted in two ways: 1. Wives started to seek to rule their husbands, refusing loving self-submission. And 2. Husbands started to tyrannize their wives, often to the point of enslaving them. Endless woe resulted. Obviously this is not true of all marriages, or perhaps not even the majority, but it certainly is for far too many.

Christian marriage is meant to restore the divine order with all its blessedness. When Christianity came, women and wifehood were elevated from their pagan degradation to the original divine intention of the marital relation of husbands and wives and the sanctification of this relationship and its glorious elevation because Christ made it the image of his own relation to the Church, with Him as the Bridegroom and the Church as his Bride.

In verse 32 of Ephesians 5, Paul refers to the union of Christ and his Bride, the Church, as a profound mystery. It is beyond unaided human understanding. And being beyond unaided human understanding, the basic reality is not that the relationship of husband and wife in Christian marriage provides an illustration of the union between Christ and the Church, since illustration denotes understanding, but that the relationship of husband and wife in Christian marriage is a human echo of Christ's relation with his Church with all its profundity. Finally, in verse 33, Paul's reemphasis on the husband's obligation to love his wife as he loves himself, and the wife's obligation to respect her husband is simply a rephrasing and summary of the whole passage.

In this passage from Ephesians which we have discussed in detail, the Apostle Paul, writing under the inspiration of the Holy Spirit, points out to husband and wife their proper relation, attitude, and conduct toward each other. Nothing truer and nobler has ever been written or said on the subject. To tamper in any way with the marriage relationship here marked out is only to cause damage to the institution, and the most terrible damage. Today we have ample evidence of such terrible damage. Many have tried, and continue to try, to modify God's Word, given through the Apostle Paul and others, on marriage. There are those who object to Paul's words regarding the self-submission of Christian wives to husbands, claiming that such self-submission is no longer up-to-date and befitting our advanced age. Apparently these people are saying that God's Word must be changed to conform with current cultural and societal standards. My response to them would be to have them consider the results of man-made changes to marriage so far in attempts to bring it up to date - utter and complete disaster with over half of marriages failed or failing.

The human composition of God's design for marriage - one man, one woman, has also come under strong criticism. As I mentioned at the beginning of this chapter, in recent years our legal geniuses have discovered a constitutional right totally contradictory to God's Word, a right totally contradictory to the Judeo-Christian foundation upon which the Founding Fathers built the nation and its government, a right that is not mentioned in the Constitution, a right that for over the first 200 years or so of our constitutional history eluded some of the most brilliant legal minds in our history, a right that, in the opinion of the radicalized secular progressive liberals in the Democratic Party, and even some in the Republican Party and Independent Party, brings God's design for marriage up-to-date with the cultural and societal standards of our advanced age. And what is that right? The imaginary constitutional right to same-sex marriage. I wonder, do you think God is grateful for the help of these radical liberals in bringing his Word, which apparently was in error, up to date with worldly standards.

What man, in his foolishness and arrogance forgets, is that human cultural and societal standards that are demonstrably contradictory to God's Word are of satanic origin, and that which is of satanic origin poses the greatest danger to a nation and its people. There is a desperate need that the majority of our people, who claim to be Christian, understand just what Scripture says on the subject of marriage, that they apprehend the critical nature of God's design for marriage, critical to the individual, critical to the family, critical to the nation, and that they recognize, at least to some degree, the marriage relationship of husband and wife as an echo of the relationship between Christ and his Church.

I have written elsewhere in this book about my opinion concerning homosexual marriage and how the Christian should relate to the homosexual community. As a Christian and follower of Jesus Christ, I am to relate to all men, including the homosexual, and perhaps especially to the homosexual, with the love and grace of God. I most certainly do not condemn them. Who am I, a miserable sinner, to condemn anyone? God alone has the authority to condemn. And so, I reach out to the homosexual in God's love, God's grace, with friendship and prayer and ask God to direct and lead them to his holy will and purpose and their highest good in Him. But I cannot give approval or support to the lifestyle or policies such as same-sex marriage. Why? Because God's Word is clear that homosexuality is a violation of God's will and order of creation. Then too, same-sex marriage is unreasonable and irrational in that it makes it impossible to accomplish the primary objective of marriage.

The primary purpose of marriage, as stated by God Himself, is to reproduce, have children, and replenish the human race. We read in Genesis 1:28 that after God created man and woman He blessed them and said to them:

"Be fruitful and increase in number; fill the earth and subdue it."

Same-sex marriage can't do that. Thus, a number of our legal, political, and religious authorities have in their ignorance approved a hybrid type of marriage in which it is impossible to accomplish the primary objective of marriage as commanded by God Himself. In the 1980s, the same-sex committed relationship was sanctioned as a "civil union," which gave the partners many of the rights (financial, medical, inheritance, etc.) reserved for married couples. However, the homosexual community demanded the so-called right of marriage in order to legitimize a relationship that is blatantly contrary to the Biblical order of marriage and blasphemy against Christ and his depiction of the husband/wife relationship in marriage as a picture, an echo, of the relationship between Himself and the Church, the Church Christ loves and sacrificed Himself for, the Church Christ cherishes and nourishes with Word and Sacrament.

For these reasons, same-sex marriage can never be considered as genuine marriage by the true Church or by those who claim to be Christian. And as I did before, I strongly emphasize that the Christian's attitude toward the homosexual is to be one that extends the love and grace of God to them, and one that ministers that love and grace to them as Christ would have us do, including our prayers that they be led to oneness in Christ and conformity to his order of creation for man and woman.

The radical secular progressive liberals would condemn me as intolerant and as homophobic. They have corrupted the word tolerance to mean something totally different from its correct meaning. To the radical, tolerance is not just acceptance, but approval and support of something. I addressed this in some detail in my first book *Divine Love / Divine Intolerance*. So for me, or for any Christian serious about their faith, in order to be acceptable to the secular progressive radical liberals, we must reject all Bible passages dealing with homosexuality and speak out in support of the homosexual lifestyle, same-sex marriage and other public policies involving homosexuality, despite the fact that to do so would be a denial of God's holy nature, God's sovereignty, and God's divine attributes - in other words a denial of God Himself and a renouncement of faith and salvation. The radical left of the Democratic Party must really hate Christians to demand this of them. I don't think even many homosexuals, perhaps the majority of them, would go that far. I ask the reader's forbearance with my raising this subject again, but I wanted to clarify my position on this hot-button issue of today.

The great text on marriage from Ephesians we have discussed, inspired by the Holy Spirit and written by the Apostle Paul, is not preached to the people often enough or thoroughly enough. And why is this? Could it be because of fear of being criticized, ostracized, condemned as a radical fundamentalist, a homophobic, a bigot, or any other number of insulting titles as mentioned above. But that should come as no surprise to the Christian. Our Lord predicted such a response in Matthew 5:11 when He said:

> "Blessed are you when people insult you, persecute you, and falsely say all kinds of evil against you because of me. Rejoice and be glad, because great is your reward in heaven, for in the same way they persecuted the prophets who were before you."

And again, in John 15: 18, 20-22:

> "If the world hates you, keep in mind that it hated me first…Remember the words I spoke to you: 'No servant is greater than his master!' If they persecuted me, they will persecute you also. If they obeyed my teaching, they will obey yours also. They will treat you this way because of my Name, for they do not know the One who sent me. If I had not come and spoken to them, they would not be guilty of sin. Now, however, they have no excuse for their sin."

May God give us strong voices who speak the truth both to those who want to hear the truth, and to those who do not want to hear the truth.

I would like to end this chapter on the Sanctity of Marriage with the account of Jesus attending the wedding at Cana given in John 2:1-11. My comments are taken from a sermon I preached on *The Three Sanctities - Life, Marriage, and Family,* on Sanctity of Life Sunday, January 19, 2020, and include comments from Lenski's Lutheran Commentary on the Gospel of John. My comments may be somewhat repetitive on occasion with previous comments, but so be it. Please consider it as increased emphasis.

Our Gospel lesson tells us of the wedding at Cana at which Jesus performed his first miracle at the outset of his ministry. We're not told why Jesus and his disciples attended this wedding, but from the description of events, it seems that Jesus' mother was a friend of the wedding party and helping them with serving the guests. Jesus and his disciples were perhaps invited as a result of Mary's relationship with the wedding party.

In her serving, Mary became aware that the wedding party was running out of wine. She came and told Jesus. Why? What did she expect Him to do? She had never seen Him perform a miracle, and it is doubtful that she expected that. Nevertheless, given all that she had heard and seen all those years past, at Jesus birth from the shepherds and wise men, what she had heard from Simeon and Anna at the temple when the child Jesus was presented to the Lord, what she saw and heard when Jesus was twelve years old and had been debating with legal scholars in the temple, who were amazed at his wisdom and understanding of the Torah, and given the fact that Mary had pondered all these things, and probably many more we don't know about, in her heart and undoubtedly still pondered them with wonder, it is understandable that she would turn to Him with this crisis and also tell the servants to do whatever He said.

It's important to understand that weddings at the time could go on for days and the wedding feast was very important. From the situation with the wine, it can be assumed that this wedding was probably much shorter and the groom's family poor. To run out of wine was more than just a minor social embarrassment. It would have been considered an act of discourtesy to the guests and a source of acute embarrassment to the groom to fail to provide wine for his guests.

We're told that:

> "Nearby stood six stone water jars, the kind used by the Jews for ceremonial washing, each holding from twenty to thirty gallons."

Ceremonial washing was necessary because according to the law, Jews became ceremonially defiled during the normal circumstances and occurrences of daily life and were cleansed by pouring water over the hands. For a lengthy feast with many guests, a large amount of water was required for this purpose.

Jesus tells the servants to fill the jars with water and they did so to the brim. Then He told them to draw some out and take it to the master of the banquet. When the master of the banquet tasted the water turned into wine by Jesus, he chided the groom for serving the poorer wine first and saving this best wine until later, when the accustomed procedure was to serve the best wine first, and then the poorer wine after the guests have had much to drink. The master of the banquet did not know where the wine came from and neither did the groom, but they surely found out from the servants who had filled the water jars when, in their amazement, they realized what Jesus had done, and certainly shared their amazement with the others.

Mary certainly knew, and we know that the disciples were astonished because we're told that it led them to put their faith in Him. And I'm sure the groom was very grateful to Jesus for saving his reputation, along with being grateful for Jesus' expensive wedding gift to him and his bride of 120 gallons of the most excellent wine ever made, much of which I'm sure was left over from the wedding feast and could be sold for a tidy sum of money, which would go far to help him and his bride set up housekeeping and start their marriage adventure in style. John ends his account by saying that this was the first of Jesus' miraculous signs, and thus revealed his glory. John always refers to Jesus' miracles as "signs," a word emphasizing the significance of the action, rather than the marvel.

Again it must be emphasized that, at this village marriage, with Jesus' first public appearance in any company, with his first miracle of his earthly ministry, with the first sign of his Messiahship, and with his first manifestation of his glory, Jesus honors the Sanctity of Marriage, and He honors marriage as it was instituted in the beginning by God in the Garden of Eden - one man, one woman, becoming one in the flesh, commanded by God to reproduce and become a member of the core of the Sanctity of Family. And again, later, Jesus would honor Biblical marriage even more by using it to describe the oneness between Himself and his followers - the Church - Christ our Bridegroom and we his Bride.

Near the beginning of the chapter, I spoke of the difference between contract and covenant. Marriage is not a contract. It is a covenant. Contracts can be broken. Covenants are not to be broken. In Scripture, they are sacred. They refer to binding relationships never to be broken. I recently ran across some additional information on covenants I would like to share. In pre-historic times, such binding covenants were referred to as covenants of salt, and still are today in some Middle East societies. Salt was the symbol of covenant relationships. Salt is composed of two elements - sodium and chlorine. If taken separately, either will kill. But if mixed together, they form an ingredient absolutely essential to life - salt.

When Jesus told his disciples, "You are the salt of the earth," He was referring to such a covenant. In their preaching of the Gospel, they would bring to the people who received the Gospel, a covenant of salt, a covenant of life.

In this chapter on the Sanctity of Marriage, I have no doubt that I have incurred the anger of many liberals, and especially the secular progressive radicals in the Democratic Party who discount Scripture in favor of their own ideology. I have used much Scripture to make my points, and whether others agree with me or not, it was necessary to do so. Again, I emphasize that when you are talking about political and spiritual corruption, you are talking about sin, and sin is a theological subject and must be dealt with carefully with systematic theological analysis and perception to bring out sin's extremely dangerous and devastating effects on individuals, families, communities, and nations.

This I have tried to do. I stand on what I have said and in my use of Scripture to say it. If anyone can prove me wrong in my commentary on the Scripture passages, I will admit it. But they must do so by using Scripture and not human philosophy or ideology.

We leave the chapter with a few more Biblical quotations on marriage I think the reader will enjoy.

> "If a man has recently married, he must not be sent to war or have any other duty laid on him. For one year he is to be free to stay at home and bring happiness to the wife he has married." Deuteronomy 24:5.

I imagine all wives would heartily agree with this passage. It shows that marital bliss was held in high regard.

> "May your fountain be blessed, and may you rejoice in the wife of your youth. A loving doe, a graceful deer - may her breasts satisfy you always, may you ever be captivated by her love." Proverbs 5:18-19.

"Fountain" refers to the wife. The passage celebrates marital love. "Doe" "Deer" Descriptive of the wife, perhaps because of the delicate beauty of the doe's limbs.

> "He who finds a wife finds what is good and receives favor from the Lord." Proverbs 18:22

"A wife of noble character who can find? She is worth far more than rubies." Proverbs 31:10

Husbands, have you told your wife lately that she is worth far more than the most precious rubies?

"How delightful is your love, my sister, my bride! How much more pleasing is your love than wine, and the fragrance of your perfume than any spice! Your lips drop sweetness as the honeycomb, my bride; milk and honey are under your tongue." Song of Songs 4:10-11

The husband describes his wife and her charms. The word "sister" is used generically and not biologically.

"My lover is radiant and ruddy, outstanding among ten thousand. His head is purest gold; his hair is wavy and black as a raven. His eyes are like doves by the water streams, washed in milk, mounted like jewels….His body is like polished ivory decorated with sapphires. His mouth is sweetness itself; he is altogether lovely." Song of Songs. 5:10-16

The wife describes her husband and his charms.

My final suggestion is that every married couple should read the Song of Songs together, also entitled in some Bibles as Song of Solomon in the Bible as strong encouragement to enjoy fully the gift of sex God has given to husband and wife.

Jesus commanding the servants

Filling the water jars

Serving the water made into wine

CHAPTER 10

THE SANCTITY OF FAMILY

"A father to the fatherless,
a defender of widows,
Is God in his holy dwelling.
God sets the lonely in families."

Psalm 68: 5-6

"If anyone does not provide for his relatives,
and especially for his immediate family,
He has denied the faith and is worse
than an unbeliever."

1Timothy 5:8

The family has been the bedrock of civilization since time immemorial. The family is the bedrock of the nation and society. A sure way to determine the health of a nation and its society is to investigate the health and welfare of its families. As someone once wisely said: "As the family goes, so goes the country."

The family environment, to a large extent, will shape the attitude, personality, and world view of the children raised in that family. Multiply this by millions upon millions and it is easy to realize just how important family status is to a nation's future, prosperity, and even survival. Unlike the not too distant past, too many people today have lost sight of the importance of family history. In today's fast-paced, mobile society, with its record number of broken families and relationships, family history loses its importance. Still however, I believe that the continuity, stability, sense of identity and belonging associated with strong family ties, values, and family history are essential to a healthy individual and a healthy society. Additionally, through such knowledge, both the good and the not so good, we come to know more about ourselves.

Scripture gives lots of attention to family structure and history. Family structure changed from Old Testament time to New Testament time, as well as from then to today. The Old Testament family was larger, more extensive and complex than that of the New Testament, and certainly than that of the typical mother, father, children nuclear family structure of contemporary western society. The Old Testament family consisted of those who shared a common blood and a common dwelling place. It included servants, resident aliens, widows and orphans who lived under the protection of the head of the family, as well as his wife (or wives and concubines if he was a polygamist) and his children.

From the beginning, when God instituted marriage in the Garden of Eden with Adam and Eve, the divine intention was that marriage should be monogamous. Polygamy, it would seem, was allowed by God for the same reason as divorce, that being a temporary concession to human weakness and hard heartedness before the coming of Christ. The New Testament leaves no room for polygamy, for otherwise the Apostle Paul's parallel between the mystical union of Christ and his Church (that's us) and the union of man and woman through marriage "in the Lord" would be altogether inappropriate. Finally, with Judeo-Christianity the foundation of western civilization, polygamy was condemned in the western nations.

In our discussion of the Sanctity of Family, historical family structures and characteristics, particularly Old Testament, will be referred to. Information on the Israelite family is taken from the "New Dictionary of Theology," edited by Sinclair B. Ferguson, David F. Wright, and J. I. Packer, Inter-Varsity Press, 1988.

The Israelite family is patriarchal. Genealogies are always given in the father's line, and women are mentioned only infrequently. It is interesting that a person's identity was expressed primarily by whose son or daughter they were. As an example, when King Saul watched the boy

David killing the Philistine Giant Goliath, he asked the Commander of his Army: "Whose son is that young man?" When the commander didn't know, Saul instructed him, "Find out whose son this young man is!"

Throughout the Bible, the Israelite husband and father, as head of the family, was responsible for the godly ordering of family life. This included the tender love and care of his wife, as covered in the last chapter (Ephesians 5:25), providing for his family as stated in 1Timothy 5:8, one of the verses used to open this chapter, and instructing, encouraging, and disciplining his children in the ways of godliness which the following passages emphasize:

> "Fathers, do not exasperate your children; instead bring them up in the training and instruction of the Lord." Ephesians 6:4 "Discipline your son, and he will give you peace; he will bring delight to your soul." Proverbs 29:17. "Do not withhold discipline from a child; if you punish him with the rod, he will not die. Punish him with the rod and save his soul from death." Proverbs 23:13-14

I hope the reader doesn't resent my emphasizing the discipline aspect. I do this because of the foolishness and ignorance of political correctness which equates spanking with physical abuse. We're not talking about beating the child here, and neither are the Bible passages above, among others. We're talking about spanking the child on the rear end. Why the rear end? Because a proper spanking on that part of the body will hurt, but it's not going to do any damage and quickly subsides. And consider this: It is less painful to discipline a child than to weep over a spoiled youth.

I remember an incident years ago when a young mother was asked if she would like to enroll her little boy who was three to four years old in a Sunday school class. She answered "No," and said that she had asked the boy and he said he didn't want to go to Sunday School. She also said that she didn't want to make him do something he didn't want to do because she wanted him to learn to make his own decisions. My thought was, "Lady, do you really expect a three to four year old to reason through a question like that and come up with a right decision? What if he doesn't want to bathe? Are you going to let him go without bathing? By the way, her three to four year old boy was a brat, undisciplined, uncontrolled, disrespectful to adults and mean to other children. If anyone deserved a good spanking, it was that boy, and perhaps attendance at Sunday School would have served to modify his behavior.

Children learn best from example; the problem is they don't know a good example from a bad example. They must be taught, and discipline is part of that learning. I loved my Dad. He was a Christian man, a loving father, and a hard worker who worked long hours six days a week to support his family. He also had a black leather belt in the closet that my older brother and I knew about. As I recall, on two occasions during our growing up years, we felt the sting of that leather belt on our posteriors. And we thoroughly deserved it. And years later we were told by our mother that our father cried after he spanked us. Dad was a member of that generation that went through the Depression and World War II, that Tom Brokaw, the news correspondent, called "The Greatest Generation," and wrote a best-selling book with that title.

My Dad and other members of the Greatest Generation would have considered the political correctness of today as foolishness and utterly stupid. And I thoroughly agree with the unknown source who labeled political correctness as "an ideology for the mentally challenged."

Back to our discussion of the family. In the Old Testament, the husband exercised an almost priestly function. He was responsible for offering sacrifices and prayers to God on behalf of himself and his family. At the Passover, which is observed in the home, the priestly duty of prayer is assigned to the father, and he is expected to be able to explain the significance of the meal to his children. The weekly Sabbath is likewise observed in families, all of whose members share in the day of rest. During New Testament times, as well as today, the context remains basically the same. The husband and father, according to Scripture, is to be the spiritual leader of the family, leading his family in devotions and prayer. The home was to be the primary schoolhouse for the children to grow in the Gospel-saving faith in Jesus Christ as Lord and Savior, become familiar with the Bible, grow to love God with all their hearts, minds, spirits, and souls, and to love their neighbor as themselves, and receive instruction in Biblical morality and ethics, primarily the Ten Commandments. The husband and father, as headmaster, is held accountable to God. The fundamental responsibility for Christian nurture and education is given by Scripture to the family even more than to the Church.

To our great devastation, the rise of secular progressive liberalism, the horrendous divorce rate, the catastrophic decline in the Sanctity of Life, the Sanctity of Marriage, and the Sanctity of Family, the vast decrease in Biblical literacy even among today's adults, and the emphasis on material and financial gain with both parents working, millions of our younger generation have not had this teaching and instruction in the home. There was a time, five or six decades or more ago, when our young folks were getting at least a modicum of such teaching in the schools, with school prayer and the teaching of Judeo-Christian morals and standards. But then, as I previously noted, some incredibly stupid judges and politicians decided that prayer in public schools, the very mention of the Bible, and the teaching of Christian morality and values was somehow dangerous to a society in a country built by our Founders on that very foundation of Judeo-Christian morality and values. Go figure what those idiots were thinking.

So, prayer in public schools, reading from the Bible, and the teaching of Christian morals and values were declared somehow unconstitutional and illegal. And now, over five or six decades later, generations of students who attended public schools did not receive instruction in Biblical morals, values, and behavior, with many of them not having received such instruction in the home either, and these former students are today's leaders in business, industry, government, education, and still, to an unfortunate degree, ignorant of what they should have learned in elementary and high school.

I believe that people are growing more and more aware that there is something dreadfully wrong in the country, with the increase in crime, corruption in politics, government, business, and corporate industry, along with riots, looting, destruction of property, and a turning away from our Judeo-Christian foundation, heritage, and tradition and the values and vision of our Founding Fathers. And they are asking "Why?" The answer is clear, and that answer is Biblical illiteracy and illiteracy in our nation's history, founding and Christian heritage. I said it before, and I say it again, that the greatest cultural disaster that has befallen our country is Biblical and historical illiteracy on the part of a multitude of our citizens, and it is the cause of all the other disasters listed above.

Our Founding Fathers would agree with this. It bears repeating that George Washington said that:

> "without God and the Bible, it is impossible to govern."

John Adams said that:

> "Our Constitution was made for a religious and moral people and that it is totally unsuitable for any other."

James Madison said that:

> "The nation's future, prosperity, and welfare rests not upon government, but upon all citizens sustaining and conducting themselves according to the Ten Commandments of God."

They understood with brilliant clarity that in a Democratic Republic which they established, where the people enjoyed a wide range of freedoms, the people must be willingly bound by a moral and ethical code of divine origin rather than one of human origin, for only such a moral and ethical code could be effective in restraining the dark and sinful impulses of human nature. That is why they emphasized the Judeo-Christian foundation they built our Democratic Republic on and the Ten Commandments as the moral and ethical code of our Democratic Republic. Biblical literacy was highly regarded as essential to good citizenship and virtually all the Founders were highly knowledgeable in Biblical teaching.

The nation is suffering terribly from its loss of Biblical literacy on the part of a vast number of its citizens. This loss is accompanied by a loss of keen appreciation of our Judeo-Christian heritage and the Biblical Ten Commandments as primary safeguards of our freedoms. This critical combined loss of knowledge and appreciation of our nation's Christian tradition and heritage has resulted in a great weakening of those safeguards to restrain the evil, dark impulses of the human nature. Have you noticed that our Constitution, which as John Adams said, was designed only for a religious and moral people, is being challenged more and more by secular progressive liberal judges and politicians, that it is being corrupted by the same, and in some cases, downright ignored?

The country's problems will not be solved by politicians, government, corporate authorities, educational authorities, human relations experts, etc. As I said before, I say again: "The country's healing and renewal will only take place when the people and our leaders adhere to God's invitation given in 2Chronicles 7:14 which reads:

> "If my people, who are called by my Name, will humble themselves and pray and seek my face and turn from their wicked ways, then will I hear from heaven and will forgive their sin and will heal their land."

When God first established the family in the Garden of Eden, it was his intention that, within the family, the covenant faithfulness of God to his people is to be mirrored in the conjugal fidelity of husband and wife. In the love and care He bestows on his wife and children, the father is to provide a model, although imperfect, of the Fatherly love and care of God Himself. And the warmth of the mother's love as she cares for and comforts her husband and children is to mirror God's tender love for his family.

We can establish a theological understanding of the family from the Biblical data available. First, it is clear that the family unit is a basic part of the structure of creation, or in other words, part of the *Order of Creation,* which was finished by God on the end of the sixth day. And let there be no doubt that family, in accordance with God's order of creation, consists of one man (husband), one woman (wife) and children. Any other family form designed by man is contrary to God's Order of Creation.

God's purpose from the beginning was that mankind should increase by families and not just as isolated individuals. Just as it was not good for Adam to be alone, so God sets the lonely in families as we're told in Psalm 68:6, one of the passages I used to open this chapter. From this perspective, we can say that childlessness, widowhood, and orphanhood are experiences which involve loneliness and a loss of community. Concerning the desolation of childlessness, we have the example of Hannah in 1Samuel 1:10-11 as follows:

> "In bitterness of soul Hannah wept much and prayed to the Lord. And she made a vow, saying, 'O Lord Almighty, if you will only look upon your servant's misery and remember me, and not forget your servant but give her a son, then I will give him to the Lord for all the days of his life.'"

The Lord answered Hannah's prayer and gave her a son - the great prophet Samuel. Concerning the desolation of widowhood, we have the account of the widow of Nain, who not only lost her husband, but now in this account, lost her only son, thus depriving her of all male support and influence and resulting in her being on her own, a disastrous situation in the society at the time. We read in Luke 7:12-15:

> "As He (Jesus) approached the town gate, a dead person was being carried out - the only son of his mother, and she was a widow…When the Lord saw her, his heart went out to her and He said, 'Don't cry.' Then He went up and touched the coffin, and those carrying it stood still. He said, 'Young man, I say to you, get up!' The dead man sat up and began to talk, and Jesus gave him back to his mother."

Concerning the desolation of orphanhood, we have the Israelites' description of themselves after they had been taken into captivity to Babylon because of their sin and unfaithfulness in Lamentations 5:1-3 as follows:

> "Remember O Lord, what has happened to us; look and see our disgrace. Our inheritance has been turned over to aliens, our homes to foreigners. We have become orphans and fatherless, our mothers like widows."

The Lord relented, and as He had promised through the prophet Jeremiah, after seventy years of captivity, the people were freed to return to Israel and rebuild their cities, Jerusalem, the wall, and the temple.

In all these examples, and many more in Scripture, the emphasis is not so much on individualism as it is on community - the community of family and the community of the nation. Thus, the first stop in a theological understanding of family is to recognize that the family as community is a basic part of God's order of creation. The second step is to recognize that the family lies at the center of God's covenant purpose. In virtually all the covenants God strikes with individuals in Scripture, family is a central feature. In Genesis 12: 2-3, God tells Abraham that He will make him into a great nation and that all peoples will be blessed through him. And in Genesis 15: 4-5, God told Abraham that his offspring would be as many as the stars in the sky. Offspring are family, and peoples also, in essence, are families.

> "I will make you into a great nation and I will bless you; I will make your name great and you will be a blessing. I will bless those who bless you, and whoever curses you I will curse; and all peoples on earth will be blessed through you." Genesis 12:2-3

> "Then the Word of the Lord came to him (Abraham)...He took him outside and said: 'Look up at the heavens and count the stars - if indeed you can count them.' Then He said to him, 'So shall your offspring be." Genesis 15:4-5

The critical importance of family in God's workings with people cannot be overstated. The fact that the family unit is a basic part of the order of creation, combined with the fact that the family lies at the center of God's covenant purposes, makes family a theological unit as well as a biological unit and social unit. To show family as a combined theological, biological, and social unit, let us consider the example of circumcision. Under the Abrahamic covenant, the sign of circumcision is administered to every male child within the context of the family. He who lacks this sign is to be cut off from his people. We read of God's instruction to Abraham in Genesis 17:10-14 as follows:

"This is my covenant with you and your descendants after you, the covenant you are to keep: Every male among you shall be circumcised. You are to undergo circumcision, and it will be the sign of the covenant between me and you. For the generations to come, every male among you who is eight days old must be circumcised, including those born in your household or bought with money from a foreigner - those who are not your offspring. Whether born in your household or bought with your money, they must be circumcised. My covenant in your flesh is to be an everlasting covenant. Any uncircumcised male who has not been circumcised in the flesh, will be cut off from his people; he has broken my covenant."

Thus, it is through membership in a covenant family that the child is related to the covenant people Israel. Just as circumcision was a sign of membership in this covenant family, so baptism is the sign of Christian membership in the Body of Christ, the family of God, the Church. Baptism through water and the Word, is a holy Sacrament establishing covenantal relationship in the family of God through Christ. I am including this information on becoming a member of the family of God because in our discussion of family, it would not do to omit the most important family we can be a part of in this life - the family of God - for whether or not we are a member of this family will determine where we will spend eternity, either in unimaginable glory in heaven with God and his family, or in unimaginable suffering in hell with Satan and his family, and that should get everyone's' attention.

Notice that both circumcision and baptism prove the above statement that family is a theological, biological, and social unit - theological in that both were instituted by God Himself, biological in that each required action affecting the physical body, and social in that each was the sign of membership in a family.

Jesus Himself submitted to John the Baptist's baptism of repentance, not because He needed it, because as the Son of God and Son of Man He was sinless and had nothing to repent of, but He did so as a deliberate act of solidarity with us sinful men and women whom He came to save.

Jesus' baptism marked the initiation of his ministry in which the saving sovereignty of God, through the Incarnation of the Son of God Who became also the Son of Man, his ministry of Word and deed, his suffering, death, and resurrection, and his sending of the Holy Spirit, all made it possible for us to become members of the family of God, both in this life and in the eternal afterlife when all of God's people will be taken into glory. In the Old Testament, to reject circumcision was to be cut off from the people of God. In the New Testament times, the times we are living in now, to reject God's Word in Christ's teaching, to reject faith in Christ as Lord and Savior, of which baptism is a sign, is to be cut off from God's family.

The importance of baptism to membership in the family of God is underlined by the fact that the Great Commission, given by the risen Christ to his disciples, prior to his ascension into heaven, included a command to baptize:

> "Then Jesus came to them and said: 'All authority in heaven and on earth has been given to me. Therefore, go and make disciples of all nations, baptizing them in the Name of the Father and of the Son and of the Holy Spirit, and teaching them to obey everything I have commanded you. And surely I am with you always, to the very end of the age.'" Matthew 28:18-20

The command "baptize in the Name of the Father, and of the Son, and of the Holy Spirit" signifies the baptism's basis and purpose to enter into a family relationship of belonging to God -in other words, being appropriated to the Father, Son, and Holy Spirit with the use of this Name. This family relationship of the believer and his/her Creator and Redeemer God cannot be overemphasized because the family relationship instituted by God in the Garden of Eden, and which we have, or should have today, is to be a reflection of the family relationship of the believer to God in Christ. Any other family relationship designed and established by man is counterfeit and heretical.

In the Apostolic teaching on baptism, the Sacrament primarily signifies union and oneness with Christ as the Divine Son of God, and in his humanity as the Son of Man, our human brother. Again, the emphasis on family. This union and oneness with our Divine God and human brother is brought out in a number of passages. In Galatians 3:27, we are told:

> "For all of you who were baptized into Christ have clothed yourselves with Christ."

The imagery is that of stripping off the clothing of sin and putting on the clothing of Christ's righteousness. Also, in the inspired words of the Apostle Paul in Romans 6:3-5 and Colossians 2:11-12, since Christ is the crucified and risen Lord, baptism signifies union with Him in his redemptive acts. This includes the concept of being laid alongside Him in his tomb and being with Him in his resurrection. However, this does not suggest that we had anything to do with those redemptive acts. We were, and are, only the beneficiaries of those acts.

> "Don't you know that all of us who were baptized into Christ Jesus were baptized into his death? We were therefore buried with Him through baptism into death in order that, just as Christ was raised from the dead through the glory of the Father, we too may live a new life. If we have been united with Him like this in his death, we will certainly also be united with Him in his resurrection." Romans 6:3-5

> "In Him (Christ) you were also circumcised, in the putting off of the sinful flesh, not with a circumcision done by the hands of men, but with the circumcision done by Christ, having been buried with Him in baptism and raised with Him through your faith in the power of God, who raised Him from the dead." Colossians 2:11-12

As mentioned before, baptism signifies union with Christ in his Body, the family of God, the Church. To be in Christ through faith, is to be one with all who are united to Him through faith. Thus, the family of God is composed of all believers who, through death, have gone to heaven to be with the Lord, all believers who live life on earth now, and all believers who in the future will live and become one with Christ through faith.

The family of God in heaven is referred to as the Church Triumphant, since they have fought the good fight against Satan and this sinful world and remained faithful to Christ until death. The family of God on earth is referred to as the Church Militant, since they are still fighting the good fight against Satan and this sinful world and remaining faithful to Christ and his promises through the power of the Holy Spirit. The family of God in heaven and the family of God on earth will be rejoined when Christ returns in glory to judge the living and the dead. At that time, the Kingdom of God which is here now, but only partially revealed, will be revealed and established in its entirety and in all its unimaginable power, glory, and magnificence, with the family of believers taken to heaven to enjoy the riches and pleasures of this Kingdom in the presence of God for eternity, while those who refused to be a member of God's family, through faith in Christ, will suffer the torments of hell with eternal separation from God.

At the outset of this discussion on the Sanctity of Family, I have devoted considerable attention to the family of God which consists of all believers in Jesus Christ as Lord and Savior. I mentioned this before, but I repeat it because, as I said, it is the most important family a person can be a member of in this life, for it will determine where a person will spend eternity.

Returning to family as established by God in Genesis, the importance of family is also attested to by the fact that in the Decalogue, the Ten Commandments of the Law, given by God to Moses on Mt. Sinai, one of those commandments dealt with family. This commandment states:

> "Honor your father and your mother, so that you may live long in the land the Lord your God is giving you." Exodus 20:12

The composition of the Ten Commandments is such that the first three commandments deal with our relationship with God. First, we are to have no other gods besides Him, the only true God, and are to love Him more than anyone or anything else. Second, we should not misuse his Holy Name, but only use it with respect and for the praise of God and the benefit and salvation of our neighbor and ourselves. And third, remember the Sabbath Day to keep it holy, and diligently devote ourselves to God's Word so that all our conduct and life may be regulated by it.

In ancient culture, honoring someone was to acknowledge their importance and example in a way that was reflected in one's own life, attitude, and value system. The Hebrew word translated into English as honor - *kabod* - literally means heaviness and weight. So, to honor someone is to live life in such a way that that person proves to be heavy or weighty in one's life. Therefore, it is not at all surprising that, after giving instructions about how to honor God in the commandments which comprise the first table of the Law, that the commandment heading the second table of the Law which addresses how we are to treat and relate to others, is the one to honor our father and our mother.

The fact that honoring one's father and mother is given priority over the other six commandments addressing our treatment and relations with our fellowmen should impress upon us the importance God gives to family. And after all, what persons have a more heavy or weighty influence on one's life than one's father and mother. God's plan for the family is that, in honoring their parents, children learn how to honor God Whom their parents honor. In a nutshell, children are to obey and honor their parents because in doing so they learn to love and worship the living God. For this reason, cursing one's parents was tantamount to shaming God, and the penalty in Old Testament Israel for cursing one's parents was death.

> "Anyone who attacks his father or his mother must be put to death….Anyone who curses his father or his mother must be put to death." Exodus 21:15,17.

Martin Luther, in his *Large Catechism*, translated by Robert H. Fischer, Fortress Press, 1959, has much to say about this commandment, and especially that word *honor*, all of it a foundational structural for parenthood and family. Luther maintains that God has given to fatherhood and to motherhood a special distinction, above all estates that are beneath it, by commanding us to not simply love our parents, but also to honor them. In our relations with brothers, sisters, neighbors, etc., God commands nothing higher than that we love them. Thus, God distinguishes father and mother above all other persons on earth, and places them next to Himself. For it is a greater thing to honor than to love. Honor our parents certainly includes love, but also to highly prize them, care for them, show respect for them, defer to them, show humility and modesty towards them, and above all, to show by words and actions that, next to God, we give them the very highest place.

To honor our parents also requires that we obey them. In Ephesians 6:2 we are commanded:

"Children, obey your parents in the Lord, for this is right."

Obedience is a byproduct of honor. The only exception is if the parent demands something of the child that is contrary to God's Word, in which case the child's responsibility to honor and obey God takes precedence over the responsibility to honor and obey the parent.

The Sanctity of the Family requires that children must be taught to revere their parents as God's representatives, and as parents and children grow older, to remember that, however lowly, poor, feeble, and eccentric the parents may be, they are still the father and mother given to them by God and are not to be deprived of their honor because of their ways or their failings. Parents who are not fulfilling their responsibilities as ordained by God, who are not providing their children with the care and love and instruction that God commands, may be difficult to love, but must still be honored for their parental status given by God, for in doing so, one honors God.

In the case of unbelieving parents, we honor them also by lifting up the Truth with them. Christians are the Lord's witnesses and ambassadors to an unbelieving world. This includes believing children being the Lord's witnesses and ambassadors to their unbelieving parents, pointing unbelieving parents to the Gospel of Salvation, to Jesus Christ as their Lord and Savior. It means discussing the truth of God's Word with them, praying for them and with them, encouraging their parents to accompany them to worship services. The children won't convert them; that's the Holy Spirit's job, but they are to share the Word and Christ with them. And one other very important point! Don't give up, no matter how hopeless it may seem. Follow Winston Churchill's advice, given in a speech at a U.S. college when he was speaking about perseverance. He told the audience: "Never, never, never, never give up!"

Again, I'm reminded of the experience of Monica, the mother of St. Augustine. St. Augustine was pretty wild as a young adult and even beyond. Monica prayed and prayed for her son to become a Christian and turn from his wild and sinful ways. She prayed not just for months or a few years, but as I remember, for decades with no result. Then one day, Augustine experienced a dramatic conversion, turned from his wicked ways, went to seminary, became a priest, then the Bishop of Hippo, and one of the most brilliant theologians, writers, and leaders of the Christian Church in history, whose impact on the Church's theology, doctrine, and outreach was incredible and remains so today. Monica lived to see her son's conversion but died within a year afterwards. She died a happy woman and a happy mother.

Caring for one's parents when they are old, sick, feeble, disabled, and unable to care for themselves is a special blessing God gives to children. It is a vital part of the Sanctity of the Family, and such care must be given, not only cheerfully, but with humility and reverence, as in God's sight, Children who have the right attitude toward their parents will not allow them to suffer want or hunger, but will place them above themselves, and will share with them all they have to the best of their ability.

Luther tells us that when we show our parents honor and obedience, it is highly pleasing to the Divine Majesty and all the angels, that it vexes all devils, and that it is the greatest work that we can do, next to the sublime worship of God described in the first table of the commandments. Even almsgiving and all other works for our neighbor are not equal to this. Thus, the greatest responsibility given by God to the husband and father is the loving, godly care, provision, protection, and instruction of his family, including his parents, and especially his children. Compared to this responsibility, being CEO of the largest corporation in the world pales in significance.

Another strong incentive for us to obey this commandment to honor our parents is that God has attached to it a wonderful promise, which St. Paul exalts and praises in Ephesians 6:2-3 where he says:

> "This is the first commandment with a promise: that it may be well with you and that you may live long on the earth."

Although the other commandments also have a promise implied, yet in none of them is it so plainly and explicitly stated. Here then we see how important God considers this commandment, and how important it is to the Sanctity of Family. He declares that it is not only an object of pleasure and delight to Himself, but also an instrument intended for our greatest welfare, to lead us to a quiet, pleasant, and blessed life. This then, is the fruit and the reward for whoever keeps this commandment. God highly exalts obedience, greatly delights in it, and richly rewards it.

In addition to honoring our biological fathers who are the authorities in our Immediate families, we are to honor our spiritual fathers in our church families, who govern and guide us by the Word of God. In 1Corinthians 4:15, St. Paul says to those in the church in Corinth:

> "In Christ Jesus I became your father through the Gospel."

Since such persons are fathers, they are entitled to honor. Yet there is need to impress upon the people that they who would bear the name of Christian owe it to God to show double honor to those who watch over our souls, and to treat them well and make provision for them. God will adequately recompense those who do so and will not let them suffer want. Those who keep their eyes on God's will and commandments dealing with the sanctity of both our temporal and our spiritual families have the promise that they will be richly rewarded for all their blessings and support given to their temporal and spiritual fathers, and for the honor they render to them. Since God promises it, and God has never lied, and will never lie, He will not lie to us in this matter either. This ought to encourage us and make our hearts melt for joy and love toward those to whom we owe honor, that we lift our hands in joyful thanks to God for giving us such promises.

In order to reestablish and strengthen the Sanctity of Family and restore it to the high position God ordained for it, parents must consider that they owe obedience to God and that, above and beyond all other concerns, demands, and duties, they should earnestly and faithfully discharge the duties of their parental office as commanded by God, and not only to provide the material support for their children, but especially to bring them up in the nurture, admonition, and instruction of the Lord, and to the praise and honor of God. I mentioned before that the father is ordained by God to be the spiritual leader of his family and will be held accountable to God for this. A major detriment to the country today, and a primary cause of the dangerous decline in the Sanctity of Family, is the failure of so many people, and primarily parents, to recognize how critically important it is to devote major attention to the spiritual, moral, and intellectual training of the young.

I think most everyone would agree that the country desperately needs more qualified and capable men and women for spiritual, political, governmental, legal, educational, and social leadership. There was a time, decades past, when our churches and schools were providing such leaders, but today not so much. Public education for the most part, as I mentioned, is a politically correct disaster; our universities and colleges, except for a brave and independent few, are bastions of secular progressive liberalism; the teachers' unions and the majority of members of the educational hierarchy give lip service to increasing the quality of education students are receiving, but that's all it is - lip service. Their primary interests are political power and money, and the vast majority of them are staunch members of the Democratic Party.

As I said before, "as goes the nation's youth, so goes the nation." This dereliction of duty by politicians, judges, so-called educators, church officials, and yes, parents, has caused a devastating decline in the nation's welfare - spiritually, politically, culturally, and internationally, not to mention the disastrous effects on the Sanctity of Family, since everything that affects the nation ultimately effects the family. We need to clean house and get back to sparing no effort, time, and expense in effectively teaching and educating students for service to God, family, country, and mankind. Trash critical race theory, political correctness, and secular progressive radicalism and get back to genuine scholarship and true education, rather than indoctrination. If this were done, God would richly bless us with his wisdom and grace so that men and women might be educated and trained to be a benefit to the nation and its people. In time, we would also have a solidly educated population who would faithfully bring up their children to be godly, moral, ethical, and effective citizens.

When God's commandments are disregarded, when the family order of creation instituted by God is ignored, and when the Sanctity of Life, Marriage, and Family is disintegrating, civil order goes by the way, public peace becomes internal conflict, riots, looting, mob violence, and loss of respect for authority all become commonplace. We complain about this state of affairs, but we refuse to see or admit that it is our own fault. We forget that, in order to solve a problem, one must first recognize the problem and own up to it.

The decline of our institutions and society didn't just suddenly happen. It has been brewing for decades. Unfortunately, the good leaders we had who saw what was happening and who tried to reverse the trends, were opposed by incompetent or downright corrupt people in leadership positions who had the backing of powerful and rich special interest groups and they were able to prevent strong reform and succeed in kicking the can down the road. The treatment of President Trump by the democrats is a perfect example of this incompetence, corruption, and lust for power. And we the people, let them get away with it. We were complacent and neglected to hold those excuses for leaders' feet to the fire as our Founders said we must do in a Democratic Republic. And so, we got what we deserved - incompetence, greed, self-interest instead of the common interest, corruption on the part of many in power, and a rabid lust for political dominance in the Democrat Party. God willing, the removal of the Biden administration and the establishment of Trump's second administration will bring positive reform and a return to our traditional values, heritage, and political integrity, and an awakening of the public to the fact that all we can expect from the radicalized Democrats is further decline in the nation's values, ethics, national and international status.

Back to our discussion of *The Sanctity of* Family. An article in the February 2019 issue of *Tabletalk*, an outreach magazine of Ligonier Ministries, Editor Burk Parsons, deals extensively with the issue of honor in the commandment to honor our father and mother, and insists that honoring one's parents is foundational for honoring God and producing a well-ordered, free society. Thus, honor is the essential quality, the backbone, of the Sanctity of Family, honor of God and honor of parents. Without honor, the Sanctity of Family loses all meaning. Comments from *Tabletalk* are included in the following section of this chapter.

C. S. Lewis, in his 1943 book *The Abolition of Man,* wrote: "We laugh at honor and are shocked to find traitors in our midst." Lewis' observation more than seventy-eight years ago falls short in assessing the widespread disregard for honor in our day. In fact, ask someone on the street to define honor and you would probably receive a blank stare. The concept of honor is, to a great extent today, ridiculed by many and treated as an irrelevant ancient relic of the past by the secular progressive liberals among us. Honor has been an extremely rare quality in the Democratic Party over the past five or six years or longer in its quest for absolute power. Additionally, many men do not show proper honor to their wives; many wives do not show proper honor to their husbands, and both find the Biblical references to submission and sacrifice entirely reprehensible.

Many children do not show proper honor to their parents, and many of the cultural heroes of young people today are unheroic, self-centered, and morally unworthy of honor - sports figures, pop stars, Hollywood celebrities, rap performers, self-made social media pundits, etc. Not all of these are dishonorable of course, but too many are, and unfortunately these are the ones our young people are attracted to. Traditional authority figures are torn down and men, especially husbands and fathers, are often pictured as idiotic fools on television shows and commercials, and the honorable men and women of the past and present who adhere to traditional values and virtues are described as out of step with progressive ways of thinking. The sociologist Peter Berger once described honor, like chastity, as obsolete in modern secular cultures. "At best," he said, "honor and chastity are seen as ideological leftovers in the consciousness of obsolete classes such as military officers or ethnic grandmothers."

That statement really (expletive deleted) me off. As one of those so-called obsolete classes - a retired military officer - I would like to inform Mr. Berger of the following. I spent a good share of my life sharing with others the personal characteristics of honor, loyalty, honesty, responsibility, patriotism, and sacrifice that the military drums into a person from day one of putting on the uniform. And you, and every American citizen that has a modicum of intelligence and discernment better hope and pray to God that those personal qualities you and others demean are not obsolete, because if they are, this nation Is headed for oblivion. If secular progressive liberals, who comprise a substantial part of the Democratic Party, ever achieve their goal of replacing our Judeo-Christian national foundation with a secular socialist foundation, then yes, those admirable personal characteristics and virtues mentioned will truly become obsolete, and what would be looming before us would be a secular age without the Judeo-Christian moral and ethical virtues that are part of our heritage, and without which, as our Founding Fathers clearly stated on numerous occasions, a Democratic Republic , which we are, cannot survive.

The supreme irony of the secular progressive liberal's claim to be liberated from the shackles of Christian theism and the Biblical moral and ethical code of divine origin is manifested by the fact that those secular progressive revolutionaries themselves depend on the virtues contained in Christian theism and the Biblical code because they realistically have no consistent concept of virtue of their own - their only seeming virtue being the non-virtue of acquiring power, and that totally.

Although I obviously disagree with Mr. Berger on the obsolescence of such personal traits as honor, chastity, and the others mentioned as being obsolete, I will give him this - they are in great danger of becoming obsolete. One important reason for this is something I discussed in a previous chapter - the establishment of the all-volunteer military. The all-volunteer military has been touted as a great success, professionally, publicly, and from a combat-readiness standpoint. And that is probably true. But there were unfavorable effects also which I discussed previously, and which I want to summarize again because of their crucial importance to our current society and culture.

The all-volunteer military was established mainly because of the violent protests during the sixties against the Vietnam War and the draft. It had wide public support, so naturally the politicians jumped aboard the bandwagon. Although it was, and is, a popular success in many aspects, there is one aspect in which it has been seriously detrimental to the nation. And that is in regard to the extensive presence within the population of those personal qualities and traits mentioned above that are drummed into a person throughout his/her military tenure. Let me repeat those qualities and traits so you can keep them in mind as you read the following. They are honor, courage, loyalty, honesty, responsibility, sacrifice, patriotism.

Prior to the all-volunteer military, with selective service and the draft in operation, I believe that some 50% to 70% of our young men, either as draftees or volunteers, had military experience. Over time, the number of individuals in the population with military experience was in the untold millions. The vast majority served their tour of duty and were discharged. However, during their military tour of duty, they lived day after day bound by those personal qualities and traits of honor, etc., etc., etc.

The military, in many respects, is like family. Ask any person who has served in the military and they will tell you that their military experience stays with them. They may shed the uniform, but they don't shed the experience. In fact, most will brag about it as a defining life experience. It's like their military experience is grafted into them. And that includes those outstanding personality traits the military embeds in them - honor, etc., etc. Not all of them, of course, but the vast, vast majority of them. Whatever they do in civilian life, whatever career they pursue, the vast majority of military veterans take those qualities and traits with them, not only benefiting the company, corporation, business, institution they are part of, but the country overall, because the survival and prosperity of a Democratic Republic is dependent on the vast majority of its citizens displaying such personal qualities and traits. Think of the incalculable value to the nation the military experience of these millions upon millions of veterans brought to it.

Now consider the fact that, with the all-volunteer military, only approximately one percent of the population experiences military service. One percent as opposed to 50%, 60%, 70%. Think of the devastating loss of those essential personal traits of honor, loyalty, honesty, responsibility, patriotism, and sacrifice to the country and its institutions and industries. The same is true of our members of Congress and government. Back during the draft, I believe that the percentage of Congressional members who had military experience was approximately 70%. Think of the tremendous advantage of this in not only those personal qualities and traits mentioned, but in the experience brought to bear on legislation concerning military matters.

Now, with the all-volunteer military, the percentage of members of Congress with military experience is approximately 14% as opposed to the 70% during the draft . The bottom line is that there are many reasons for the overall decline in the quality of leadership and the steep decline in patriotism and respect for our nation's history, traditions, and heritage on the part of too many citizens. As previously mentioned, the dismal state of our educational system is one of the primary causes, but I submit that the drastic lack of military experience and its indoctrination in the aforementioned personal characteristics and traits, is also one of the major causes.

One other comment concerning the all-volunteer military. From 1776 to the 1970s, the United States military was proudly referred to as a "citizens military." The standing force was kept relatively small, with the draft giving us the option to build up rapidly in times of crisis. Today with around 99% of the population not choosing to benefit their life's experience with military experience, our military can hardly be called a citizen's military anymore. It more resembles a mercenary military.

However, I understand the rationale given by all-volunteer military proponents that, with the advances in weapon systems and mobility, we no longer have the time to build up the force in times of crisis that we had during the draft.

I thank the reader for indulging my desire to again emphasize this subject which I consider to be of great importance to defining our nation's culture and society.

As a result of the decline in the social / cultural environment of the nation, we rarely hear the word honor today. Yet, the word is prominent in Scripture and the Bible commands us to honor certain people. In addition to the command to honor father and mother which involves family, we are told in Revelation 4:11 that first and foremost we are to honor God:

> "You are worthy, our Lord and God, to receive glory and honor and power, for you created all things, and by your will they were created and have their being."

In Leviticus 19:32 we are told to honor the elderly:

> "Rise in the presence of the aged, show respect for the elderly and revere your God. I am the Lord your God."

Is the writer of Leviticus associating God with the elderly? If so, it would make sense since Scripture tells us that God is "from everlasting to everlasting." In 1Peter 2:17, we're told to honor rulers:

> "Show proper respect to everyone: Love the brotherhood of believers, fear God, honor the king."

In 1Timothy 5:17, we're told to honor church leaders:

> "The elders who direct the affairs of the church well are worthy of double honor, especially those whose work is preaching and teaching."

In Philippians 2:29, the Apostle Paul tells us to honor all those who serve Christ faithfully like his dear friend Epaphroditus, his fellow worker and fellow soldier in Christ, whom he was sending to Philippi: Paul tells them and us:

> "Welcome him in the Lord with great joy, and honor men like him, because he almost died for the work of Christ, risking his life to make up for the help you could not give me."

In addition to honoring these individuals, we are also told by Scripture to honor certain God ordained institutions such as the Sabbath Day and marriage: Concerning the Sabbath:

> "If you keep your feet from breaking the Sabbath and from doing as you please on my holy day, if you call the Sabbath a delight and the Lord's holy day honorable, and if you honor it by not going your own way and not doing as you please or speaking idle words, then you will find your joy in the Lord, and I will cause you to ride on the heights of the land and to feast on the inheritance of your father Jacob. The mouth of the Lord has spoken." Isaiah 58:13-14.

And concerning marriage:

> "Marriage should be honored by all, and the marriage bed kept pure, for God will judge the adulterer and all the sexually immoral." Hebrews 13:4.

Biblical teaching on honor transcends any particular time and culture. Honoring the Sabbath, marriage, father and mother, the family, reflect God's eternal character and commandments. These institutions were established at creation, and thus they have enduring significance and importance.

Finally, the Bible describes certain actions as honorable or dishonorable. Concerning honorable actions:

> "It is God's will that you should be sanctified: that you should avoid sexual immorality; that each of you should learn to control his own body in a way that is holy and honorable." 1Thessalonians 4:3-4.

And concerning dishonor:

> "Although they knew God, they neither glorified Him as God nor gave thanks to Him, but their thinking became futile and their foolish hearts were darkened. Although they claimed to be wise, they became fools….They exchanged the truth of God for a lie…Because of this, God gave them over to shameful lusts. Even their women exchanged natural relations for unnatural ones. In the same way, the men also abandoned natural relations with women and were inflamed with lust for one another. Since they did not think it worthwhile to retain the knowledge of God, He gave them over to a depraved mind, to do what ought not to be done." Romans 1:21-28.

Scripture makes it clear that homosexual activity comes from dishonorable and sinful passions. Furthermore, it is a violation of God's Order of Creation for both the individual and the family. I mentioned this before, and also what the Christian response to the homosexual community should be. I want to repeat this to make sure that the reader does not get the impression that I am condemning the homosexual. Who am I to condemn anyone since I am a miserable sinner saved only by grace? Although Christians cannot approve of the lifestyle or support it since it is forbidden by Scripture, they are still obligated by Scripture to reach out to the homosexual in Christian love and grace with the Word of God and its assurance of God's love, forgiveness, and renewal. And one other thing: Since the homosexual is, like the Christian and all people a human being created in the image of God, he/she is to be treated with honor. To refuse to do so is to refuse to honor God Himself. In our dealings with our fellowmen, and especially with those we disagree with, we have a tendency to forget that God fashioned all human beings in his image, and when we honor others, no matter who they are, we honor God. We can, and must, honor the adversary, but not honor what separates us if it is contrary to God's Word.

Honor was once the barometer, the yardstick, for measuring virtue, honesty, and the righteousness of both men and nations. It was foundational to healthy human relationships and vital for the maintenance of order in a civil society. The book of Proverbs in the Bible tells us that the wise will receive honor, but that honor is not fitting for a fool:

> "The wise inherit honor, but fools He holds up to shame." Proverbs 3:35.

> "Like snow in summer or rain in harvest, honor is not fitting for a fool." Proverbs 26:1

Honor may not be fitting for a fool, and God may hold fools up to shame, but since even fools are created in the image of God, we humans, as difficult as it may be, are to treat them honorably. To fail to honor those around us, whether superior, inferior, or equal to us professionally or socially, is to engage in rebellion against God. This is why rebellion against parents was such a grievous sin in the Old Testament. It was not only a refusal to honor fellow humans, but a refusal to honor God's ordained representatives and authority for the family, and therefore a rebellion against the Sanctity of Family God established. Consistent rebellion against this parental authority called for the death penalty. The importance of this is indicated by the fact that the Apostle Paul included disobedience to parents among the grave offenses committed by even the pagan nations, the ungodly.

As God is due honor by virtue of his being our God so also our superiors in other areas - church, government, school, workplace, etc., are due honor by virtue of their having authority instituted by God. When we honor our fellowmen in their positions of authority and leadership, we honor the God who placed us all where we are.

Scripture not only talks about honoring God, honoring people, and giving and receiving honor, but also tells us that honor brings blessings. Blessing in the Bible implies well-being in all of life. The prime example in this chapter on family is the blessing tied to the commandment to honor our father and our mother, which is "living long and having things go well with us." In the Psalms, the Lord's favor and blessing are associated with honor, an example being Psalm 84:11 which says:

"For the Lord God is a sun and shield; the Lord bestows favor and honor; no good thing does He withhold from those whose walk is blameless."

In Proverbs, honor is associated with riches, life, and righteousness, an example being Proverbs 21:21 which follows:

"He who pursues righteousness and love finds life, prosperity, and honor."

The fact that honor is a blessing and that it brings blessing we can see in our daily lives. If we treat people with courtesy and honor them appropriately, beginning with family, we will have a healthier, more stable, and more fulfilling family life, healthier and more fulfilling friendships, and overall a more fulfilling life. Granted that sometimes we honor others, and we are not blessed or rewarded for it. Nevertheless, ultimately, to bestow honor brings blessing, if not in this lifetime, then in the life to come. As Scripture encourages us to do, we are storing up treasures in heaven and we know that, in the end, our labor is not in vain. We have Scripture's Word on it:

"Therefore, my dear brothers, stand firm. Let nothing move you. Always give yourselves fully to the work of the Lord, because you know that your labor in the Lord is not in vain." 1Corinthians 15:58.

Honor is a blessing both in this age and in the age to come. Over the centuries, the concept of honor has served to constrain utter brutality and the bounds of evil. The Christian concept of honor emerged as a great correction to the pagan concepts of honor that shaped the ancient world. St. Augustine rightly observed that the ancient Romans were morally constrained and shaped by their aspiration to honor, both individual and imperial.

Tabletalk magazine, referred to earlier in this chapter, contains an article entitled *What if Honor is Lost Altogether?* authored by Dr. R. Albert Mohler Jr., Professor of Christian Theology at Southern Baptist Theological Seminary and teaching fellow at Ligonier Ministries. His question is one of great importance to our people and our country today given the decline in our Judeo-Christian tradition, the increasing influence of a secular progressive socialist ideology in the Democratic Party with its emphasis on dominant political power, and its deemphasis on such traits as honor, virtue, integrity, bipartisanship, and patriotism.

Dr. Mohler claims that the radical secular progressive liberals amongst us, with their ideology of cultural deconstruction fueled by Marxist critical theory and its many permutations, insist that human liberation (in our case, racial liberation) can come only by overthrowing the very idea of honor. They refer to wars of honor and honor codes as evidence of patriarchy, elitism, and moral coercion. Certainly, history teaches us that honor can be corrupted and misrepresented just as any other virtue. Sin is quite capable of turning virtue into vice, and we human beings, as sinful creatures, are able to dishonor even the virtue of honor. And even we Christians often fall short of God's command both to show honor where honor is due, and to live honorable lives before the world.

John Calvin, another great Reformer along with Luther, defined honor with theological clarity. He claimed that "honor, rightly understood and applied, should produce reverence, obedience, and gratitude." Reverence to whom? God! Obedience to whom? God! Gratitude to whom? God! I submit that these three virtues - reverence, obedience, and gratitude - in essence describe a Christian family, community, and nation. They are the glue that holds family, community, and nation together and provides stability to societies and culture. And honor is an essential ingredient to virtue.

Yet, the secular progressive liberals, again a major faction of the Democratic Party, claim that we are living in a post-Christian era and culture that sets itself against the Judeo-Christian foundation of the nation of which these three virtues, among others we have talked about, are essential qualities. They insist that our Judeo-Christian foundation must be replaced with a modern secular foundation friendly to socialism, and this again reveals their ideology as ungodly, un-American, and unhinged.

Dr. Mohler further claims that "a world without honor is a world without any culturally compelling notion of what it means to be a good person, worthy of honor. It is a world without any culturally compelling notion of what it means to be an honorable society. A world without honor is a world without virtue - a world that has traded light for darkness. A world without honor is a cruel world of crumbling institutions, weakening societies, moral relativism, and a raw lust for power." Does this sound familiar? Look around and see the fracturing of the family, the perversion of marriage, the political intrigues of governments and political organizations unrestrained by honor and its virtues.

In a world without honor, the powers that be become deadly powers indeed. I would add one other characteristic of a world without honor to Dr. Mohler's list, and that is the widespread cheapening of life, evidenced by abortion on demand. With this addition, Dr. Mohler's description of a world without honor as a world of crumbling institutions, weakening societies, moral relativism, and lust for power closely resembles the theme of this book - corruption of the three Sanctities - Life, Marriage, and Family, the trashing of our history, tradition, and heritage, and the replacement of our Judeo- Christian foundation with a secular socialist foundation, all championed by the secular progressive radicalized Democrat Party of today. Dr. Mohler's list, with abortion added to it, not only describes a world without honor, but also a nation without honor, a community without honor, and an individual without honor. We will consider these characteristics individually in the following. And again, since a lack of honor is a lack of virtue, I use the two words in a synonymous manner. And instead of the world, I will relate my comments to the prevailing culture which directly affects the nation, its families and individuals. First, it must be understood that virtue and morality, associated with honor, are theological terms. In our democratic republic, virtue and morality are synonymous with the Biblical code of morality and ethics. Therefore, as Dr. Mohler asserts, without the Biblical definition of honor, virtue, morality, and ethics, an individual, a community, a nation, has no solid, proven criterion for determining whether they are honorable or dishonorable. Without virtue, an individual, a community, a nation, trades light for darkness - the light of God's theological Biblical code of morality and ethics for the darkness of human ideological morality and ethics which is corrupted by the sin which infects all human beings.

Without virtue, we live in a culture of crumbling institutions. We see that today in the decline of the church's authority, the corruption of our political, educational, and societal institutions, and the lack of respect for our nation's history, tradition, and heritage.

Without virtue, we experience a weakening in society. This is certainly apparent in the loss of confidence on the part of the vast majority of the population in the leadership of the institutions listed above. It is also accompanied by an emphasis on material gain and status, and a deemphasis on service and sacrifice. Finally, this weakening of society is manifested by confusion and concern, on the part of a vast number of citizens, over the direction the nation is taking nationally and internationally.

Without virtue, there is an increase in moral relativism, an ideology that refutes the moral and ethical authority of the Bible, refutes the existence of absolute truth, and insists that what is moral and ethical depends on the conditions and circumstances present at the time. This is nothing but pure humanism that claims so-called human wisdom as paramount.

Without virtue, we live in a culture characterized by a raw lust for power. We see this on behalf of nations, on behalf of political organizations, on behalf of unions, and on behalf of individuals. We see it clearly today in the radicalized Democrat Party which has renounced the priority of bipartisanship in the conduct of national politics as intended by our Founders and designed in our Constitution. They have pursued approval of legislation in a purely partisan manner, and revealed their raw lust for power by announcing their intention to pass legislation that would assure them a dominance of political power for the foreseeable future.

Without national, community, and individual virtue, we see a fracturing of the family, and the corruption of the Sanctity of the Family which Dr, Mohler warned against and which is the central theme of this chapter.

Without national, community, and individual virtue, we see a perversion, a corruption of the Sanctity of Marriage, which was the dominant theme of the previous chapter, and without virtue, we see not only a cheapening of life, but a rejection of the Sanctity of Life and creation of human life in the image of God, which was the dominant theme in two previous chapters. Without national, community, and individual virtue, we see the political intrigues of government unrestrained by the demands for honor. Again, we see this today in the priority being given to political party interests rather than to the national interest, and to political party welfare rather than to the common welfare.

With the above narrative describing the characteristics and effects of a loss of individual, community, and national honor and virtue, it should be readily apparent that our country is suffering today from these dishonorable characteristics and effects, and the results have been, and continue to be, devastating to what used to be the American way of life based on the Christian precepts. The source of this loss of honor and virtue is, not completely but primarily, the ungodly, un-American, and unhinged radicalized secular progressive liberalism of the Democratic Party, which has become a dangerous internal threat to the nation and its historical and traditional values.

Dr. Mohler asserts that "a world without honor would be a world in which a husband and father would no longer seek to deserve honor from his wife and children, in which parents would no longer be bound by honor to remain together in marriage, in which there would be no earthly explanation for why anyone, given the opportunity, would not lie, cheat, steal, destroy, disparage, defile, commit adultery, or even murder.

The Apostle Paul gives us the answer as to how to maintain honor and virtue and guard against losing them in Philippians 4:8 where he tells the Church at Philippi:

"Finally, brothers, whatever is true, whatever is noble, whatever is right, whatever is pure, whatever is lovely, whatever is admirable — if anything is excellent or praiseworthy — think about such things."

Paul understood how one's thoughts can influence one's life and behavior. What a person allows to occupy his/her mind will sooner or later determine their speech and action. Paul's exhortation to think about such things he mentions is followed by a second exhortation to put it into practice. The combination of virtues listed in the above passage is sure to produce a wholesome thought pattern, which in turn will result in a life of moral and spiritual excellence. On the other hand, in a world, a nation, a community, a family without honor and virtue, nothing is noble, right, pure, lovely, admirable, excellent, or praiseworthy in their genuine sense. In such a world, nation, community, family, no one aspires to honor, no virtue survives, and no one is safe.

Although honor may be becoming more and more obsolescent in our institutions and society today, we must never let it disappear from our hearts, our home families, our church families, and we must always strive to honor our neighbor - that is, our fellowmen, and above all, honor our Lord and God. Concerning those who refuse to honor the Lord, they would do well to remember God's promise concerning his Son given in Philippians 2:9-11 as follows:

"Therefore, God exalted Him (Jesus) to the highest place and gave Him the Name that is above every name, that at the Name of Jesus every knee should bow, in heaven and on earth and under the earth, and every tongue confess that Jesus Christ is Lord, to the glory of God the Father."

The day is coming when every person who refuses to honor the Lord, whether on this earth or in hell, along with all Christians in heaven and on earth will, willingly or unwillingly, bow at the Name of Jesus and confess that Jesus Christ is Lord. Lord, your people ask you to hasten that day.

Before I close this chapter on the Sanctity of Family, I want to make some additional comments on the family which alone is greater than the temporal family we have which consists of father, mother, and siblings, and that is the family of believers, our church family. The secular progressive radicals want desperately to reduce, or if possible, eliminate the influence of the Church and its families on government, education, society, and culture in order to pave the way for its secular progressive and socialist agenda. They know that if the Church ever wielded its spiritual power and the support of its congregational families against them, they could never hope to win the cultural battle. In fact, the Church and its true leaders, not government and politicians, are the only hope of our citizens for preserving our Christian heritage and our religious freedom, along with other freedoms.

The theological term for this Church family is the "Communion of Saints," which is found in the classical Creeds. For example, the third article of the Apostles' Creed reads:

> "I believe in the Holy Spirit, the holy Christian Church, the Communion of Saints, the forgiveness of sins, the resurrection of the body, and the life everlasting."

The term was included in the creed to express the belief that the living and the dead believers were united in the Body of Christ, the Church. Over time, the word "saint" acquired different meanings. In medieval theology, a saint was either a person whose name appeared in the Bible as a believer in Christ, a martyr, or a Christian whose earthly life had exhibited an outstanding degree of holiness. It was not until the Protestant Reformers, who followed God's Word in the New Testament, that the word "saint" was given the Scriptural meaning of any true believer in Christ.

The doctrine of the Communion of Saints, the family of believers, is defined according to both time and space. In time, it is taken to mean the fellowship of Christians in every age, past, present, and future. We Christians alive on this earth are in fellowship as family with our brothers and sisters in Christ who have gone to heaven. They are the Church Triumphant, the Church at rest, and we on this earth are the Church

Militant, the Church still at war with Satan and his kingdom, with this world of sin, and with our own sinful nature. The Church today has the sacred duty to preserve the faith given it by our Lord and Savior through the Holy Spirit and inherited from the Apostles, the Church fathers, and our faithful family in Christ who have gone before us and transmit it unimpaired and in all its truth and purity to future generations. Just as temporal families pass on a legacy to future family generations, the Christian family passes on the legacy given it by Christ, which is his Word and Gospel of Salvation, to future generations.

The Communion of Saints, defined according to space, means that all true believers are united as family and are in fellowship together regardless of location, nationality, language, ethnicity, or culture. All denominations are obliged to make allowance for the existence of true believers outside their respective denominations.

The Communion of Saints, the family of all true believers throughout time and space, in heaven and on earth, is expressed in the prayer given during the Sacrament of Holy Communion which includes the following statement:

> "Therefore, with angels and archangels and with all the company of heaven we laud and magnify your glorious Name…"

True Christians should never doubt that they are members of God's family, and resist all efforts by Satan, one's own conscience, and the secular progressives who oppose the Christian Church and its powerful influence on society and culture, to convince them otherwise. Membership in God's family is through faith alone and not works, although works are important and serve as a sign of a living and active faith. Jesus Himself confirms the believer's membership in God's family when he encouraged his disciples, and us, to refer to his Father as our Father. In the Lord's Prayer, which He taught to the disciples and us, the opening statement is "Our Father Who art in heaven." After his resurrection when He appeared to the women, He told them:

> "Go instead to my brothers and tell them, 'I am returning to my Father and your Father, to my God and your God.'" John 20:17.

In this passage, Jesus confirms that his Father is our Father and that , in his humanity as Son of Man, He is our brother. What better confirmation could the Christian have that he/she is a beloved member of God's family. The character of God as Father is revealed preeminently in the teaching of Jesus recorded in the Gospels. In Jesus teaching, God is emphasized as Father of the individual believer even more than as Father of the nation, thus giving priority to the concept of family. Jesus' emphasized his followers' oneness with Him and the Father, and the Father's love for them. Speaking of his post-resurrection, He told them:

> "Before long, the world will not see me anymore, but you will see me. Because I live, you also will live. On that day, you will realize that I am in my Father, and you are in Me, and I am in you. Whoever has my commands and obeys them, he is the one who loves me. He who loves me will be loved by my Father, and I too will love him and show myself to him." John 14:19-21.

Jesus used the intimate Aramaic term "Abba" for the Father and invited his followers to do the same. This term was a decisive change from the remote and highly formal modes of divine address employed by the Jews of the day. Some interpreters have overstressed the informality of the term as equivalent to "Daddy." A better interpretation would be "Papa," a name a respectful son would have given his father in every stage of life, with its connotation of affection and respect. The Gospel shows that Jesus used "Abba" in addressing his Father and encouraged his disciples to do so. There are some who consider this as one of the most important features of his teaching.

"Abba" is expressive of an especially close relationship with God. There are many, even some who call themselves committed Christians, who do not want that close of a relationship with God for some reason. Perhaps they think that such a relationship would put too much pressure on them to become a saint. But if they are true Christians, they are already saints. Or perhaps they are still too attached to this world and its allurements and haven't placed every aspect of their lives under Christ's control through the Holy Spirit. At any rate, one thing is sure and confirmed by Scripture, and that is that God the Father wants such a close relationship with each of his children through Christ.

The Apostle Paul uses "Abba" to emphasize the believer's oneness with God as his child and a member of his family. In Romans 8: 15-16, Paul tells the Christians at Rome, and us:

> "For you did not receive a spirit that makes you a slave again to fear, but you received the Spirit of sonship. And by Him we cry, 'Abba. Father.' The Spirit Himself testifies with our spirit that we are God's children."

And in Galatians 4:6 we are told:

> "Because you are sons, God sent the Spirit of his Son into our hearts, the Spirit who calls out, 'Abba, Father.' So, you are no longer a slave, but a son; and since you are a son, God has made you also an heir."

That word "sonship" in Romans 8:15 has the underlying meaning of adoption. Adoption was common among the Greeks and Romans, who granted the adopted son all the privileges of a natural son, including inheritance rights. Christians are adopted sons and daughters into the family of God by grace through faith in Christ. Christ, however, is God's Son by nature, begotten of the Father and co-equal with the Father and the Holy Spirit in divinity, as we are told in the second article of the Nicene Creed as follows:

> "And in one Lord Jesus Christ, the only begotten Son of God, begotten of his Father before all worlds, God of God, Light of Light, very God of very God, begotten, not made, being of one substance with the Father, by Whom all things were made...."

Being members of God's family, the concern of God for the individual believer (that's you and I) is that of a father for his child. This is clearly shown in Jesus' Parable of the Prodigal Son. The Father, representing God, was heartbroken when his son, representing us, asked for his inheritance, and when the Father had given it to him, the son left home, went to another land and wasted it all in riotous living. A famine came upon that land, and the son was starving to death. Finally, he came to his senses, and asked himself "how many servants does my Father have, and they all have plenty to eat? I will return to my Father, tell him I am no longer worthy to be called his son, and ask him to hire me as one of his servants."

When the Father saw his son in the distance returning to him, he gathered up his robe, ran to meet him, threw his arms around him, kissed him, had him clothed in the best robe, put a ring on his finger, sandals on his feet, killed a fattened calf, and conducted a feast of celebration for his son's return, rejoicing and saying: "this son of mine was dead and is alive again, he was lost and is now found." In this parable, which is a favorite of many, Jesus gives a stirring and dramatic account of God the Father's love for each of the sons and daughters of his family who are his through faith in his Son, our Savior, Redeemer, and Brother. And this brings up a couple of final points concerning the Fatherhood of God.

There is a tendency to refer to God as Father of all humanity. Since God is Creator and all human life is created in the image of God, there is a sense in which He is Father of all. However, the Fatherhood of God as Creator is fundamentally distinct from his redemptive Fatherhood of the Church, the Body of Christ, of which every true believer is a member. Being created by God does not make one a member of the family of God. Sin separated all humanity from God. Only God's redemptive Fatherhood in sending his Son to take on our humanity, becoming fully human as well as fully divine, paying the full and terrible price to redeem us from our sins with his holy, innocent, and bitter suffering and death on the cross, his resurrection, and the believer's confessing Christ as Lord and Savior makes one a member of the family of God.

The title "Fatherhood of God" inevitably led to feminist calls within the Church to address God as "Mother," or "Parent," as well as, or instead of, Father. This arose from a series of misunderstandings that calling God Father only was chauvinistic and discriminatory. However, according to Biblical revelation, our address to God as Father is a gracious privilege announced by Jesus Himself, as previously mentioned, and not some human theory about Him that is open to revision. God the Father is not human, but Spirit as Scripture tells us. But to make Him personal to us human beings, the Holy Spirit, who inspired the writers of Scripture, had them refer to God as Father.

Moreover, the character of God revealed in Scripture is not simply masculine, for the Biblical images are of One who cares, pities, nurtures, cherishes, and protects, qualities that certainly are associated with motherhood as well as fatherhood, and not of a chauvinistic deity. And it is his love that is supremely evident in his invitation to us to call him "Out Father," and "Abba."

This chapter on the Sanctity of Family has been extensive and rightly so. God's comment in the Garden of Eden that "it is not good that man should be alone" is as appropriate today as it was then. Community, family, are as essential to man's spiritual and mental health as food and drink are to his/her physical health. As mentioned at the outset, family is the bedrock of society, as well as civilization as a whole. The two greatest families, and one could accurately say, the two genuine families, are the ones discussed in this chapter - the temporal family we have here on earth, and the family of God we have both here on earth and in heaven.

I have gone to lengths to describe both families in view of their critical importance to the nation's past, present, and future, and the Founders numerous references to the human family and the family of God as they understood it from the basis of Judeo-Christianity. Readers may think that I went to too great lengths, especially with the family of God, and I am thankful for their forbearance, but I thought it necessary since a discussion of family and its importance would, in my mind, be incomplete without it. Also, the family of God is usually addressed by people in a generic manner, without a clear understanding of what exactly the family of God is, how a person is brought into the family of God, and the future of those who are members of the family of God in this life and the next.

Since our nation was established on the foundation of Judeo-Christianity, it is highly desirable, if not mandatory, that citizens have at least a partial knowledge of the family of God, and such knowledge requires a fairly thorough application of systematic theology which I have tried to provide. Then too, the main themes of this book, The Sanctity of Life, The Sanctity of Marriage, and The Sanctity of Family, are predominantly spiritual in nature and require adequate theological explanation and application. Again, I express my gratitude for the reader's forbearance, and I will do so again at the end of this book.

Not all of us are members of the family of God, as referred to, but virtually all of us are members of a temporal family here on earth. A fulfilled life can be described as being fulfilled in both families. And the first step in that fulfillment is honor - honoring God our Divine Father and honoring our human father and mother. Over the centuries, there have been scoundrels, deceivers, and false prophets who have tried to diminish the influence of these two great families and change them into something other than what God created them to be. Thankfully, they failed. However, we still have scoundrels, deceivers, and false prophets of the radical secular progressive left with us today who are still trying to replace the riches of our Judeo-Christian heritage and capitalist economy with the rags of secular Marxism and socialism. They are so captive to their ideology that they cannot see, or refuse to see, that our heritage and economy has made us the most powerful, free, benevolent, generous nation in history, with an affluence that gives our families the high standard of living that is the envy of the rest of the world, while socialism around the world has caused immeasurable and unimaginable suffering, poverty, loss of freedoms, family dissolution, institutional corruption, and societal decay.

Why is the radical left today so determined to rewrite history? Because furtherance of their secular progressive socialist agenda demands increasing government control and power, with restrictions on freedom and increased censorship of a free people. The 1619 project is a radicalized view of American history that trashes America's Founders and its founding. I read where President Trump, prior to leaving office, established an eighteen member commission - the 1776 report - to refute the revisionist history, and reinstate the truth concerning the nation's Founders and founding. I read that, within hours after inauguration, the Biden administration deleted the 1776 report from the White House website and ended President Trump's commission with an executive order. My response: Disgust, confusion to the enemy, and a pox on their racist, socialist, ungodly, un-American, and unhinged ideology and policies. Many of these scoundrels, deceivers, and false prophets of today, seeking to replace our Judeo-Christian heritage and capitalism with secularism and socialism have apparently found a home in the Democratic Party. Hopefully, President Trump, now at the beginning of his second administration, will reestablish the 1776 commission.

I have included a multitude of Bible passages and theological narrative on those passages, as well as numerous quotes and references to the Bible from our Founding Fathers and many other eminent individuals that show clearly that the Founders built this nation on the foundation of Judeo-Christianity and insisted that if that foundation were ever allowed to crumble, the nation as a Democratic Republic could not survive.

I'm sure readers are getting a bit tired of my repeating this statement over and over throughout this book, and I thank them for their patience. However, if there was ever a statement that needed to be repeated over and over again, this is it, because apparently a large multitude of our citizens have either forgotten it or were never taught it to begin with and are therefore vulnerable to deception by the secular progressive radicals I mentioned above.

Given the extensive Biblical illiteracy existing today, many reading this book may have no working knowledge of this Christian God who the vast majority of our Founding Fathers worshipped, prayed to, and trusted during the terrible years of the Revolutionary War and afterwards when planning, designing, and laying the foundation for the most exceptional nation in history. Therefore, before closing the book with an Epilogue, I would like to add two relatively short chapters, one concerning the character, and one concerning the personality of this Christian God who defines and undergirds our nation according to both our Founders and a multitude of other grand persons involved in our history. And perhaps doing so will serve to raise the reader's awareness of the evil extent of the secular progressive radical liberals' efforts to remove this God from our government and the public square.

George Washington

John Adams

James Madison

The Apostle Paul of Tarsus

Reformer Martin Luther.

Reformer John Calvin

St. Augustine of Hippo

CHAPTER 11
THE GOD WHO WEEPS

"I long to redeem them but they speak lies against
Me. They do not cry out to Me from their hearts,
but wail upon their beds….I trained them and
strengthened them, but they plot evil against Me.
They do not turn to the Most High…".

Hosea 7: 13b-16a.

"How gladly would I treat you like sons and give you
a desirable land, the most beautiful inheritance of
any nation. I thought you would call me 'Father' and
not turn away from following me. But like a woman
unfaithful to her husband, so you have been unfaithful
to me, O house of Israel," declares the Lord.

Jeremiah 3:19-20.

In the chapter on family, I discussed our spiritual family as well as our temporal family, and our spiritual Father as well as our temporal human father. It is sometimes difficult for us humans to think of God as our Father in the intensely personal terms that Jesus spoke of, as our "Papa" who loves us with an intensity we are incapable of understanding. Scripture speaks repeatedly of God the Father's love for us; yet we fail to comprehend this in the human terms with which we define our human father's love for us, which are the only terms we can relate to with our human intellectual limitations. After all, God's thoughts are as high above our thoughts as the heavens are above the earth. Then too, God is God, Sovereign Creator of the heavens and the earth and all they contain, omnipotent (all-powerful), omniscient (all-knowing), and omnipresent (unrestricted by time of space), whose glory, majesty, and magnificence fill the universe and space. No wonder it is so difficult to conceive of Him as "Papa."

Nevertheless, Christianity alone among all belief systems gives us a God who intensely desires an intimate fellowship with his human creation. In fact, we are God's special and highest creation, created as human in his image, so that we could have that close fellowship with God our Creator.

Scripture tells us that God is love, that love is the primary attribute of all God's attributes, the attribute from which all the others flow. And that brings up a question. As our loving Father, does God have feelings? Does God experience emotions such as sadness, sorrow, grief, joy, happiness, disappointment, and pride with his children as human fathers do? Is Almighty God the Father emotionally vulnerable to his human children's actions and attitudes as human fathers are? Numerous Scripture passages assure us that He most certainly does experience such emotions. Understand of course, that the Holy Spirit inspired the writers to describe God's emotions in human terms, for if divine terms were used, it would be far beyond our understanding.

I entitled this chapter *The God Who Weeps,* because it is immensely comforting to me to know that the God I worship not only has all those attributes described above, but is a Father God Who rejoices with me, laments with me, laughs with me, and weeps with me. So, let's consider God's vulnerability to his children, his family, to us as our Heavenly Father, and its similarity to the vulnerability of our human fathers to the actions and behaviors of their children, their family. And perhaps this will help us view and relate to God not only as our Almighty, everlasting, sovereign God and Lord, but also as our ABBA, our Divine "PAPA." I will only consider a few of the many passages that reveal God's emotions.

In the book of Hosea, we find God baring his heart, speaking with deep sorrow. In Chapters 1-3 God speaks of Israel as an unfaithful wife. But then in Chapter 11, He speaks of Israel as a wayward son. In Hosea

11:1-2 God speaks of his love for Israel, and his disappointment and hurt. As you read this passage and the following ones, try to place yourself in God's position. I'm sure every human parent will be able to sympathize to some extent.

> "When Israel was a child, I loved him, and out of Egypt I called my son. But the more I called Israel, the further they went from Me. They sacrificed to the Baals and they burned incense to images."

The passage initially traces God's choice of Israel back to Egypt, his delivering them from slavery and the exodus out of that country, having given birth to the nation. He refers to Israel as "my son," and therefore to Himself as Israel's Father. God also referred to Israel as his son in Exodus 4:22-23 when God instructed Moses to tell Pharaoh:

> "This is what the Lord says: 'Israel is my firstborn son, and I told you, let my son go, so he may worship Me.'"

And in Deuteronomy 32:6, God refers to Himself as Father when through Moses He tells the people:

> "Is this the way you repay the Lord, O foolish and unwise people? Is He not your Father, your Creator, who made you and formed you?"

In verse 2 of our Hosea passage, God says that the more He called his son Israel, the further they went from Him. Parents of teenagers can certainly relate to the frustration that is apparent in these words. There seems to be an immutable law that when children reach their teens, they must assert their independence, and show how much smarter they are than their parents. I still remember my doing this, and my disgusting behavior which my parents put up with for only one reason - love. Although my father, on one occasion, reminded me that as long as I lived at home and they supported me, there were rules I had to obey; otherwise, there was the door, and I could leave. Thankfully, I had enough common sense to abide by those rules, except for a few occasions which I thoroughly regret.

But the challenge Israel presented to God as his son was greater than simply asserting their independence. God tells us that his son sacrificed to the Baals and burned incense to images. The Baals were idols, heathen gods of fertility, the worship of which involved disgusting and abominable practices. Images referred to other idols, lesser gods that the heathen worshipped. Israel had disobeyed God their Father's command to cut down all idols, the false gods of the heathen peoples they were to conquer, destroy all references and monuments to them completely in the fire. Israel failed to do so, the idols were a temptation to them, and their worship of them was nothing less than a refutation of God their Father's sovereignty and authority over them. Like many human fathers, God the Father had to suffer the indignity and sorrow of having his children turn away from Him, seeking other authority figures to whom they would more willingly give their loyalty and service.

In Hosea 11:3, God the Father's heartbreak becomes more evident:

> "It was I who taught Ephraim to walk, taking them by the arms;
> but they did not realize it was I who healed them."

The name Ephraim refers to the northern kingdom of Israel. After the reign of Solomon, the Kingdom of Israel was split in two, ten tribes belonging to the northern kingdom, often referred to as Ephraim, the main tribe of the ten, and the other two tribes of the southern kingdom referred to as the Kingdom of Judah, the largest of the two. The picture of a father teaching his child to walk is one of the most tender of sights. Again, consider that this is the Sovereign, Almighty, Everlasting God recalling with tenderness and love how He supported, cared for, and taught his children, and lamenting in sorrow that they didn't even realize, or remember, that it was He who healed their injuries, hurts, and wounds they suffered in battle or accidents. How many times have human fathers and mothers bandaged a child's wound, kissed and comforted the child with the assurance that all would be well.

In verse 4, God the Father remembers:

> "I led them with cords of human kindness, with ties of love; I
> lifted the yoke from their neck and bent down to feed them."

Again, the picture of a loving God as Father, leading, guiding, counseling, and yes, disciplining his children with cords of human kindness and with ties of love. It is interesting that God here relates his kindness with human kindness, perhaps an expression of solidarity with human fathers and mothers with whom He shares the ties of love and the joys, blessings, and heartaches of parenthood. God's statement that He lifted the yoke from their neck could well refer to his freeing them from the yoke of slavery in Egypt through Moses and the Exodus. And his comment that He bent down to feed them to his supplying the miraculous food of manna from heaven during those forty years in the wilderness.

In verse 7 God the Father continues to express his sorrow when He says:

> "My people are determined to turn from Me."

Time and time again, during all those years of wandering in the desert, the people murmured and complained against God and Moses. God their Father more than met their every need with grace and love; yet, whenever God delayed meeting a need for a little while in order to test and build their faith, the people would grumble and complain to Moses saying:

> "Why did you bring us out of Egypt where we had plenty of food and water and other delicacies, to die in this desert."

Did they not realize that a complaint against Moses, God's representative and mediator, was a complaint against God Himself? And how soon they forgot the incredible suffering they endured while slaves in Egypt.

In Hosea 7:13b-16a, God expresses his heartache over his children turning against Him. Again, many a human father could relate to God the Father's lament:

> "I long to redeem them but they speak lies against Me. They do not cry out to Me from their hearts...but turn away from Me. I trained them and strengthened them, but they plot evil against

Me. They do not turn to the Most High; they are like a faulty bow."

God the Father likens his rebellious children to a faulty bow, made for warfare, but useless and unable to be used for that purpose because of its faulty construction, or in the case of his children, their faulty stubbornness, unfaithfulness, and rebelliousness.

In verse 7b, God the Father in frustration says of his stubborn and rebellious children:

"Even if they call to the Most High (Me), He will by no means exalt them."

Like human parents dealing with stubborn and rebellious children, God the Father's emotions go from one extreme to the other. In the above statement, He says that even if they call to Him, He will not restore them to the high and exalted position they had before in his love, support, and blessing. Then, in the very next verse, verse 8, He seems to reverse that statement and words of love and longing shine through his deep sorrow, disappointment, and anger. Again, He laments:

"How can I give you up, Ephraim (Israel)? How can I hand you over, Israel? How can I treat you like Admah? How can I make you like Zeboiim? My heart is changed within Me; All my compassion is aroused."

The reference to Admah and Zeboiim are to cities of the plain destroyed when Sodom and Gomorrah were destroyed because of their sinfulness and corruption. Comparing Israel to these cities emphasizes the extent of the evil of their sinfulness and rebellion.

In the passage above, it is as if God the Father is conducting a gracious debate within Himself concerning Israel, his son's case, a debate between justice and mercy, in which God's nature plainly inclines to mercy's side. Let's consider the justice side and the mercy's side in this debate. The justice side is referred to by the comments "give you up" and "hand you over," which emphasizes that the severity of Israel's sin deserved the punishment described in Deuteronomy 21:18-21 as follows:

"If a man has a stubborn and rebellious son who does not obey his father and mother and will not listen to them when they discipline him, his father and mother shall take hold of him and bring him to the elders at the gate of his town. They shall say to the elders: 'This son of ours is stubborn and rebellious. He will not obey us...'. Then all the men of his town shall stone him to death. You must purge the evil from among you."

After God the Father asks, "how can I give you up?" "how can I hand you over," "how can I treat you like Admah and Zeboiim," the justice side, He says that his heart is changed within Him and that all his compassion is aroused. That is the mercy side in the debate.

After the Father said, "My people are determined to turn from Me," you would think his next comment would be something to the effect that "Now I am going to destroy them and never show mercy anymore," or "Let my son Israel be given up as an incorrigible, rebellious son to the elders to be stoned, to be destroyed like those cities of the plain." But No! Instead, we're told that God the Father's heart is changed, that God's compassion is aroused, God's mercy overcomes his anger, frustration, and disappointment, and the compassionate Father asks Himself: "How can I do it?" "How can I give my son Israel over to the condemnation he deserves?" "How can I cast off my stubborn and rebellious son, for though he be stubborn and rebellious, he is still my son?"

"There were times when he was a dear son, a pleasant and faithful child. Israel has been a people near to Me; there are yet some good among them. They are the children of the Covenant; if they be ruined, the enemy will triumph. It may be that they will yet repent and reform, and therefore how can I turn from them, cast them off, and consign them to destruction, even though they remain stubborn and rebellious for a time and I remain angry. So, I will wait awhile, and see if they will repent, return, and reform."

In the debate God has with Himself in our Hosea passage between justice and mercy, mercy wins the day against judgment. In Hosea 11:9 God says:

"I will not carry out my fierce anger, nor will I turn and devastate Ephraim (Israel). For I am God, and not man — the Holy One among you. I will not come in wrath."

And in Psalm 78:36-39 we're told:

"But then they would flatter Him (God) with their mouths, lying to Him with their tongues; their hearts were not loyal to Him, they were not faithful to his covenant. Yet He was merciful; He forgave their iniquities and did not destroy them. Time after time He restrained his anger and did not stir up his full wrath. He remembered that they were but flesh, a passing breeze that does not return."

Although Israel has been unfaithful and unreliable, God will not be untrue to the love He has shown toward them. God declares that the reprieve for Israel shall be lengthened out yet longer. Israel was to be punished and disciplined, but not destroyed. God would mitigate the sentence and reduce the intensity of it. He would show Himself to be justly angry, but not implacably so. Israel would be punished, and justly so, but not consumed.

I wonder how many times God has said this about our country, these United States — "I will not carry out my fierce anger, nor will I turn and devastate them." There have been times in our history, and currently we are living in such a time, when we have to a great extent turned away from the Christian foundation and heritage our Founders gave us, failed in our primary responsibility to our God to believe, to obey, and to remember, failed to honor our Christian tradition and heritage which was honored and affirmed by Presidents, Congresses, and Supreme Courts until fairly recently as history goes.

God's words: "For I am God and not a man - the Holy one among you. I will not come in wrath," are words of encouragement to Israel, and to us, to hope for mercy and compassion. Whereas man's anger commonly lords it over other men, God, as Sovereign Lord over all things, both visible and invisible, is Lord even over his anger. God, in his wisdom, gave us the solution to the dilemma of tension between justice and mercy, a solution that honors both his just nature against sin and his loving nature for his human creation. And that solution is his Son, the GodMan, Savior and Redeemer, Jesus Christ.

Man's compassions are nothing in comparison with the tender mercies of our God, whose thoughts and ways are as much above ours as the heavens are above the earth. As I mentioned at the outset, there are a multitude of Scripture passages, in addition to the passages in Hosea, that emphasize the grace, mercy, compassion, patience, and long-suffering of our God towards sinners (that's all of us) who have corrupted his Sanctity of Life, Sanctity of Marriage, and Sanctity of Family. God's grace is available through his Son the Redeemer and the working of the Holy Spirit to even the most hardcore sinners among us. In Jeremiah 3:12-15, God tells Israel and us through the prophet:

> "Go, proclaim this message toward the north: 'Return faithless Israel, declares the Lord, I will frown on you no longer, for I am merciful, declares the Lord, I will not be angry forever. Only acknowledge your guilt - you have rebelled against the Lord your God, you have scattered your favors to foreign gods under every spreading tree, and have not obeyed Me, declares the Lord. Return, faithless people, declares the Lord, for I am your husband. I will choose you - one from a town and two from a clan - and bring you to Zion. Then I will give you shepherds after my own heart who will lead you with knowledge and understanding.'"

"Merciful" here is also translated as loving. Here, plainly spoken, is God's Fatherly heartbreak over Israel's unfaithfulness and rebellion, and his readiness to pardon sin and graciously receive repenting sinners. All that God asks is that sinners acknowledge their sin and rebellion and repent of it. God's words: "For I am your husband," refers to the Covenant of Grace between God and his children, his family, which is symbolized by and compared to the Covenant of Marriage. In the passage, God promises to give his people shepherds, that is, leaders, after his own heart who will lead them with knowledge and understanding - that is, with wisdom, the wisdom of his Word. The phrase: "shepherds after my own heart," is probably a reference to King David who God called "a man after my own heart." It is well with a people, a nation, when their leaders are men and women after God's own heart, who seek his will through his Word in their dialogues, deliberations, and decisions, who make it their priority to provide for the people first rather than themselves, and to do all they can for the common good and welfare of the people at large.

Our Founding Fathers clearly understood the absolute necessity of having such leaders in a Democratic Republic in which people select their leaders by vote. I believe it was George Washington who, in his farewell address to the nation, warned the people to consider with the utmost care the candidates for office, and select leaders of character, faith, integrity, virtue, honesty, knowledge, and wisdom.

In Jeremiah 3:19-20, referred to at the beginning of the chapter, we have God the Father again lamenting over his stubborn and rebellious children. One can imagine the tears of sorrow being shed by Him as He laments over his wayward children:

> "I Myself said: 'How gladly would I treat you like sons and give you a desirable land, the most beautiful inheritance of any nation! I thought you would call Me 'Father' and not turn away from following Me. But like a woman unfaithful to her husband, so you have been unfaithful to Me, O House of Israel,' declares the Lord."

This passage refers to another situation similar to that in Hosea. The Lord's statements: "How gladly would I treat you like sons," and his hope that they would call Him "Father," expresses his desire for the closest fellowship with his people - the fellowship of family. He wants to bless them with prosperity and the most beautiful inheritance of any nation. God had joined them to Himself by covenant, just as a marriage covenant, but like an unfaithful wife, they had broken that covenant and dealt treacherously with God who had always dealt kindly and faithfully with them. Treacherous dealings between humans is bad enough, but dealing treacherously with God is the highest form of treason and wickedness.

God has blessed us tremendously with a most desirable land and the most beautiful inheritance of any nation - the inheritance of one nation under God, with liberty and justice for all, with a government of the people, by the people, and for the people, and a nation that, under God's direction, guidance, and counsel, has gained and held the status as the most powerful, free, rich, generous, and benevolent nation in history. Yet now, today, we face a question that not many decades ago we would never have thought possible - the question of whether we can retain that status. We have strong enemies without who seek the removal of United States world leadership and its status as a world superpower. But the most dangerous enemy is the enemy within, those government, corporate, educational, and other institutional leaders who seek to remove the Judeo-Christian foundation our Founders built the nation on and replace it with a secular progressive socialist foundation, and at the same time remove the Biblical code of morality and ethics which has so richly blessed our nation over the centuries and brought it world-wide respect and admiration, and replace it with a code of situational morality and ethics which, in effect, paves the way for immoral and unethical conduct.

Historically, their political ideology of secularism, progressivism, and socialism and the policies that flow from that ideology have caused the devastating decline of nations, economic bondage and crushing poverty, the loss of individual and national incentive to grow and prosper, and the growth of a population dependent on government benefits.

The enemy within is composed of, not entirely but mostly, the secular progressive liberal radicals within or associated with the radicalized Democrat Party. May God open the eyes and understanding of our people to see and thoroughly reject their ungodly, un-American, and unhinged ideology and policies and replace those enemies within with leaders who possess the attributes the Founders emphasized - Christian wisdom, character, integrity, and virtue. Scripture is filled with examples of such leaders, one of which was Levi whom God referred to in Malachi 2:4-7:

274 | Darrell J. Ahrens

> "And you will know that I have sent you this admonition so that my covenant with Levi may continue," says the Lord Almighty. "My covenant was with him, a covenant of life and peace, and I gave them to him; this called for reverence and he revered Me and stood in awe of my Name. True instruction was in his mouth and nothing false was found on his lips. He walked with Me in peace and righteousness and turned many from sin."

There, in a nutshell, is a model of a religious, presidential, congressional, institutional, and cultural leader deserving of the title.

I mentioned that not all in the Democratic Party have been corrupted by the ungodly, un-American, and unhinged radicalism of secular progressive liberalism. There are those, although apparently a minority and hesitant to speak out due to fear of being criticized or ostracized by the party, who nevertheless remain faithful to the policy of political bipartisanship and free enterprise given us by the Founders. It is to be hoped that their example will have the effect on the radicals in the Democratic Party of awakening them to the critical danger they and their policies pose to the nation's political, economic, and social well-being, and bring about a deep regret for the damage done to the nation, a change of attitude and reversal of policies leading to a renewal of the political, economic, and social exceptionalism of the nation our Founders established, a renewal similar to that of the Israelite people Scripture tells us about in Jeremiah 3:21and 25:

> "A cry is heard on the barren heights, the weeping and pleading of the people of Israel, because they have perverted their ways and have forgotten the Lord their God. 'Let us lie down in our shame, and let our disgrace cover us. We have sinned against the Lord our God, both we and our fathers; from our youth till this day, we have not obeyed the Lord our God.'"

The choice is clear. We either honor our Christian heritage and traditions or we put them aside and honor secular progressive liberalism. The secular progressive liberals trust in human wisdom to guide government, educational, and social institutions to solve national, international, and social problems. Our Founders and their successors trusted in and sought God's wisdom to lead them to the right solutions and God's counsel in making the right decisions to bring about those solutions. As I mentioned, this Christian heritage of our Democratic Republic has been a centerpiece of America's exceptionalism from the beginning, and it is a profound tragedy that we have leaders today that either do not accept American exceptionalism or are willing to trash it for the sake of secularism, progressivism, and socialism.

Again, I refer to Gary Demar and his book *America's Christian History, The Untold Story* , American Inc. 1995, who on page 192 quotes Robert C. Winthrop (1809-1894), Speaker of the Thirtieth Congress, who put the choice of societies by man in exceptionally clear and relevant terms when he said:

> "All societies of men must be governed in some way or other. The less they may have of stringent State Government, the more they must have of individual self- government. The less they rely on public law or physical force, the more they must rely on private moral restraint. Men, in a word, must necessarily be controlled, either by a power within them, or by a power without them; either by the Word of God, or by the strong arm of man; either by the Bible, or by the bayonet. It may do for other countries and other governments to talk about the state supporting religion. Here, under our free institutions, it is Religion which must support the State."

Abraham Lincoln understood the inseparable connection between religion and liberty when he said:

> "Only the nation under God will enjoy the blessings of true liberty."

Our Founders were right! Human wisdom alone cannot solve national problems, stop national decline, and reverse it. And the reason is that it is only human. And being only human, man's intelligence and knowledge alone does not equate to wisdom. The Psalmist tells us:

"The fear of the Lord is the beginning of wisdom; all who follow his precepts have good understanding."

According to the Psalmist, without the fear (a holy respect for) the Lord, one doesn't even have the beginning of wisdom. Wisdom is often understood in terms of knowledge and education. It is not! We have no shortage of educated fools. Wisdom is knowing how to use knowledge and education in a way that both honors God, benefits mankind, and enables one to reach their highest good. The Psalmist also described the fallacy of human wisdom as follows:

"Lowborn men are but a breath, the highborn are but a lie; if weighed on a balance, they are nothing; together they are only a breath." Psalm 62:9.

How can man's so-called wisdom alone, which is but a breath, a lie, and nothing, contend with and resolve the big somethings we face in religion, politics, economics, education, and culture? The answer is "it can't!" Human wisdom, which is counterfeit wisdom, leads only to confusion and chaos. The Psalmist, however, does not leave it there. In the same Psalm 62, verses 5-8, he assures us of the wisdom, strength, knowledge, understanding, and help freely available to us to enable us to overcome and resolve those big somethings that we face both as a nation and as individual citizens of this great nation. The Psalmist tells us:

"Find rest, O my soul, in God alone; my hope comes from Him. He alone is my rock and my salvation; He is my fortress, I will not be shaken. My salvation and my honor depend on God; He is my mighty Rock, my Refuge. Trust in Him at all times, O people; pour out your hearts to Him, for God is our Refuge."

In this chapter, I have attempted to present God's character in human terms such as feelings, emotions, joy, sorrow, laughter, tears. Hence the title: *The God Who Weeps*. The passages from Hosea and Jeremiah are only a few of many in Scripture that present God as One who feels, emotes, rejoices, grieves, etc. Hopefully the passages selected help the reader to understand and appreciate more fully God the Father's response to his people Israel, whom He refers to as his son, and his grief and sorrow over their sin, stubbornness, and rebellion. And perhaps that fuller understanding and appreciation will translate to a fuller understanding and appreciation of God the Father's response to his family today (that's us), and his grief and sorrow over our sin, stubbornness, and rebellion when we stubbornly demand our own way, and rebel against his will and purpose.

Shawn Carney, President of *40 Days for Life,* in their Spring 2021 publication *Day 41,* Volume 5, issue 1, stated that America and other western nations are living as if God does not exist. He says that the dictatorship of relativism is prevalent and, as a result, we can all believe anything we want, and refers to the unprecedented attacks on the dignity of the human person in the womb, the redefinition of marriage, and the blatant denial of the scientific reality of gender as examples. He further claims that, in our insanity, we deny God, science, and reason and quotes Dostoevsky who, in *The Brothers Karamazov,* said: "If God does not exist, everything is permissible." He also says, in regard to some people saying that the world has gone mad, that is what can be expected from a world without God or basic gender identity, and quotes G. K. Chesterton who said: "If you deny the supernatural, it is only a matter of time before you deny the natural."

I have no doubt that with our nation's precipitous decline in church attendance and Biblical literacy, the attempts to remove God from government and the public square, the corruption of the Sanctity of Life, Sanctity of Marriage, Sanctity of Family, and our living as if God does not exist is causing our God every bit as much grief and sorrow as his stubborn and rebellious family of Israel did throughout their history. I am sure that God is weeping as many tears over us as He wept, and continues to weep, over them.

God was real to our Founding Fathers. They weren't angels, but neither are you and I. But virtually all of them witnessed to their faith in the God of the Bible, humbled themselves before Him, sought his guidance, direction, and counsel in all deliberations and decisions. And they built the nation and established its moral code on the Rock of his precepts, ordinances, and laws contained in the Bible. In doing so, they gave to the citizens of this land a heritage of supreme greatness and value - the heritage of life, liberty, and the pursuit of happiness.

And what is the heritage that the secular progressive liberal radicals want to replace the heritage of our Founders with? The heritage of death, bondage, and the pursuit of hopelessness. The overwhelming death of the genocide being conducted against the most innocent and helpless among us - babies in and out of the womb, the bondage of economic socialism with its quashing of individual incentive, imagination, and ambition, and the hopelessness of a life in which God does not exist, or in which God is irrelevant. One can only hope and pray that the majority of our citizens will wake up and vote every secular progressive radical liberal Democrat and their supporters out of office and replace them with men and women of faith, integrity, honesty, virtue and common sense who hold to and promote the heritage of our Founding Fathers. If this is done, hopefully God our Father will no longer have to grieve and weep over his wayward America.

Having considered the character of the Christian God who weeps for his human creations, we now go on to consider the personality and attributes of this Christian God who is our Father and our friend.

The God Who Weeps

CHAPTER 12
THE PERSONAL GOD

*"The Lord is my Shepherd, I shall not be in want. He makes
me lie down in green pastures, He leads me beside quiet
waters, He restores my soul. He guides me in paths of
righteousness for his Name's sake. Even though I walk
through the valley of the shadow of death, I will fear no evil,
for You are with me; your rod and your staff, they comfort
me. You prepare a table before me in the presence of my
enemies. You anoint my head with oil; my cup overflows.
Surely goodness and love will follow me all the days of my
life, and I will dwell in the house of the Lord forever."*

Psalm 23

*"The Lord is compassionate and gracious, slow to anger,
abounding in love…He does not treat us as our sins
deserve or repay us according to our iniquities. For as high
as the heavens are above the earth, so great is his love
for those who fear Him. As a father has compassion on his
children, so the Lord has compassion on those who fear Him…"*

Psalm 103:8,10,11,13.

In this chapter we will consider the Christian God's nature, attributes,
and personhood. Throughout Scripture, God is presented as a personal
God. The Passages above give emphasis to the personhood and
personality of the Christian God. Our Founding Fathers believed in a
personal God. There are those who say that our Founders were a bunch

of Deists. A Deist is one who believes in God but insists that God is not personal nor involved in the affairs of men. They are Biblically, theologically, and experientially wrong. As I recall, only a couple of our Founders were thought to be Deist - Thomas Jefferson and Benjamin Franklin. Virtually all the rest were devout followers of the Christian faith. Yet, Thomas Jefferson, in addition to believing that the teachings of Jesus Christ are the highest form of truth and wisdom and the foundation of our Constitution, also referred to Jesus Christ as Lord and Savior, the central doctrine of the Christian faith. And Benjamin Franklin, in his own words, acknowledged God's workings in the affairs of men. During the Constitutional Convention, according to William J. Federer in his *America's God and Country,* Encyclopedia of Quotations, Amerisearch, Inc., 2000, page 248, the representatives were engaged in bitter debate over how each State was to be represented in the new government. The debate became so bitter some of them got up and walked out. Finally, when they reconvened, it was Benjamin Franklin who brought order to the convention floor with these words:

> "In the beginning of the contest with Great Britain, when we were sensible of danger, we had daily prayer in this room for Divine protection. Our prayers, Sir, were heard, and they were graciously answered...And have we now forgotten that powerful Friend? Or do we imagine that we no longer need His assistance? I have lived, Sir, a long time, and the longer I live, the more convincing proofs I see of this truth — that God governs in the affairs of men. And if a sparrow cannot fall to the ground without His notice, is it probable that an empire can rise without His aid? We have been assured, Sir, in the Sacred Writings, that 'except the Lord build the house, they labor in vain who build it.' I firmly believe this, and I also believe that without His concurring aid, we shall succeed in this political building no better than the builders of Babel.... I therefore beg leave to move that henceforth prayers imploring the assistance of Heaven, and its blessing on our deliberations, be held in this Assembly every morning before we proceed to business, and that

one or more of the clergy of this city be requested to officiate in that service."

Would God that everyone in Congress today take Ben Franklin's comments to heart.

Franklin insisted that God governs in the affairs of men. The secular progressive liberals of the Democrats do not want God to govern. They want their secular, progressive, socialist ideology to govern. To those secular progressives who claim to believe in a personal God, I again pose the question: "How can you claim genuine faith in a personal God when you give strong approval and support to policies and laws that show insult and contempt for both his Person and his Word by corrupting the Sanctity of Life, the Sanctity of Marriage, and the Sanctity of Family?"

As I mentioned on occasions throughout this book, Christians of genuine faith in their Lord and Savior who have invited this personal God to be Sovereign Lord of their life are children and family of a God who desires to govern and bless our lives with intimate fellowship, who wants to share with each of us the joys of our successes, gains, and accomplishments which He gives us, and share our failures, sorrows, and losses, which come from living in a sinful world, with his comfort, encouragement, assurance, and strength to press on with his guidance, direction, and counsel. And when we stumble, backslide, and fall into sin, this personal God does not leave us or forsake us, but waits patiently for us to respond to the Holy Spirit's leading to turn back to Him in confession and repentance so He can forgive us, restore us, and renew us as He promises to do for the sake of His Son Jesus. In Ezekiel 36:25-28, the Prophet tells us what God promises to those who turn away from their sinful and ungodly attitude and dealings and turn to Him. He says:

> "I will sprinkle clean water on you, and you will be clean; I will cleanse you from all your impurities and from all your idols. I will give you a new heart and put a new spirit in you; I will remove from you your heart of stone and give you a heart of flesh. And I will put my Spirit in you and move you to follow my decrees and be careful to keep my laws. You will live in the land

284 | Darrell J. Ahrens

I gave your forefathers; you will be my people, and I will be your God. I will save you from all your uncleanness…"

The divine love of God continuously seeks us out. Like an earthly father, our personal God, as our Heavenly Father, is sad when his children do not get along and are bitter towards one another. In 1Peter 3:8-12, our personal God the Father tells everyone, even politicians:

"Finally, all of you, live in harmony with one another; be sympathetic, love as brothers, be compassionate and humble. Do not repay evil with evil or insult with insult, but with blessing, because to this you were called so that you may inherit a blessing."

And then the Prophet continues with God's warning:

"Whoever would love life and see good days must keep his tongue from evil and his lips from deceitful speech. He must turn from evil and do good; he must seek peace and pursue it. For the eyes of the Lord are on the righteous and his ears are attentive to their prayer, but the face of the Lord is against those who do evil."

Concerning the Personhood of this Christian God that our Founders were, and we are, called upon to worship and obey, Scripture tells us that God is Trinity, three persons in one Godhead - God the Father, God the Son, and God the Holy Spirit. God the Father and God the Holy Spirit are Spirits; however, God the Son is both Spirit, fully divine as God, and flesh, fully human as man - the GodMan, Son of God and Son of Man. The three Persons of the Trinity are co-equal in sovereignty and divinity as one God. It was necessary for God the Son to take on our humanity and become fully human as well as fully God so that, as man, He could live the perfect, sinless, life in our place, so that as man, He could be the perfect, sinless, sacrifice for all humans, so that as man, He could suffer and die in our place for the forgiveness of our sins and our salvation. All this He had to do as human, not using his divine powers to avoid suffering and the cross. He lived our life for us, the sinless life we could not live, and died our death for us, the innocent death we could not die because all have sinned and fallen short of holiness. By his resurrection from the dead, Jesus' suffering and death were declared all sufficient to satisfy the demands of justice against humankind's sins, past, present, and future, including yours and mine. And Jesus, as Son of Man and Redeemer, was given by the Father all authority in heaven and on earth and under the earth, and He will come again in glory at the end of the age to judge both the living and the dead, consigning those who reject Him as Savior to hell, and taking his believers with Him to heaven where He will establish his Kingdom of Glory in its fullness which will last forever and ever.

When we speak of being in God's family, we think of God as Father; when we speak of our salvation and redemption, we think of God the Son, who as also Son of Man is our Savior, Redeemer, and our brother; and when we speak of our Teacher, Guide, and Counselor, we think of God the Holy Spirit, who has brought us to saving faith in Jesus Christ as Lord and Savior, and who sanctifies and sustains us in that faith.

The Personhood of God involves personality, and this can best be understood by considering the personal attributes of God. As mentioned before, He is omnipotent (all-powerful), omniscient (all-knowing), and omnipresent (all-present), as well as transcendent (above all creation), and immanent (pervading all creation). These attributes God alone possesses, sets Him apart from all creation, and are thus non-relative. Other attributes God possesses are relative, shared by man, but to a far less degree, whereas with God, they are supreme in their nature, extent, and quality. Such attributes are love, mercy compassion, patience, justness, grace and on and on. Again, the emphasis in this chapter is on God being personal, with self-consciousness, will, purpose, and the capability of feeling, choosing, and having reciprocal relationships with other personal and social beings. Scripture is literally filled with accounts of God's relationships with his human creations, from Adam in chapter 1 of Genesis, the first book of the Bible, to John in chapter 1 of Revelation, the last book of the Bible. God's capability of feelings and emotions was discussed in the previous chapter with examples given in the Old Testament books of Hosea and Jeremiah. Other examples abound, also in the New Testament, such as Jesus' feeling of deep sorrow as He lamented the coming utter destruction of Jerusalem in 70 A.D.

> "O Jerusalem, Jerusalem, you who kill the prophets and stone those sent to you, how often I have longed to gather your children together, as a hen gathers her chicks under her wings, but you were not willing. Look, your house is left to you desolate." Matthew 23:37-38.

And then we have the passage that describes how *The God Who Weeps* was literally manifested to the people. When Jesus went to Bethany where his friend Lazarus had died four days previously, He was met by Lazarus' sisters and the group of mourners who were with them. We're told:

> "When Jesus saw her weeping, and the Jews who had come along with her also weeping, He was deeply moved in spirit and troubled. 'Where have you laid him?' He asked. 'Come and see, Lord,' they replied. Jesus wept." John 11:33-35.

Take note that this is Jesus, God Himself, weeping over the death of his friend, even though knowing that He would shortly raise him from the dead, turning the weeping and mourning of the sisters and friends of the family into deep joy. So much does our Creator God share the feelings and emotions of his human creations. And this capability of feeling and emotion extends to all three Persons of the Trinity. Passages documenting the feelings and emotions of the Father and the Son are noted. God the Holy Spirit's capability for feeling and emotion is also expressed in Scripture passages that exhort us not to "grieve the Holy Spirit."

The Holy Spirit, the Divine Evangelist, our Counselor and Guide, grieves whenever we humans sin against God. One of many examples is Isaiah 63:9-10 where we're told:

> "In all their (Israel's) distress, He (God) too was distressed, and the angel of his presence saved them. In his love and mercy, He

redeemed them; He lifted them up and carried them all the days of old. Yet they rebelled and grieved his Holy Spirit. So, He turned and became their enemy and He Himself fought against them."

Notice in this passage God's dealings with his people. He takes their distresses upon Himself. In his love and mercy, He redeemed them. He lifts them up and carries them. Still, despite all this, they continue to rebel against Him and grieve the Holy Spirit.

It is clear from this passage, and from so many other passages of Scripture, that God wants us to share every aspect of our lives with Him, our distresses, our joys and sorrows, our highs and lows, our successes and failures, our hopes and dreams, our goals and everything in-between. During a discussion on prayer, I once had a friend tell me that he only prayed over the big things in life. He didn't want to bother God over the little things. I assured him that, according to Scripture, in the sharing of every aspect of our lives with God, there are no little things. This is the most intimate type of fellowship, the fellowship God desires with you and me and all his human creations. In fact, Scripture strongly suggests that this is the fundamental reason God created us humans in his image in the first place - for such fellowship.

We have evidence of God's desire for fellowship throughout Scripture in the examples of God's choosing. A few examples follow. We're told in Genesis 5:24 that the prophet Enoch walked in close fellowship with God; then he was no more because God took him away. Enoch was taken to heaven by God without experiencing death. We're told that Noah had close fellowship with God, and because of the righteousness of his faith, he and his family were the sole survivors of the flood. God chose close fellowship with Abraham because of the righteousness of his faith and chose him to be father of the great nation He was creating, and to be a blessing to all people. God chose Moses for intimate fellowship as his deliverer of his people from slavery, as his lawgiver to the people, and as the only person whom God would meet with face-to-face. God chose David to be King of Israel, covenanted with him that one of his descendants would rule over a Kingdom that would last forever, and referred to David as "a man after his (God's) own heart." That's fellowship. Scripture gives us numerous other examples of God's close fellowship with individuals, the same fellowship He desires with you and me.

In the passage quoted above from Isaiah we're told that God continued to share in all the peoples' distress, save them, redeem them, lift them up, and carry them, and yet they continued to rebel against Him and grieve his Holy Spirit until finally He turned and became their enemy and He Himself fought against them. Does this mean that He stopped loving them, stopped seeking their return to Him so He could forgive them, restore them, and renew his fellowship with them. No! His turning away, becoming their enemy, and fighting against them was a form of judgment, not punitive judgment, but judgment meant for good, awakening them to the disastrous path they were on, bringing them to their senses, and turning them back to Him. In previous narrative, I used the example of God sending his people into captivity to Babylon for seventy years, before allowing them to return to their homeland and rebuild, in order to cure them of idolatry, which it did once and for all.

There is a crucial lesson here for everyone, and that is if a person consistently and continually refuses God's offer of fellowship, refuses God's reaching out to the person through the Holy Spirit with love, grace, mercy, and compassion, and stubbornly continues to grieve the Holy Spirit, that person will eventually make God their enemy and have God fighting against them. But again, God loves that person and wants that person in his family, and God will fight against any enemy who is trying to prevent a person from turning to Him, even if that enemy and the person is ourself.

And know this! For a person to make God their enemy who fights against them is the worst possible situation a person can find themselves in during this life, and if persisted in until death, the most appallingly foolish and utterly stupid decision of a lifetime because of its horribly dire eternal consequences.

Concerning the dominant theme of this book, the political and spiritual corruption of the Democratic Party and others who follow its party line, it is my contention that the situation described above is the precise situation the secular progressive liberal radicals are in today. Their policies, which result in the corruption of the Sanctity of Life, Sanctity of Marriage, and Sanctity of Family, in effect consist of direct refusal of God's offer of fellowship and the grieving of the Holy Spirit. How can God have fellowship with a person or group whose policies and actions are in direct opposition to God's Word and will? How can God have fellowship with a person or group whose policies and actions continually grieve the Holy Spirit? The bottom line is that, through its ungodly, un-American, and unhinged policies, the radicalized secular progressive liberals of today have made God their enemy and are engaged in battle against God's Word, God's will, God's purpose, and God's order of creation. And until the Democrat Party purges this evil from its midst, it is of no godly use to itself, its members, or the nation. In fact, it is an enemy of our Founders, their successors, and the nation's Judeo-Christian heritage.

Returning to our discussion of God's nature, personhood, and attributes, the fact that God has personality is indicated in several ways in Scripture. One of these ways is the fact that God has a Name, a Name which He assigns to Himself and by which He reveals Himself. In the following passage, God reveals his Name to Moses. Moses said to God:

> "Suppose I go to the Israelites and say to them, 'The God of your fathers has sent me to you,' and they ask me, 'What is his name?' Then what shall I tell them? God said to Moses, 'I AM WHO I AM! This is what you are to say to the Israelites, I AM has sent me to you.'" Exodus 3:13-14.

By naming Himself, God demonstrates that He is not an abstract, unknowable being, or a nameless force. It is most unfortunate and indeed tragic that many people's concept of God is as an abstract, unknowable being, or a nameless force. The Name in Hebrew is *YAHWEH* and is not used to merely refer to God or to describe Him. It is also used to address Him. Many passages invite us to call upon Him. The Name is to be spoken and treated respectfully. According to Exodus 20:7:

"You shall not misuse the Name of the Lord your God, for the Lord will not hold anyone guiltless who misuses his Name."

The great respect accorded to the Name is indicative of the personality of God. Hebrew names were not mere labels to distinguish one person from another. In our impersonal society, this may seem to be the case. Names are seldom chosen for their meaning; rather parents choose a name because they like it, or it is currently popular.

The Hebrew approach was quite different. A name was chosen very carefully with attention to its meaning and significance. The name was considered as an embodiment of family to the person bearing it, and when spoken would often be followed by the term, "son of," or "daughter of." In the chapter on family, I used the example of King Saul who, when he observed the boy David going to fight the Philistine giant Goliath, did not ask, "Who is that boy?" but asked, "Whose son is that?"

There are numerous passages in Scripture that refer to God having physical features such as hands or feet, eyes, ears, mouth. How are we to regard these references? It seems best and most helpful to treat them as attempts to express the truth about God through human analogies. With our limited human intellect, we can only understand human terms, and thus our understanding of God in this life is partial. In fact, Scripture tells us that:

"Now we see but a poor reflection as in a mirror; then we shall see face to face. Now I know in part; then I shall know fully, even as I am fully known. "1Corinthians 13:12.

In heaven, the Christian will see the Lord directly and clearly and know the Lord to the fullest extent, similar to the way the Lord knows us fully and infinitely.

Relating God in human terms are called *anthropomorphisms,* after the Greek word anthropos for human. There are also passages where God appears in human physical form, and these are called *theophanies,* one of the most profound being in Genesis 18:1-5 as follows:

"The Lord appeared to Abraham near the great trees of Mamre while he was sitting at the entrance to his tent in the heat of the day. Abraham looked up and saw three men standing nearby. When he saw them, he hurried from the entrance to his tent to meet them and bowed low to the ground. He said, 'If I have found favor in your eyes, my Lord, do not pass your servant by. Let a little water be brought, and then you may all wash your feet and rest under this tree. Let me get you something to eat, so you can be refreshed and then go on your way, now that you have come to your servant.' 'Very well,' they answered, 'do as you say.'"

Abraham immediately recognized the three men as heavenly beings. In Genesis 18:3, one of the men is identified as the Lord Himself, and in Genesis 19:1 the other two men are identified as angels. In discussing God's nature, the omnipotence, omniscience, and omnipresence of the Lord are emphasized, along with his transcendence, immanence, sovereignty, spirituality, and invisibility, while the anthropomorphisms are treated as human analogies to express truths about God in human terms, and the theophanies as temporary manifestations of God in human form to accomplish a specific purpose of God.

In Biblical times, and even today, the doctrine of God's spirituality serves to counter the practice of idolatry and nature worship. God, being Spirit, cannot be represented by any physical object or likeness. And the fact that God is not restricted by time or space also countered the idea that God could be contained or controlled.

A further indication of the personal nature of God is the activity in which He principally engages. His relationships and activity are primarily with persons rather than with nature, which is the case with many religions. The emphasis of our personal God is his concern with leading, sharing, and shaping the lives of his children individually, socially, and as a community of faith. His goal for each of us is that we reach our highest good in Him, by fulfilling the works He ordained for us from the foundation of the world, by fulfilling his good and perfect will and purpose for each of us through the leading of the Holy Spirit. In the earliest account of his relationship with man in Genesis 3, God comes to Adam and Eve, talks with them and fellowships with them and the impression is given that this was a regular practice. Thus, right from the beginning, we see God both in spiritual terms as Almighty God, and in anthropomorphic (human terms), as a Person who relates to other persons, and as having all the capacities associated with personality. He knows, feels, wills, and acts. Also, our passages from Hosea and Jeremiah in the previous chapter show this clearly.

Because God is our Heavenly Father, the relationship we have with Him has the characteristics of warmth, respect, love, and faith. God is not an unknowable power or force that automatically provides for our needs. He is a knowing, loving, good Father. He can be approached and spoken to, and He in turn speaks to us in various ways, primarily through his Word. In fact, Scripture invites, encourages us, enjoins us, commands us to approach our God in prayer with our joys, sorrows, concerns, and requests.

> "Let us then approach the throne of grace with confidence, so that we may receive mercy and find grace to help us in our time of need." Hebrews 4:16. "Do not be anxious about anything, but in everything, by prayer and petition, with thanksgiving, present your requests to God. And the peace of God, which transcends all understanding, will guard your hearts and your minds in Christ Jesus." Philippians 4:6-7.

Our relationship with God is not a one-way street. Most certainly God is a Being most worthy of our utmost respect and reverence, and all our praise and worship. But He does not simply receive and accept what we offer. He is a living, reciprocating Being, constantly working to bring us to our highest good in Him and to the success He planned for us from the beginning, long, long, before we were even born. He is not One of whom we merely hear, but the One the Holy Spirit constantly works to have us meet and know in a personal relationship.

We are not to think of God as someone to be manipulated and used. There are many, including ourselves, who are tempted at times to think of God as such. Yes, as stated, we are invited by God to bring all our requests and supplications to Him, but we are to do so in an attitude of humility, asking that He respond according to his will. After all, God knows our needs and what is in our best interests better than we do, and whether He should respond with a yes, no, or not yet. The idea that God is simply there to solve our problems, meet our needs, and fulfill our wish list is not faith, but sin.

God is the beginning and the end in Himself, not a means to an end. He is of inestimable, incomprehensible value to us for Who and What He is in Himself, not simply for what He does or can do. In Exodus 20:3 we have the first of the Ten Commandments which reads:

> "You shall have no other gods before Me."

In the verse preceding this verse we read:

> "I am the Lord your God, who brought you out of the land of Egypt."

We are wrong if we interpret these passages to mean that the Israelites were to put God first because of what He had done for them - delivered them from slavery in Egypt, and that out of gratitude they were to make Him their only God. No! Rather, what He had done for them was the proof of Who and What He is. Certainly, we are to continually express our praise and thanksgiving to God for what He has done, and continues to do, for us. But it is because of Who and What God is - Creator, Redeemer, Counselor, Provider, Protector, Refuge, Strength, and beloved Papa, that He is to be worshipped as the only True God, loved and served supremely and exclusively. Our God, as a Person, is to be worshipped, loved, and served for Who and What He is, not for what He can do for us.

When we consider the attributes of God, the first one that invariably comes to mind is love. Many regard it as the basic attribute, and in a previous chapter, I referred to it as the attribute from which all the other attributes flow. There is Scriptural basis for considering love as the very nature or definition of God. An example is 1John 4:8 and 16 as follows:

> "Whoever does not love does not know God, because God is love...And so we know and rely on the love God has for us. God is love. Whoever lives in love lives In God, and God in him."

1Corinthians 13 is referred to as the love chapter. I quoted part of it in the previous chapter on the Sanctity of Marriage. If you haven't read this chapter, I suggest you do so. It will open your eyes to what love really is. In fact, everyone, especially married couples, should make it a habit to review this chapter on love periodically. If everyone did this, and strove to put it into practice, what a different world this would be.

The love of God and the love described in 1Corinthians 13 is, of course, the highest form of love - agape love, the love of intelligence, wisdom, purpose, and sacrifice. In the chapter on marriage, I quoted from Ephesians 5 God's commands to husbands and wives. Both are to love their spouses with the agape love, but to the husbands alone, God gives the command to love their wives just as Christ loved the Church (that's us) and gave Himself up for her. How did He give Himself up for her? He went to the cross and laid down his life for her (us). If it comes to it, husbands are to lay down their lives for their wives. That's sacrificial love, agape love.

When you consider what God commands of husbands and wives and read the chapter on love in 1Corinthians 13, your response will be, "I can't do that; it is just too much." Of course you can't! Nor can I! Not on our own. We're sinners, and our sins of self-pride, self-interest, hypocrisy, and the sinful tendency to give priority to our needs, wants, desires, and goals gets in the way of sacrificing for our wives. God understands our weaknesses, and to overcome those weaknesses He has given us the Holy Spirit. The Holy Spirit, through Christ, gives us strength to conquer our sin and obey God's commands, even his command to love with the agape love described in 1Corinthians 13 and Ephesians 5.

The Lord assured the Apostle Paul of this strength that overcomes our weaknesses. The Apostle Paul suffered a weakness of the flesh which he called his thorn. When he appealed to the Lord three times to take it away, the Lord's response to him was:

> "My grace is sufficient for you, for my power is made perfect in weakness." 1Corinthians 12:9.

And we know that Paul learned the truth of this from his statement in Philippians 4:13 where he said:

> "I can do everything through Him (Christ) who gives me strength." Philippians 4:13.

God's love cannot be fully comprehended with our limited human intellect. God's love fills the universe and all that is. God's love is the source of his eternal giving and sharing of Himself. The perfect love among the persons of the Trinity - Father, Son, and Holy Spirit, binds them together as One True God. In John 14:31 Jesus said:

> "The world must learn that I love the Father and that I do exactly what my Father has commanded Me."

And in Matthew 3:17 we're told that at Jesus' baptism, the Holy Spirit in the form of a dove descended on Him, and the Father's voice from heaven said:

> "This is my Son Whom I love; with Him I am well-pleased."

Before there were any created beings, perfect love existed within the Trinity. And not only that, but since God is not limited by time or space, that love extended to the creation that existed in God's mind and that He would bring into being at his appointed time. The love of God is from everlasting to everlasting. And this brings up a profound reality, an amazing paradox. And that is simply this: You cannot do anything to make God stop loving you!

God loves you for the duration. God's highest good and greatest desire for each of his human creation is to bring them into his family and kingdom through faith in his Son, our Savior Jesus Christ, and bless them with the glory and eternal life we inherit through that faith. As long as you draw breath in this life, God will work to bring you to that highest good for you through the Holy Spirit, no matter how bad you are, how sinful you are, or what despicable deeds you have done. With your sincere confession and repentance, God's forgiveness, restoration, and renewal are always there for you. As we are told in 1 Timothy 2:3-4:

"...God our Savior who wants all men to be saved and to come to a knowledge of the Truth."

"Wait a minute", you say! "How can God send someone He loves to hell?" The answer is, "He doesn't." If that someone continues to grieve the Holy Spirit by refusing God's grace, forgiveness, and salvation, right up to the moment they close their eyes in death, and then open them to find themselves in the torment of hell, they have no one to thank but themselves. God didn't send them there. They sent themselves there.

Just a few of the many characteristics of God's love for us are *benevolence, grace, mercy, and persistence.* You may say that these are also characteristics of human love, and you are right. As I mentioned before, the difference is in both quality and dimension. The quality of God's love is absolutely pure, all-encompassing, unselfish, and self-giving. The dimensions - the height, depth, and breath of God's love, are far greater than either human reason or imagination can comprehend. Let's briefly consider each of these characteristics.

Benevolence: This describes God's concern for the welfare of those whom He loves. God unselfishly, benevolently, mercifully, and persistently seeks our ultimate welfare, our highest good, and we must be brought to the realization that this ultimate welfare and highest good can only be found in Him. Of the numerous Bible passages that speak to this, the best known is probably John 3:16 which says:

"For God so loved the world that He gave his only Son, that whoever believes in Him should not perish, but have eternal life."

Statements of God's benevolence are also numerous in the Old Testament, an example of which is Deuteronomy 7:7-8, in which He tells Israel:

"The Lord did not set his affection on you and choose you because you were more numerous than other peoples, for you were the fewest of all peoples. But it was because the Lord loved you and kept the oath He swore to your forefathers that He brought you out with a mighty hand and redeemed you from the land of slavery."

God's love for us is an unselfish interest in us for our sakes, not his. God does not need anyone or anything. He is Sovereign Lord of the heavens and the earth and all they contain. The fact that Almighty God is a personal God and would want fellowship with his creation man, a fellowship based on mutual love, is a mystery unfathomable. In John 15:9-12, Jesus makes it clear that love is the basis for this relationship and fellowship between God and man. Jesus says:

> "As the Father has loved Me, so have I loved you. Now remain in my love. If you obey my commands, you will remain in my love, just as I have obeyed my Father's commands and remain in his love. I have told you this so that my joy may be in you and that your joy may be complete. My command is this: Love each other as I have loved you."

Jesus identified the highest example of love when He went on to say:

> "Greater love has no man than this, that a man lay down his life for his friends."

Yet Jesus did not lay down his life only for his friends, those who loved Him. He also laid down his life for his enemies, those who hated, despised, and rejected Him. This is truly the greatest love, dying for our enemies as well as for our friends, concerned for our enemy's welfare and highest good as well as our friend's welfare and highest good.

This self-giving, unselfish, benevolent quality of the divine love is spoken of by the Apostle John in 1John 4:10:

> "This is love: not that we loved God, but that He loved us and sent his Son as an atoning sacrifice for our sins."

And in Romans 5:8 the Apostle Paul tells us:

> "But God demonstrates his own love for us in this: While we were still sinners, Christ died for us."

Grace: Here is another attribute of God and his love, the full meaning of which is again incomprehensible to the human intellect and truly amazing. In fact, that is the subject and title of one of the most treasured hymns ever written - *Amazing Grace*. The meaning of grace - *charis* in the Greek - is unmerited favor. God's grace leads Him to deal with us not on the basis of our merit or worthiness, or what we deserve, for we are all sinners and deserve only condemnation, but on the basis of his goodness and generosity. God's grace means that He supplies us with undeserved blessings and favors, even the greatest blessing of salvation, while requiring nothing from us but faith, and even this faith is a blessing from God through the Holy Spirit. Our free-will was corrupted by the fall into sin and does not enable us to come to saving faith on our own volition. God graciously provides the Holy Spirit to prompt us, lead us, strengthen us, and enable us to come to faith in Christ as our Lord and Savior, and receive through that faith the greatest blessing of all - forgiveness of our sins, salvation, unity with God in Christ, and eternal life.

The Rev. Dr. Martin Luther, the great Reformer, in his explanation of the third article of the Apostle's Creed, says this concerning the Holy Spirit:

> "I believe that I cannot by my own reason or strength believe in Jesus Christ my Lord, or come to Him, but the Holy Spirit has called me by the Gospel, enlightened me with his gifts, sanctified and kept me in the true faith."

The grace of God is prominent and reaches its apex in the New Testament with the coming of Christ. The Apostle John tells us in John 1:14,16-17 concerning Jesus Christ:

> "The Word became flesh and made his dwelling among us. We have seen his glory, the glory of the One and Only, who came from the Father, full of grace and truth." "From the fullness of his grace we have all received one blessing after another. For the law was given through Moses; grace and truth came through Jesus Christ."

Also, numerous passages in the Old Testament speak of the graciousness of God, an example of which is Exodus 34:6 where we are told:

"The Lord, the Lord, the compassionate and gracious God, slow to anger, abounding in love and faithfulness, maintaining love to thousands, and forgiving wickedness, rebellion, and sin."

And in Ephesians 1:7-8, the Apostle Paul tells us:

"In Him (Christ) we have redemption through His Blood, the forgiveness of sins, in accordance with the riches of God's grace that He lavished on us with all wisdom and understanding."

Note the element of abundance of grace in all these passages. God is not a stingy god who gives just barely what he must and conserves the rest. Our personal God is a generous God of amazing grace who gives abundantly. There are passages which are even more explicit in relating salvation to the extravagant gift of God's grace. In Ephesians 2:6-9 we're told:

"And God raised us up with Christ and seated us with Him in the heavenly realms in Christ Jesus, in order that in the coming ages He might show the incomparable riches of his grace, expressed in his kindness to us in Christ Jesus. For it is by grace you have been saved, through faith - and this not from yourselves, it is the gift of God - not by works, so that no one can boast."

The words "in the heavenly realms in Christ Jesus" emphasizes our union with Christ.

If God gave to all of us what we deserve, no one would be saved. Everyone would be lost and condemned to hell. We are saved by Christ alone, through faith alone, by grace alone, the grace of a loving and personal God who weeps for those who reject his grace. Every aspect of our life -spiritual, secular, political, work, pleasure, leisure, and all other should be lived in gratitude to this God of amazing grace, in steadfast faith and in obedience to his Word as the final authority in faith and life.

Mercy: God's attribute of mercy is his loving compassion for us, his tenderness of heart toward us. If justice sees us as sinful, guilty, and condemned, mercy sees us as miserable, helpless, and needy. In Psalm 103:13 the Psalmist says:

> "As a father has compassion on his children, so the Lord has compassion on those who fear Him; for He knows how we are formed, He remembers that we are dust."

And in Psalm 86:5-6 the Psalmist says to the Lord:

> "You are forgiving and good, O Lord, abounding in love to all who call to you. Hear my prayer, O Lord; listen to my cry for mercy. In the day of my trouble, I will call to you, for you will answer me."

God's mercy is vividly apparent throughout Scripture. It is seen in his pity and concern for the people of Israel who were in the bondage of slavery to the Egyptians. In Exodus 3: 7-8 we're told that He heard their cry and knew their sufferings.

> "The Lord said: 'I have indeed seen the misery of my people in Egypt. I have heard them crying out because of their slave drivers, and I am concerned about their suffering. So, I have come down to rescue them from the hand of the Egyptians and to bring them up out of that land…'"

God's mercy is also clearly seen in the compassion that Jesus felt during the multitude of occasions when people suffering from spiritual and physical sickness and disease came to Him. Frequently we are told that Jesus was moved with compassion for the person or persons before He healed him, her, or them. In Matthew 9:35-36 we're told:

> "Jesus went through all the towns and villages, teaching in their synagogues, preaching the good news of the Kingdom and healing every disease and sickness. When He saw the crowds, He had compassion on them, because they were harassed and helpless, like sheep without a shepherd."

Mercy is the outworking of God's benevolence and grace. Mercy is a dominant characteristic of a personal God who weeps. Mercy is also one of the evidences of genuine faith on the part of God's people.

Persistence: Persistence is God's long-suffering, his withholding final judgment and continuing to offer grace and salvation over a person's lifetime. This withholding of judgment and offer of grace and salvation ends only when one closes their eyes in death. But right up to that moment, the Holy Spirit continues to prompt, encourage, lead, and witness to the unbeliever to turn from their unbelief, and in faith, confess Jesus Christ as Lord and Savior to the glory of God the Father, and receive the grace, forgiveness of sins, and eternal life that God wants to give them.

The great example of this long-suffering patience and persistence of God is the account of one of the two criminals crucified with Jesus given us in Matthew 23:39-43:

> "One of the criminals who hung there hurled insults at Him (Jesus): 'Aren't you the Christ? Save yourself and us!' But the other criminal rebuked him saying, 'Don't you fear God,' he said, 'since you are under the same sentence? We are punished justly, for we are getting what our deeds deserve. But this man has done nothing wrong!' Then he said, 'Jesus, remember me when you come into your Kingdom.' Jesus answered him, 'I tell you the truth, today you will be with Me in paradise.'"

The man was a hardened criminal with a sinful, wicked life that was about to come to an agonizing close. But there was something about Jesus, his words and acts on the cross, that softened that criminal's heart, and the Holy Spirit used that to witness to that criminal and bring him to faith in Christ, evidenced by his words to his fellow criminal and his expression of faith and request to Jesus. And the genuineness of his faith was attested to by Jesus when He assured the criminal that his request to be remembered would be honored that very day.

God's persistence and long-suffering were clearly shown in his faithfulness to Israel. As previously discussed, the Israelites repeatedly rebelled against God. During the Exodus, when things got tough in the desert, they criticized Moses for bringing them out to the wilderness to die, and even expressed their desire to return to Egypt, forgetting all those years of suffering under the intense cruelty of the slave masters from which God had delivered them. They rejected the leadership of Moses, God's chosen one to be their deliverer and mediator. Even when they were settled in the Promised Land by the grace of God and the victories He gave them over the nations through Joshua, they continued to rebel against Him by taking up the evil practices of the heathen nations around them. They intermarried with them against God's command, they worshipped their idols with its disgusting and abominable rituals. God would have been fully justified in destroying them; yet He did not cut them off and continued to reach out to them through the Prophets.

God's persistence and long suffering were not limited to his dealings with Israel. Concerning the flood in Genesis, the Apostle Peter tells us in 1Peter 3:20 that God waited patiently all that time that the ark was being built for the people to respond to his grace and repent. But they refused God's offer of grace and forgiveness and all humankind was destroyed in the flood except for Noah and his family.

The Apostle Peter also tells us that the long delay in Christ's return to earth in glory to judge both the living and the dead, and to usher in the eternal state, is due to God's forbearance and his desire that everyone come to repentance. In 2Peter 3:9 he tells us:

> "The Lord is not slow in keeping his promise, as some understand slowness. He is patient with you, not wanting anyone to perish, but everyone to come to repentance."

Like our personal God and Father, we are to exercise persistence and patience with others, our human family, our brothers and sisters in Christ, and our fellowmen. And yes, even our enemies. When Peter came to Jesus and asked Him, in front of the other disciples, how often he should forgive a brother who sinned against him, and suggested seven times, probably thinking that this would impress Jesus and the other disciples since the Jewish standard at the time was to forgive three times, Jesus answered him, "I tell you, not seven times, but seventy seven times."

This number has been interpreted as 77, 70x7, or times without number. Times without number is considered by most to be what Jesus meant since it more closely describes the persistent, relentless, nature of the love that is to be characteristic of a follower of the Lord.

The Apostle John insisted that the absence of practical acts of mercy, concern, and compassion, which would include the failure or refusal to forgive, is an indication that one's supposed Christian experience is not genuine, and that God's love does not abide in that person.

> "Anyone who claims to be in the light but hates his brother is still in the darkness. Whoever loves his brother lives in the light, and there is nothing in him to make him stumble." 1John 2:9-10.

One final point in our consideration of some of the attributes of our personal God and Father. And that is the question of whether there is any tension among any of the attributes? The one point of potential tension usually mentioned is the relationship between the love, grace, and mercy of God and the justice of God, his just nature. Sin is anathema to God and punishable by death. God cannot just overlook sin or forgive sin without restitution being made. That would be a violation of his just nature and divine status. And God cannot violate his just nature and be God. So how does one reconcile God's attributes of mercy and justice? On one hand, God's justice seems so severe and harsh, requiring death for not only individuals but large groups of people. On the other hand, God is incredibly and supremely merciful, gracious, patient, forgiving, and long-suffering.

The answer to how do we reconcile God's attributes of mercy and justice is we don't have to. As briefly mentioned before, God has already done that for us through Jesus Christ our Lord and Savior. Christ suffered the holy, innocent, bitter sufferings and agony of the cross in payment for yours and my sins and the sins of all humanity, past, present, and future. That's justice! And for his sake, we are forgiven, cleansed, restored and reconciled to God our Father every time we confess our sins and repent of them, for as Scripture tells us, the Blood of Christ just keeps cleansing us. That's love, mercy, and grace. And concerning God's supposed severe and harsh justice, Scripture shows that such justice usually came upon individuals and groups after their sin, rebellion, and depravity had reached such extremes that there was no other hope for their turning back to God.

A prime example of God's incredible patience with sinners is given in Genesis 15, where God tells Abraham that his descendants will be enslaved by a foreign nation (Egypt) for four hundred years before God would free them and bring them to the land He was promising them (the land of Canaan) as their inheritance. The reason for the long delay was that the sin of the Amorites (representing the many heathen nations of Canaan) had not yet reached its full measure. And what was the sin of those heathen tribes? Archaeology, artifacts, and ancient texts tell us. Their worship was polytheistic and included child sacrifice, idolatry, religious prostitution with both male and female prostitutes, and divination. God was patient with those wicked Canaanite nations, giving them more than four hundred years to repent and turn from their abominable ways before bringing them to justice and giving their lands to the Israelites.

There is no tension between God's attributes. They are in harmony with one another. Thus, God's justice is a loving justice, a justice that is motivated by love and seeks to restore love and reconciliation if at all possible. Love is not fully understood unless it is seen as including justice. Love and justice work together in God's dealing with man. Christ on the cross is the perfect example of this. Perfect justice for our sins in Jesus suffering and death. Perfect love in his purchasing our forgiveness and salvation through that suffering and death. Love without justice is only mere sentimentality.

Unfortunately, much of what passes for love today is nothing but sentimentality. More and more we read about secular progressive liberal Democratic prosecutors who refuse to indict criminals, even repeat criminals, guilty of what they consider lesser offenses. I'm sure they think of themselves as merciful and compassionate; however, the reality is that it is not mercy and compassion they are showing those criminals but hate and encouragement for them to continue pursuing a criminal career. And then they and others like them wonder why the crime rate is increasing at an alarming rate, or worse, they deny that the crime rate is increasing in the face of irrefutable evidence. Like the saying goes, "You just can't cure stupid!"

Again, love and justice work together harmoniously and with all the other attributes of God. God is both just and loving to the highest extent, and the greatest, irrefutable proof of this is the cross of Christ.

God's love and justice are of crucial importance concerning the Sanctity of Life. Where is the justice for that baby created in the image of God being butchered in the womb? Where is the love for that baby created in the image of God being butchered in the womb? There is none. There is no justice, no love, for that most innocent and helpless of God's creations. For these babies, there is only the torture and death of abortion, which by the way, as I have repeated over and over, is a major policy of the radicalized secular progressive liberal Democrat Party which, with their few Republican in name only allies, can lay claim to some 63 million murdered babies in the womb and some out of the womb. And not only that, but they insist that abortion be allowed right up to the moment of birth. All this alone, without even considering their other radicalized economic and social policies, justifies the labeling of the Democrat Party of today as an ungodly, un-American, unhinged organization, a modern day pariah of American politics.

In the listing of the Ten Commandments, the eighth commandment is "Thou shalt not bear false witness against thy neighbor." Martin Luther, in his *Small Catechism,* gives the answer to the question, "What does this mean?" as follows:

> "We should fear and love God that we may not deceitfully belie, betray, slander, nor defame our neighbor, but defend him, speak well of him, and put the best construction on everything."

To bear false witness is to lie. God has commanded his people to be honest in all situations. They are to be truthful both in what they clearly state and in what they imply. To lie is to sin. Which brings up a question! Is there ever a time when it is not a sin to lie? A time when the significance of the end justifies using the means of falsehood, misrepresentation, lying? A typical example people in the past used was that of a family hiding Jews during World War II. The Nazis come to the door and ask: "Are there any Jews here?" If the head of the household says to himself, "I am a devout Christian, I must not lie for it is a sin," and tells the Nazis, "Yes, there are Jews here," they will be taken away to death in a concentration camp. If he says, "No, there are no Jews here," they will live. Is lying in this case a sin or not?

Interesting question, and one which the renowned Lutheran theologian Dietrich Bonhoeffer, who was martyred by the Nazis, addressed. His response was most interesting. First of all, what would Jesus have us do? Would Jesus have the person avoid lying at all costs and turn the Jews over to the Nazis? I don't think anyone would answer yes to that. Well then, would lying in this case not be a sin? Bonhoeffer's response was "No!" Sin is sin, and lying is a sin. But in extremely rare cases like that described, it is the right thing to do, and therefore is forgiven sin.

Then too, remember the case of Rahab the harlot of Jericho, in Joshua 2, who hid the two Israelite spies who had come to spy out the defenses of Jericho from her townspeople who wanted to find them and kill them. When she was asked if she had seen them, she said they had left the city and if they hurried they might still catch them. Later, she had the two spies lowered from her home built in the wall of the city so they could escape and return to the Israelite encampment. Her lie enabled the two spies to escape and Rahab was richly blessed by the Lord for her act. She and her whole family were saved when the Israelites attacked and totally destroyed Jericho, and she became a member of God's family, an Israelite mother, and is listed in the human lineage of Jesus, Son of God and Son of Man.

Just as God's people are to be honest in their dealings with others, so they are to be thoroughly honest in their presentation and use of the Word of God. Here too, there are those who are quick to rationalize that the end justifies the means. I once had a highly respected lawyer tell me that for people new to the faith, or being introduced to the faith, it would be best not to emphasize or go into too much detail about the Lord's suffering and crucifixion on the cross since that could have an initial impact of offending them. He thought it best to wait until later when they were more grounded in Jesus' teachings, and then cover the Lord's atonement, suffering, and death in greater detail.

I countered this with two points. First, in many cases, later never comes. And although the extent of the horror and brutality of Christ's physical, spiritual, and mental sufferings and death cannot be fully comprehended with our limited understanding, there are unfortunately many Christians who do not even have a partial understanding of his sufferings and death. And secondly, I told him that the sufferings, death, and resurrection of Jesus Christ is the very core of the Christian faith. To minimize it is to minimize the faith, and without it, there is no faith, just another religion.

In 2Corinthians 4:1-2, the Apostle Paul condemns deception and distortion concerning the Word of God. He says to those in Corinth:

> "Therefore, since through God's mercy we have this ministry, we do not lose heart. Rather, we have renounced secret and shameful ways; we do not use deception, nor do we distort the Word of God. On the contrary, by setting forth the Truth plainly we commend ourselves to every man's conscience in the sight of God."

Since time immemorial, highbrow and lowbrow scoundrels and those in-between, have with cunning and deceit tampered with, misrepresented, and distorted God's Word for personal gain or to be able to falsely use it to justify a policy, decision, or goal that is contrary to that Word. This is especially true of the powerful and influential among us - the first who come to mind are secular progressive radical liberal politicians, corporate and educational authorities, and celebrities. The Apostle Paul, In the above passage, assures the Christians at Corinth that he and his companions have renounced the disgraceful, underhanded ways of others, and that they refuse to change, alter, or modify in any way God's Word, but give the people clear and open statements of the Truth as given them by Jesus and the Apostles. Paul went on in later verses to assure the people that he and his companions preach only Jesus Christ as Lord and themselves as their, the people's, servants, and not like the false teachers who were puffed up with self-importance. What we, and especially every person in authority over others must understand, just as the vast majority of our Founders and their successors understood until recently, is that the personal God of Truth is to be best served by his people by their presentation of the Truth - the Absolute Truth.

In April 1944, a year before the Nazis hanged him, Bonhoeffer, whom I mentioned before, wrote:

> "What is bothering me incessantly is the question of what Christianity really is, or indeed what Christ is for us today."

Keep in mind that Bonhoeffer wrote this during the greatest war in human history, a war that devastated a goodly portion of the world, a war that cost millions upon millions of human lives with incomprehensible, worldwide suffering, loss, and destruction. In view of it all, Bonhoeffer's question is understandable. But it is also a question for all time and for everyone. It is a question that each of us must ask ourselves, "Who is Christ to me today?" "What does discipleship involve for me today?" Compared with this question, everything else in life is a distraction. Why is that? Because everything else in this life will pass away. Naked we came into this world from dust, and naked we leave this world to return to dust. But how we answer that simple all-important question about Jesus while we are in this world will decide where we spend the next life - eternity - either in heaven or in hell.

It is so easy to be distracted from this all-important question. That's why I have, in one way or another, repeated it a number of times in this book. Satan will try repeatedly to keep us from seriously considering that question. And so many other important things compete for our full attention - family, job, career, school, goals, finances, circumstances, conditions, and on and on. Those who are in positions of power and influence, political, corporate, or other, are near totally involved in keeping that power or increasing it. They don't have time to ponder that all-important question and fail to consider the fact that when they die, all that power and influence disappears like dust in the wind. And even if, after they die, they are honored by numerous ceremonies and accolades, they aren't going to be around to see or hear them. Power is one of the strongest addictions, and like the saying goes, "Power corrupts, and absolute power corrupts absolutely."

And this is precisely what the current leadership and the secular progressive radical liberal faction of the Democrat Party want - absolute, dominant power. Scripture, as well as history, reminds us that absolute political power is extremely dangerous, and is the cause of the majority of the death, destruction, genocide, poverty, and misery that have spanned the ages. What the radicals do not understand is that absolute power, whether political, economic, military or other, cannot bring about enduring change. Power can force people to change, but eventually they will rebel. Only love can move people to willingly change. Power can control behavior, but only love can move the heart. And according to author Brennan Manning in his book *The Signature of Jesus*, no power on earth can so move the heart as suffering love, and the perfect expression of such suffering love is "God's love for us in the dying figure of Jesus on the cross pleading for someone to moisten his burning lips."

As one pastor put it, life is hard for a Christian, but to be anything else is too dull. I imagine that the Christian life is going to get harder. The fact that, for the first time in our nation's history, Christians are starting to be persecuted does not bode well for the future. And this persecution is being conducted against those Christians who insist on being faithful to God's Word and Jesus' teachings and who refuse to approve of, or give support to, activities, beliefs, and lifestyles that are in violation of Biblical teachings and standards.

I'm sure this persecution will grow worse since that is the normal progression of persecution, with more and more demand that Christians compromise their faith and submit to cultural and societal standards. And the persecutors will consist of the powerful, so-called elites of the country - religious authorities who, in order to keep peace and their status, have accepted the radicals' demands for compromise of God's Truth; politicians who have corrupted themselves both politically and spiritually for the sake of wealth and power, and who, puffed up with self-pride, consider themselves as rulers rather than servants of the people; ostentatious, liberal professors who mock religious and conservative values; and millions of citizens who, because of the appalling degradation of our public education system over the past five or six decades, are too Biblically and historically ignorant to fully comprehend the gross violation of both Scripture and the Constitution that such persecution is. Hopefully there will remain enough Biblically and Constitutionally literate and wise leaders and citizens left who are able to resist, condemn, and defeat such persecution of Christians. Our country's destiny depends on it.

I close this chapter devoted to our personal God by referring for the second time to the parable in Matthew 7:24-27 with which Jesus closed his *Sermon on the Mount.* Jesus said:

> "Therefore, everyone who hears these words of mine and puts them into practice is like a wise man who built his house on the rock. The rain came down, the streams rose, and the winds blew and beat against that house; yet it did not fall, because it had its foundation on the rock. But everyone who hears these words of mine and does not put them into practice is like a foolish man who built his house on sand. The rain came down, the streams rose, and the winds blew and beat against that house, and it fell with a great crash."

Our Founding Fathers had the great wisdom, insight, and brilliance to build this first experiment of a nation with a government of the people, by the people, and for the people, on the rock of Judeo-Christianity, and it has withstood the strongest storms of human, natural, and spiritual origins for over two hundred forty-nine years. Yet, the radicals of the Democrat Party, and those who are allied with them, want to replace this rock formation of Judeo-Christianity with a sand formation of secular progressive socialist liberalism, an act of ungodliness, un-Americanism, and terminal stupidity that would progressively diminish and eventually destroy the United States of America as the world's most benevolent and generous superpower.

We must pray that our personal God give us both true leaders and a multitude of godly citizens who will stand fast against this insidious evil.

Thomas Jefferson

Benjamin Franklin

Reformer Martin Luther

Theologian Dietrich Bonhoeffer

Jesus and friends

*Jesus ministering to Samaritan
woman at Jacob's well*

Jesus washing disciples' feet.

Three views of our personal God

CHAPTER 13
EPILOGUE

Our nation is in peril. The danger of losing our national identity, and with it the national soul, has never been greater. There are those who would strongly disagree, citing historical times of crisis such as past wars, primarily the Civil War, and past social and cultural upheavals such as the Depression and Civil Rights movement as greater perils. Also, there were other political / paramilitary organizations that sought to overthrow our Democratic Republic and its institutions, such as the America Nazi Party and the American Communist Party, but these were fringe organizations and not really a major threat to the nation.

Our Founding Fathers maintained that if the United States was ever destroyed as the Democratic Republic, which they gave us, the causes for its destruction would come from within, and not from without. And this is the crux of why our country is in peril today. Even during the past major crises of local and World Wars, Depression, Civil Rights violence, Vietnam War violent protests, the nation's identity, or again its soul, remained fundamentally unchanged from a Judeo-Christian foundation, a Biblical code of morality and ethics, and a history, tradition, and heritage accepted, admired, and respected by virtually all the citizenry as well as by millions of people abroad. Even during the Civil War, the greatest internal threat to the nation's stability and survival up to that time, the issue was slavery, but other than that, both Northerners and Southerners honored the nation's history, tradition, and heritage and basically shared the same goals and objectives for life. Confederate and Union soldiers alike prayed to the same God, wanted to get back to the farm or to the profession they were pursuing before the war intervened, find a wife, raise a family, and advance financially, professionally, and socially.

This is no longer the case. With the serious spiritual, political, educational, societal, and cultural deterioration over past decades, there are many, too many, of our citizens who prefer a secular foundation for our country instead of the Judeo-Christian foundation our Founders gave us, a human code of morality and ethics based on moral relativism, rather than the Biblical code which came from God, a socialist economy rather than a capitalist economy, and who insist that the nation is racist and imperialistic, ignoring the fact that the nation has expended an incalculable fortune in blood and wealth saving other nations from defeat by totalitarianism, including two World Wars, major war in Korea and Vietnam, and other conflicts in various parts of the world, and then expending multiple billions of dollars helping those nations to rebuild, all the while making no imperialistic demands except, as Secretary of State Colin Powell told a French diplomat, just enough land to bury our dead who had died defending those foreign nations.

Today we also have too many citizens, as well as too many illegal aliens, whose primary interest is not the country's welfare, but how much they can get from the country's treasury. I believe it was Thomas Jefferson who said that when citizens discovered that, with the vote, they could pressure their congressional representatives to provide them largess from the national treasury, it would be the beginning of the end of our Democratic Republic. Too many people have taken President John Kennedy's statement: "Ask not what your country can do for you; ask what you can do for your country." and have turned it around to read: "Ask not what you can do for your country; ask what your country can do for you." Unlike the past, too many people today are not so much interested in finding work as they are in finding government subsidies, government handouts, government welfare payments, fulfilling Jefferson's prophecy. Too many people are asking, "What can the country give me?"

And our government leaders are exacerbating the situation. There's talk of our democrats in congress promoting legislation to provide welfare payments to illegal immigrants, free health care to illegal immigrants, free school tuition to illegal immigrants, etc. Legal immigrants resent this, and who can blame them? They came to this country, worked hard to support themselves and family, and studied hard for their citizenship. My sister-in-law was one of those. It wasn't easy by any means, and it took her eight years, but the day finally came when she proudly walked to the front to receive her citizenship papers. And we, her husband, my wife, and I rejoiced with her. I'm hoping that if the above legislation to give all those freebies to illegal immigrants passes, the immigrants who did everything right, and those who are doing everything right, will rise up in mass protest and let the politicians know exactly how they feel and use the ballot box to retaliate.

Why would politicians, primarily Democrats, propose such legislation in the first place? And here we get to corruption, plain and simple. They know that if they throw the doors wide open to illegal aliens, those illegal aliens are sure to vote Democrat in elections for the foreseeable future. So, the more illegals, the better. Wait a minute, you say. They can't vote. They are illegal and not citizens. Oh, did I forget to mention that the Democrats are considering legislation to allow illegal aliens to vote. Yes, I know! That's contrary to the Constitution and the national interest. But to the current crop of Democrats, not all of them, but too many of them, who are secular progressive radicals, the Constitution is a plaything, and party interest takes priority over national interest every time.

G. K. Chesterton, in his wise commentary on society and culture, made the statement:

> "Once God is abolished from society, the government becomes god."

And that is precisely what the secular progressive radicals in Congress want - a government as god, and the citizens as wards of the state. Unfortunately, our former democratic president was either incapable or unwilling to provide strong resistance to the radicals' agenda, or worse yet, from his statements and attitude, it could well be that he agrees with them. What the country desperately needs is strong leadership in the form of that addressed by J. Oswald Chambers, the great Christian pastor and author, when he said the following:

"The leader must be one who, while welcoming the friendship and support of all who can offer it, has sufficient resources to stand alone, even in the face of fierce opposition, in the discharge of his or her responsibilities. He or she must be prepared to have no one but God."

Of our recent presidents, in my opinion, President Ronald Reagan and President Donald Trump during his first administration and now at the start of his second administration, exemplified the type of leadership J. Oswald Chambers described.

In the 1950s, no one of either political party could have conceived of Supreme Court decisions that would substantially remove the expression of Christian faith out of public life, take the schools out of the hands of local citizens, safeguard obscenity, create protected classes of society, and establish elective abortion as law. These massive changes, and others, in American life and institutions, beginning in the early 1960s, were wrought upon the country from the top, primarily by secular progressive liberal Democrat regimes that used government, and the least representative organs of government - the courts - to carve the larger society in their own image.

These ungodly, un-American, unhinged forces are at work today, even stronger, in trying to carve America into their secular, socialist image. A central problem and danger in government and the judiciary today is a lack of reverence and honor for our Christian heritage, the Constitution, and for the wisdom, values, and vision of the nation's Founding Fathers. Too many in all the branches of government do not feel bound by the Constitution. This includes some of our Congressional leaders who will resort to any means, underhanded or not, to get partisan legislation passed. This includes submitting such legislation in bills numbering in the thousands of pages which everybody knows that nobody has read but couldn't care less. Apparently, this tactic was going on even in the early days, since James Madison denounced it with this comment:

"It will be of little avail to the people that the laws are made by men of their own choice if the laws be so voluminous that they cannot be read, or so incoherent that they cannot be understood."

Angelo M. Codevilla, author of *The Character of Nations,* stated the following:

"When politics is reduced to the question of who is to get what, when, and how? the results are ever more demanding constituents, ever higher taxes, ever weakening civic responsibility, and the transformation of citizens into subjects. A political agenda of redistribution engenders partisan warfare and violence."

Mr. Codevilla is correct, and his words describe perfectly the agenda of the secular progressive radicals - high taxes, weakening civic responsibility on the part of citizens, turning citizens into subjects of the government, and redistribution of income and assets. Codevilla also said that:

"Citizenship is full partnership in a regime, not to be exploited and manipulated."

That statement should be printed, framed, and hung on the wall of every member of the House of Representatives and the Senate.

Why are so many young Americans, and some not so young, excited about socialism. Why do they approve of the redistribution of income, and quite willingly subject themselves to government in order to receive a portion of that redistributed income. Whatever happened to the old-fashioned work ethic? As I mentioned before, the spiritual, political, educational, and societal deterioration of our nation over past decades has a lot to do with it. We undoubtedly have millions of young and middle-aged adults who have never had a course in American history in high school or college, who are either illiterate or nearly so in our nation's Judeo-Christian foundation, illiterate concerning our Founding Fathers and the nation's founding, illiterate concerning our nation's heritage and exceptionalism and the reasons for that exceptionalism. Also, as I mentioned, the drastic increase in Biblical illiteracy and the large decline in church attendance have been major contributors to the nation's deterioration.

A large share of those millions of citizens have probably never received Christian instruction, experienced a church family, or even a temporal traditional family with two parents, a father and a mother. Therefore, it is not surprising that a person with such a background, without the benefits listed above which help to instill within a person the basic Christian worldview, would find socialism, even with the corresponding loss of some freedoms, attractive. And to be honest, even many of us who were blessed with the benefits listed above, might find certain aspects of socialism desirable. The attractiveness of socialism, however, is deceptive, and in its tyrannical forms of Fascism, Naziism, Communism and other forms of dictatorships, has caused unimaginable misery, poverty, suffering, devastation and death to untold millions of subjects. And giving in to the siren song of socialism results in not just forfeiting a few freedoms here and there but forfeiting one's freedoms overall. Those secular progressive radicals who are working to change our nation into a secular socialist state are indeed enemies of the state.

In order to remake or refashion a nation and society, you must first destroy or change that nation's and society's heritage and replace or weaken the foundation upon which they are built. The secular progressive radicals understand this, and thus their priority is to destroy, weaken, or at least make irrelevant, the Judeo-Christian foundation our Founders built the nation on and prepare the way for replacing it with a secular foundation. Further, the radicals understand that, without religious authority, morals and ethics are hard to define and almost impossible to justify. Our Founders understood this, and that is why they insisted that religion and morality were absolutely essential for the survival of a Democratic Republic. I have quoted statements by Washington, Adams, and Madison to support this. The vast majority of laws regulating behavior are based solidly on religious principle. If the radicals remove the religious principle, our Biblical code of morality and ethics, the Ten Commandments, loses its authority and the way is open for establishing a human code of morality and ethics based on moral relativism. A sign of the secular progressive radicals' goal of replacing our Judeo-Christian foundation and Biblical code of morality and ethics with a secular foundation and code is the persecution of Christians which is becoming more and more common for the first time in our national history. I touched on this at the conclusion of the last chapter and would like to expand on that discussion here.

Again, the Christians being persecuted are those who refuse to compromise and corrupt God's Word by accepting and supporting those cultural and societal standards of today that are in direct violation of God's Word and moral precepts.

David Horowitz is a New York Times bestselling author whose latest work is *Dark Agenda, The War to Destroy Christian America,* reviewed by Newsmax magazine. In the 1960s, during the Vietnam War, Horowitz was a leader in the far-left radical liberal activist group. When the group sanctioned violence against the U.S., Horowitz broke away from them, became a conservative, and today is one of the nation's leading and most respected conservative thinkers and speakers. His *David Horowitz Freedom Center's* primary objective is restoring America's popular culture consistent with its Judeo-Christian traditions, heritage, and values.

In his book, Horowitz maintains that Christianity, once the backbone of America's civilized society, is under cruel and relentless attack. He warns that left-wing activists, working in tandem with Democrats and radicals, are attempting to tear down our religious freedoms, and are waging war against Christians in courts and the media. Their goal is to destroy Christianity in America and establish a new millennium in which Christianity is banished.

Horowitz argues that Judeo-Christian values are at the very root of America's democracy and success. If such values are rejected, all our freedoms could perish. Here Horowitz is in total agreement with our Founding Fathers and a multitude of other historic national and international figures. I have emphasized throughout this book that our Founders and the vast majority of their successors emphasized that, in a democratic society with the freedoms enjoyed by the people, the people must be bound by a common loyalty to a transcendent authority rather than a human authority. This transcendent authority for the United States and all other western nations was the Christian God, the Ten Commandments, and the teachings of Jesus Christ.

Loyalty to this transcendent authority, its teachings and its moral / ethical code, undergird the development of western civilization into the most religiously, politically, economically, educationally, technologically, culturally, and powerfully advanced civilization in human history. Conversely, it has been a fatal weakening in loyalty to this transcendent authority that has caused a precipitous decline in the power and influence of western civilization over the past six or seven decades.

Our Founders firmly believed that in a democratic society, without the precepts of Christianity, there could be no true morality or ethics for individuals or for the nation. The secular progressive liberal left rejects these Christian precepts as authoritative; however, without them, any democratic society will drift into anarchy. History has shown this, and our own national experience is currently proving it true.

If anyone had predicted fifty or more years ago that the day would come when Christians would be persecuted in the United States, they would have been laughed at or considered daft or crazy. Our Christian heritage and foundation were solidly established in the hearts and minds of the overwhelming majority of our citizens. The devastating decrease in church attendance and Biblical literacy in the population have resulted in multitudes being totally unaware of our Lord's prophecy concerning such persecution as a prelude to the signs of the end time. In Luke 21:12-19 Jesus prophecies:

> "But before all this, they will lay hands on you and persecute you. They will deliver you to synagogues and prisons, and you will be brought before kings and governors, and all on account of my Name. This will result in your being witnesses to them. But make up your mind not to worry beforehand how you will defend yourselves. For I will give you words and wisdom that none of your adversaries will be able to resist or contradict. You will be betrayed even by parents, brothers, relatives and friends, and they will put some of you to death. All men will hate you because

of Me. But not a hair of your head will perish. By standing firm, you will gain life."

For the secular progressive radical left, law is the highest good, because law, like public opinion, can be manipulated, shaped, and corrupted to pave the way for a political agenda. Our seven justices who gave us legalized abortion clearly proved this. For the conservative, morality is the highest good, and morality is higher than law. Why? Because we are one nation under God, and there are some things that are not negotiable with God, and his moral / ethical code is one of them. And why is this? Because it reflects his holiness, his nature, his created order, and these are not to be compromised by man, nor is man to assume that God's moral code changes over time. It is eternal and unchanging, just as God is eternal and unchanging. Moses, writing under the inspiration of the Holy Spirit, makes this clear in Numbers 23:19:

> "God is not a man, that He should lie, nor a son of man, that He should change his mind."

This passage describes the immutability of God and the integrity of his Word. Neither the means nor the end of any endeavor are justified if they contradict God's moral law. This, of course, would include the majority of the secular progressive radical's liberal policies and agenda. In its essence, the culture war afflicting the United States today is a battle between legality and morality, the legality corrupted by the secular progressives and the morality commanded by God. For the Judeo-Christian world, including the U.S., law is very, very important, but Bible based morality is ever more important.

Alexis de Tocqueville, in his classic work, *Democracy in America,* said this:

> "There is not a country in the world where the Christian religion retains a greater influence over the souls of men than in America. America is still the place where the Christian religion has kept the greatest real power over men's souls, and nothing better demonstrates how useful and natural to man it is, since the

country where it now has widest sway is both the most enlightened and the freest."

Bill Hecht, in his *Two Wars We Must Not Lose,* said that:

"The reason for the unparalleled success of this great country is that so many of the underlying principles upon which our nation was founded are based firmly on Judeo-Christian teachings of morality, compassion, and justice."

And James Madison's speech in 1789 on behalf of the First Amendment to the Constitution made clear that it was introduced to protect several States' religious arrangements and meant to foster the practice of religion and in no way inhibit it.

Paul Johnson in *God and the Americans,* summed it up as follows:

"Hence, though the Constitution and the Bill of Rights made no provision for a state church - in fact, quite the contrary - there was an implied and unchallenged understanding that the Republic was religious, not necessarily in form, but in its bones, and that it was inconceivable that it could have come into being, or continue to flourish, without an overriding religious sentiment pervading every nook and cranny of its society."

Are these statements true today? The Bible was considered the rule of life by the vast majority of Americans during approximately the first 150 years of our existence as a nation. Christianity is no longer the basis for life and law in the western world. This is a tragedy of monumental proportions, since it was its Christian principles and motivations that propelled Western Civilization to the highest power, wealth, accomplishments, discoveries, and influence of any civilization in history. How it has fallen! Today, many western nations are dangerously close to paganism.

As far as the United States is concerned, our nation's ways, to a great extent, no longer reflect the Founding Fathers' wisdom, values, and vision. I don't believe that our country has fallen as far from their Judeo-Christian roots as other western nations. But that is the trend, and that trend must be reversed if we are not to follow those nations with their post-modern, secular-progressive, moral relative, humanistic ideology which brings confusion between the sacred and the sinful, between grace and permissiveness, and a lack of Biblical understanding of sin.

Right and wrong are realities, and it is vitally important to correctly discern between the two. Otherwise, everyone feels justified in going their own way and doing their own thing, regardless of the effects on others or society as a whole, with the result being confusion and chaos. This is precisely where secular progressivism, humanistic liberalism, and post-modernism fail miserably to provide a solid foundation for the spiritual and physical realities of life. Our Founding Fathers understood with clarity that the only source of such a solid foundation was the Biblical code of morality and ethics - the Ten Commandments primarily - which the western nations, including the United States, have removed from the public venue.

George Washington and the other Founders taught that the American system is built on the foundation of Biblical religion and morality. They insisted that the future and the prosperity of the nation depended on its citizenship conducting themselves and relating to one another according to the Ten Commandments. Removing those from the public square and from our schools five or six decades ago was, as I mentioned repeatedly, an act of appalling ignorance and stupidity on the part of politicians and the courts and, combined with the deterioration in the nation's institutions over that period of time, the effects have been devastating to the stability, confidence, and status of the country, nationally and internationally. To a great extent, our country is no longer a nation that walks humbly before God and strikes fear in the hearts of its enemies.

And what about our politicians and judges today? Do they not realize and understand the devastating effects removal of those Ten Commandments from the public venue and schools have had on people's sense of right and wrong, their behavior and lack of conscience? Do they not realize the devastating effects on the national character and conscience? I cannot believe that there are no politicians and judges who

324 | Darrell J. Ahrens

recognize these devastating effects and agree that removal of those Ten Commandments was a national disgrace. And if there are, then my question is where are the efforts to restore those Ten Commandments in the public venue and schools? Where are the politicians and judges with the wisdom and guts to stand up and say, "A terrible mistake of gigantic proportions was made in their removal to the great detriment of the nation, and it is the right thing to do to rectify that mistake and restore those Ten Commandments to the public venue and the schools." Or do they think it is better to let bad law remain than for the judiciary or politicians to suffer embarrassment in admitting to mistake?

St. Augustine once said:

> "In order to discover the character of any people, we have only to observe what they love."

The hierarchy of love among most Americans was once "God, Family, Country." With the drastic decrease in church attendance and Bible literacy over the past few decades, it is doubtful that love of God is the first priority of many of citizens today. With the divorce rate over 50% and the deemphasis on the Biblical order of family, it is doubtful if family is the second love of the majority of citizens today. And with the decline in overall patriotism and a growing unwillingness to serve country, it is doubtful if country is the third love of the majority of citizens today.

The political and societal condition of America today is much like that of Israel in the Old Testament described in Psalm 82:5 as follows:

> "They (the judges and rulers) know noting; they understand nothing. They walk about in darkness; all the foundations of the earth are shaken."

And from Ecclesiastes 10:2-3, written by King Solomon, considered by many to have been the wisest man who ever lived:

> "The heart of the wise inclines to the right, but the heart of the fool to the left. Even as he walks along the road, the fool lacks sense and shows everyone how stupid he is."

To the right…to the left in the above passage can stand for the greater and the lesser good, or for good (right) and evil (left).

God's words to Israel in Psalm 50:16-17 could well apply to our nation today:

> "What right have you to recite my laws or take my covenant on your lips? You hate my instruction and cast my words behind you."

And also in Psalm 81:11-12:

> "But my people would not listen to me; Israel would not submit to me. So, I gave them over to their stubborn hearts to follow their own devices…"

But God follows his words of rebuke with words of hope in Psalm 81 verses 13-14 and that hope is ours also today:

> "If my people would but listen to me, if Israel would follow my ways, how quickly would I subdue their enemies and turn my hand against their foes."

There are many in America today who grieve over the condition of the country just as Israelites faithful to God grieved over what was happening to their country. In Psalm 139:20, the Psalmist says to God:

> "They speak of you with evil intent; your adversaries misuse your Name."

In Psalm 119:53, the Psalmist laments:

> "indignation grips me because of the wicked, who have forsaken your law."

In Jeremiah 8:18, the prophet is brokenhearted:

> "My joy is gone; grief is upon me; my heart is sick within me."

And in Psalm 119:134,136, the Psalmist again laments:

> "Redeem me from the oppression of men, that I may obey your precepts. Streams of tears flow from my eyes, for your law is not obeyed."

God is not a neutral bystander. Sometimes it may seem that way, but Scripture assures us that God is always in control. There are times, however, when God will pull back and withhold blessing, allowing us to experience the consequences of our sin until we earnestly repent and seek his forgiveness. Such a time is described in Hosea 5:15-6:1. In Hosea 5:15 we read of God's response to Israel's wickedness:

> "Then I will go back to my place until they admit their guilt. And they will seek my face; in their misery they will earnestly seek me."

And in Hosea 6:1, we read of the peoples' response to God's turning away:

> "Come, let us return to the Lord. He has torn us to pieces, but He will heal us; He has injured us, but He will bind up our wounds."

I believe we are in such a time period now. God has not forgotten us or left us. But I think He has turned his face from us, waiting for our national repentance for turning away from Him and his Word and our Judeo-Christian heritage, waiting for our return to Him. In Isaiah 59:2, the great prophet also spoke of such a time:

> "Your iniquities have separated you from your God; and your sins have hidden his face from you, so that He will not hear."

What do you, the reader, think? Do you think our nation is ready for repentance, for turning back to God and his Word as absolute truth and authority for life in all its aspects, including politics? Personally, I don't think so! Many of our leaders and citizens want this, but too many do not. We have too many leaders, as well as citizens, who meet the criteria described in Psalm 36:2-3 as follows:

"For in his own eyes, he flatters himself too much to detect or hate his sin....he has ceased to be wise and to do good."

Like the saying goes, "The most powerful addiction is self-addiction." Due to the extensive, widespread Biblical illiteracy of past decades, we have a preponderance of leaders and citizens who do not understand what grace and righteousness are. We have a situation like that spoken of by the prophet in Isaiah 26:10:

"Though grace is shown to the wicked, they do not learn righteousness; even in a land of uprightness, they go on doing evil, and regard not the majesty of the Lord."

Justice and righteousness are the cornerstones of government and society.

The corruption of these two cornerstones today is extensive. Rampant among our political and cultural institutions today, and even some of our churches, is the denial of God's Word as the inspired absolute truth and the authority for faith and life in all its categories. They consider man as his own determinant authority and God must be made over in man's image. They insist that God must abide by man's concepts of justice, peace, and sustenance in this world. Man's naive idea of righteousness is fairness, and sin is a minor infraction that we all commit occasionally. And hell, and even Satan, no longer exist in the minds or understanding of many today.

In Biblical times, God used prophets to speak to a rebellious people and to insist that God is God and man is his creature, responsible to Him and to his morality and order of creation. We need to hear again that kind of prophetic voice in our midst that speaks with the authority of the very Word of God, and not with the straw and mush of secular progressive radical liberalism.

I am reminded of a commentary from Lutheran Hour Ministries entitled *Marked by the Cross,* author unknown. The theme was during the trial of Jesus Christ before the Roman Governor Pontius Pilate, when Pilate followed a custom of releasing one prisoner to the people at Passover time. The only prisoner that he had, other than Jesus, was

Barabbas, a notorious murderer, thief, and hardened criminal. Pilate, wanting to release Jesus, and sure that the crowd would not choose someone like Barabbas, asked the crowd: "Who do you want me to release to you, Barabbas, or Jesus, with whom I find no offense and who is called the "King of the Jews?" And the crowd, in their hatred for Jesus, responded, "Release Barabbas." The author of the commentary expertly used this gross miscarriage of justice to make his point concerning our generation as follows:

> "In our generation, we have seen the crowd calling for abortion rather than life. In our generation, we have seen the crowd calling for the rights of criminals rather than the rights of victims. In our generation, we have seen the crowd speaking up for immorality rather than the Sanctity of Marriage and the Family. Indeed, when the crowd shouts nowadays, we can almost always be sure that it is for some Barabbas type of cause."

I think we as a nation have come to a crossroads that requires adherence to Thomas Jefferson's wise statement concerning corruption, which was previously quoted but which deserves being repeated:

> "When once a republic is corrupted, there is no possibility of remedying any of the growing evils but by removing the corruption and restoring its lost principles. Every other correction is either useless or a new evil."

So how do we remove the corruption in politics and restore the Republic's lost principles? One suggestion that has come up periodically over the years and which is gaining in popularity today, is term limits for Congress, which I have come to support. People ask, "Why didn't the Founders establish term limits?" To answer that requires a short review of our early history. Initially, our members of Congress were not elected by the citizens of their states. They were selected by the state authorities. It was George Mason, who at Virginia's constitutional ratifying convention in 1788, made the case for a citizen legislature, that is, a legislature voted into office by the citizens of their state.

His reason for wanting a citizen legislature, with members elected by their fellow citizens, was grounded in reality and elegant in its rationale and wisdom. He said:

> "Nothing so strongly impels a man to regard the interests of his constituents as the certainty of returning to the general mass of the people, from whence he was taken, where he must participate in their burdens."

Mason's rationale was accepted and election of our members of Congress approved. The reason term limits were not established at the time was because there was no need for them. There was no such thing as a career politician; in fact, the term was unknown. The common practice was for elected officials to fulfill their duties and responsibilities, and when their terms expired, they returned to their farms, their businesses, and other professions.

The term "public service" was meaningful back then because elected officials received a pittance of salary from the federal government, their primary income coming from their profession as doctor, lawyer, farmer, merchant, etc. Also, Congress was not in session all year, but only periodically to handle political, legislative and budgeting matters, and then adjourn until the next session or until a need arose for an emergency session. Then too, members of Congress were only paid while Congress was in session.

Today, of course, we have a full-time Congress and career politicians. I'm sure that if our Founders could have foreseen the political situation as it exists today, they would certainly have established term limits. Nothing corrupts like power, wealth, and celebrity. For a politician, as the time in office grows, so grows the temptation and opportunity to acquire all three. I'm not saying all politicians are corrupt, not by any means. We have many that are squeaky clean and who serve their nation, state, and constituents with honor, honesty, and sacrifice. However, to the country's detriment, there are too many others who are corrupt. It never ceases to amaze me how an elected member of Congress can begin a career on a legislator's salary, and not too many years in the future, end up as a multi-millionaire.

Since it would have to be our congressional representatives to introduce legislation for congressional term limits, it's probably never going to happen unless the public outcry for term limits is so great that they can't ignore it. In my opinion, 12 years, that is two terms as a Senator, and 8 years, that is 4 terms for a member of the House of Representatives, would best fit the country's needs and allow plenty of time for the new legislator to become experienced and effective, and have a good amount of time to serve as such.

I wish every member of the three branches of government - executive, legislative, and judiciary, would carry in their wallet, purse or somewhere on their person, and refer to it often, the prayer for wisdom that King Solomon prayed when he became king, found in 1Kings 3:7-9:

> "Now, O Lord my God, you have made your servant king in place of my father David. But I am only a little child and do not know how to carry out my duties. Your servant is here among the people you have chosen, a great people, too numerous to count or number. So, give your servant a discerning heart to govern your people and to distinguish between right and wrong. For who is able to govern this great people of yours."

And this word from God I would also like to hang on the wall of every member of Congress, given by the prophet Isaiah:

> "Woe to those who make unjust laws, to those who issue oppressive decrees." Isaiah 10:1

Dennis Prager, President of Prager University and author, in commenting on government, said:

> "Since it lacks the self-control apparatus that is a major part of religion (specifically Judeo-Christian morals and standards) the Left passes more and more laws to control peoples' lives. That is why there is a direct link between the decline in Judeo-Christian standards and the increase in government laws controlling human behavior."

Proverbs 29:18 says basically the same thing:

> "Where there is no revelation, the people cast off restraint; but blessed is he who keeps the law

Let's consider for a moment that self-control apparatus Prager mentions, and the ignorance of God in our passage, which could also be called Biblical illiteracy. In a society where ignorance of God, Biblical illiteracy, is extensive, people are bound by a code of morality and ethics they consider to be of human origin. And if that is the case, why should they be bound by that code. After all, we are fellow humans, and who is to say that the code other humans came up with, which I'm bound by, is any better than the one I devise for myself and follow. In such a society, everyone has their own standards of morality and ethics which are bound to differ substantially, and the result would be mass confusion and chaos unless the government comes up with laws to restrict people from deciding for themselves what is proper and improper behavior, and strictly enforces those laws. This is especially true with totalitarian governments who, at the first sign of a desire for freedom among the people, take action to squash that desire, often brutally.

On the other hand, in a society where knowledge of God and Biblical literacy is common and the Biblical code of morality and ethics - the Ten Commandments - are still the normal standard for social behavior, the people know that that code is of divine origin, given by a transcendent authority, and not of human origin. The people feel bound by this transcendent authority, and who is this transcendent authority? For lack of a better term, let's refer to Him as God. Whether people believe in God or not, they are, to a great extent, inhibited from crime and other anti-social behavior by the self-control pressure emanating from this transcendent authority. Thus, Prager's comment that "there is a direct link between the decline in Judeo-Christian standards and the increase in government laws controlling human behavior" is demonstrably correct.

Our Founding Fathers clearly understood this along with their keen understanding of human nature, and again, that is why they continually emphasized that, in a Democratic Republic where people enjoyed wide freedom in their activities and behavior, the Judeo-Christian foundation upon which they built the nation, and the Biblical code of morality and ethics, especially the Ten Commandments, that accompany that foundation, were absolutely critical to the nation's future, security, and prosperity, and if they were ever lost or discarded, the nation would fall.

One can only wonder at the actions of those who removed the Ten Commandments from our public institutions and schools. Were they ignorant fools? Fools yes, because what they did was the epitome of foolishness. They used "separation of church and state" as their justification, a phrase, as mentioned previously, that is not in the Declaration of Independence, the Constitution, or any other of our founding documents. In a previous chapter, I discussed in considerable detail the misunderstanding, the misinterpretation, and the wrong and downright unethical use of this phrase over the years, a favorite phrase of those who are trying to replace our Judeo-Christian national context with secular progressive liberalism. I also think there is something else involved with their insistence that God and any mention of God be removed from government buildings, schools, and other public buildings, and that is their fear that if they admit there is a transcendent authority, then they become morally responsible to that transcendent authority, and this would put limits and boundaries on their activities and behavior that are unacceptable to their ideology.

Their attitude is like that of one teacher of Darwinian evolution, whom I will not identify, who said:

> "I know that evolution is scientifically impossible, but I'm still going to teach it because it is morally comfortable. As long as I believe I am nothing but an animal, I can live any way I choose. But as soon as I admit there is a Creator, then I become morally responsible to that Creator, and frankly, I don't want to be morally responsible to anyone."

Thomas F. Torrance, in his *The Apocalypse Today*, spoke of the secular progressive radical's attitude toward religion in America today when he said:

> "The world likes a complacent, reasonable, religion, and so it is ready to revere some pale image of Jesus, some anemic Christ and Messiah. The world, and those who are of this world (including some pastors and religious officials) seek to bend the will of God to serve the ends of man, to alter the Gospel and shape the Church to conform to the fashions of the time."

Torrance's words serve as a warning to America today, lest we lose the battle to secular progressivism, because as I said before, if they cannot destroy the nation's foundation of Judeo-Christianity, they will seek to make it irrelevant, exactly what Torrance's statement warns about. To guard against this, we must never dare to interpret what God clearly says in his Word with our own, or others, conception of what He says. We must never change God's Word by one iota, because just as God doesn't change his mind, as the above passage tells us, so God's Word doesn't change. That which is confusing to us we attempt to interpret by means of other passages of Scripture. It is a primary method of hermeneutics (the art and science of Biblical interpretation) to interpret Scripture with Scripture.

The belief in American exceptionalism comes from the underlying Judeo-Christian values in American life. The secular progressive radicals in the Democratic Party do not believe in American exceptionalism because they do not accept the underlying Judeo-Christian values in American life. Again, their attitude towards religion, and in particular the Christian faith and those who are serious about it, is that religion may be fine for commoners so long as they do not get passionate about it and keep it out of public places.

Is America exceptional? Certainly our Founding Fathers thought so. And virtually all our leaders since the Founders have thought so. I can think of only a few presidential exceptions - Woodrow Wilson, Barak Obama, and possibly Joe Biden. Until approximately the 1960s, the attitude of the majority of Americans, as well as many across the world was that of Charles Malik (1906-1987), Lebanon's former Ambassador to the United Nations, who spoke of American exceptionalism as follows:

> "The good in the United States would never have come into being without the blessing and power of Jesus Christ. Whoever tries to conceive the American word without taking full account of the suffering and love and salvation of Christ is only dreaming. I know how embarrassing this matter is to politicians, bureaucrats, businessmen, and cynics; but whatever these honored men think, the irrefutable truth is that the soul of America is, at its best and highest, Christian."

May Ambassador Malik rest in peace. Back to the question, "Is America exceptional?" America is the first experiment in government "of the people, by the people, and for the people." It is an amazing fact of history , which I spoke of previously but bears repeating, that John Wycliffe, the great Bible translator gave convincing evidence of America's exceptionalism when, before his death in 1384, he translated the Bible into English and wrote in the flyleaf of his own translation these words:

> "This Bible is translated and shall make possible a government of the people, by the people, and for the people."

These words were immortalized almost 400 years later by our Founding Fathers with the birth of our nation. And since then, our nation became the most powerful, influential, affluent, generous, benevolent, and free nation in human history. Exceptional? I would say so! How about you?

American exceptionalism has been described as the belief that America often knows better than the world what is right and wrong. This infuriates the American left, the secular progressive liberals, just as fundamental Christianity infuriates them. But until the past few decades, history shows that more often than not, America did know better the right from the wrong, based on our Judeo-Christian conscience, and led other nations in pursuance of the right. This in no way absolves the nation from episodes and events of the past that were scandalous and downright shameful; for example, our treatment of the African American population both during slavery and afterward, our treatment of the original inhabitants of the land - the Indian population, the incarceration of our Japanese American citizens during World War II, and others. On balance, however, the good America has done far outweighs the not so good, and the generosity of America has extended around the world. So sorry, Mr. Wilson, Mr. Obama, Mr. Biden! Although your presidencies were not exceptional, the country of which you were president has proven to be, and to some extent still is, exceptional.

St. Augustine made a comment to the effect that we were created for fellowship with God, and until we have that fellowship, we have an emptiness to our souls. When people stop believing in God, they become so desperate to fill that emptiness that they believe in anything or they become so cynical about that emptiness that they believe in nothing. In an article in the weekly Washington Times, dated May 12-18, 2003, Dennis Prager stated:

> "The breakdown of belief in the God of the Bible has led to the demise of the belief in the Sanctity of Human Life."

I would add to Mr. Prager's demise of the belief in the Sanctity of Human Life the demise of the belief in the Sanctity of Human Marriage and the demise of the belief in the Sanctity of the Human Family, the three sanctities which are the theme of this book. Concerning the Sanctity of Life, I devoted four chapters to it, including the chapters on Roe v. Wade and Psalm 139 because it is the greatest of the sanctities that God gives us, and from it flows everything else.

The chapters on the Sanctity of Life make clear the horrible nature of abortion. Abortion is the greatest abasement and corruption of the nation's soul. Abortion on demand for any reason, or for no reason in particular, precludes all notions of family as God designed it. Abortion puts one person's choice above natural and religious responsibility. Abortion trains everyone to disregard the most fundamental responsibility of all - life.

In killing a human being, a murderer demonstrates his /her contempt for God as well as for his /her fellowman and forfeits his /her life as a result. In Genesis 9:5b-6 we are told:

> "And from each man too, I will demand an accounting for the life of his fellowman. Whoever sheds the blood of man, by man shall his blood be shed; for in the image of God has God made man."

God Himself is the great defender of human life which is precious to Him because He created man in his image, and because man is the earthly representative and focal point of God's Kingdom. In the theocracy of Israel, those guilty of premeditated murder were to be executed.

Those who conduct abortions and those who support abortion should seriously contemplate the above passage. At the moment of conception, the image of God is given to that new creation. Therefore, it must be emphasized again and again that abortion at any stage of pregnancy is a direct attack on the image of God, and thus an act of contempt for God, an act of arrogance against God, a denial of God's sovereignty over life, and a claim of the person's sovereignty over the life in her womb. One frequently hears women say, "Don't tell me what I can or can't do with my own body!" The fact is that it is not their body. That created life in the womb is connected to their body, but it is not part of their body.

From conception to full-term, when the child is aborted, all God's plans for that child are aborted also, all his blessings reserved for that child, the child's accomplishments, successes and failures, the child's joys, pleasures, sorrows, marriage, parenthood, and the legacy of a life well-lived - all gone in an instant through abortion. How does the abortionist and those supporting abortion justify this when called to give an account of their life when Christ returns to judge the living and the dead? As I mentioned in the chapter dealing with abortion, the only hope is to turn away from the abominable practice, repent of it, seek God's forgiveness for Jesus' sake, who suffered the full punishment for the sin of abortion as well as for all sins on the cross, accept his forgiveness and thank Him for it, and live a renewed life as God's dear child.

Do not deceive yourself by thinking you can support abortion and still be a devout Christian. How can a person purposely go on violating God's Word concerning life, reject God's sovereignty over the life in the womb that He created and redeemed, and for which He ordained a future, and still be a devout Christian? The answer is - he /she can't. Slavery was the great sin of the 19th century. Abortion is the great sin of the 20th and 21st centuries. Why? Because both deny the value of human life in God's image. Scripture often associates life with light. Two examples are:

> "For with you is the fountain of life; in your light, we see light." Psalm 36:9.

> "In Him (Jesus) was life, and that life was the light of men." John 1:4.

With abortion, there is nothing but darkness, the darkness of death. May God bring light to those who are engaged in this satanic practice and who support it so our land may be cleansed of its horror and stigma.

I'll start my concluding remarks on the Sanctity of Marriage with Benjamin Franklin's advice:

> "Keep your eyes wide open before marriage and half-shut afterwards."

Good advice! Eyes open before marriage to insure you are making the right choice and not acting simply on feelings and emotion. Eyes half-shut afterwards because not long after the honeymoon, you will start discovering the flaws in that perfect spouse you have chosen.

The Sanctity of Marriage was established in the Garden of Eden when God joined Adam and Eve together as husband and wife. This joining together in marriage was to be permanent until death. Jesus, in his discussion of marriage with the Pharisees, told them:

> "At the beginning of creation God made them male and female. For this reason, a man will leave his father and mother and be

united to his wife, and the two will become one flesh. So, they are no longer two, but one. Therefore, what God has joined together, let man nor separate." Mark 10:6-9.

The Founding Fathers treated marriage as a preeminent part of the divine order of nature and order of creation and as the foundation of private morality. Since the Founders believed that a Democratic Republic form of government was possible only among virtuous people, they revered marriage as few people have, before or since. Their generation considered men's and women's interests as fundamentally the same and regarded marriage as the divinely ordained and supremely good and effective way to organize life. To the Founders, marriage also meant a monopoly of lawful sex. Every colony and town had their laws against fornication and adultery, and husbands were obliged to support their wives and pay their debts. Divorce could be granted only in outrageous cases - mainly adultery. Alexis de Tocqueville made an astute observation concerning marriage when he said:

"There is hardly a way of persuading a girl that you love her when you are perfectly free to marry her but will not do so." (Women, take note!)

Today, the Sanctity of Marriage has become for many more of a temporary contract of convenience instead of a sacred trust. Rather than the divinely ordained supremely good and effective way to organize life, marriage is considered by many as not all that preferable to alternate lifestyles. Couples living together outside of marriage today is commonplace with no stigma attached as in previous years. It is doubtful if most people today even know the meaning of the word fornication - sex outside of marriage.

Thanks to no-fault divorce, another supremely stupid decision with unintended consequences made by our politicians and judges, it is estimated that 50% or more of marriages today end up in divorce. Were these politicians and judges so dumb that they didn't realize that if divorce was made so easy, the divorce rate would head for the stratosphere? The effect has been devastating to children. Divorce is so common that it has been estimated that a white child has only a 30% chance of reaching the age of 18 with both natural parents. A black child has only a 6% chance. In addition to divorce, the fact that so many mothers now work has resulted in children getting some 40% less time with their parents than they did a generation ago.

For many, Scripture passages on marriage and divorce are old-fashioned and no longer apply to our modern, sophisticated times. They do not have the wisdom to know that God's Word is timeless. It never becomes outdated and is authoritative for every period of history. Jesus Himself said:

> "Heaven and earth will pass away, but my words will never pass away." Matthew 24:35.

Let's take a look at just one of those passages on marriage and divorce in the book of Malachi. Apparently, unfaithfulness and divorce were major sins in his day also. God tells the people through his prophet:

> "You flood the Lord's altar with tears. You weep and wail because He no longer pays attention to your offerings or accepts them with pleasure from your hands. You ask 'Why?' It is because the Lord is acting as the witness between you and the wife of your youth, because you have broken faith with her, though she is your partner, the wife of your marriage covenant. Has not the Lord made them one? In flesh and spirit, they are his. And why one? Because He was seeking godly offspring. So, guard yourself in your spirit, and do not break faith with the wife of your youth. 'I hate divorce,' says the Lord God of Israel....So guard yourself in your spirit, and do not break faith." Malachi 2:13-16.

What affects marriage affects the family. The two are inseparable. Following are my concluding remarks on the Sanctity of the Family. In that chapter, I gave strong emphasis on the fact that God has ordained the husband and father as the spiritual leader of his family. There are many Scripture passages that extol the godly man, husband, and father, especially in the Psalms. The following is just one of them:

"Blessed is the man who fears the Lord, who finds great delight in his commands. His children will be mighty in the land; the generation of the upright will be blessed. Wealth and riches are in his house, and his righteousness endures forever." Psalm 112:1-3.

The Psalmist gives a eulogy to the godly man. The godly man brings blessings to his children and is himself blessed through them. "His children will be mighty in the land," that is, they will be persons of influence and reputation.

Erwin L. Lucker, Editor-in-Chief of the Lutheran Cyclopedia, Concordia Publishing House, 1954, maintained that God made the home and family the center of worship and religious training. This was also emphasized in the chapter on the Sanctity of Family. Why? Because the home conveys not only physical life but is the primary institution of God to insert the life in Christ into each generation. Scripture backs up Lucker's claim as the following passages show:

"For I have chosen him (Abraham) so that he will direct his children and his household after him to keep the way of the Lord by doing what is right and just…" Genesis 18:19 "These commandments that I give you today are to be upon your hearts. Impress them on your children. Talk about them when you sit at home, and when you walk along the road, when you lie down and when you get up." Deuteronomy 6:6-7.

The Cyclopedia goes on to say that the home and family is the cradle of personality, the most potent teaching agency, the chief unit in evangelism, the best barrier against evil, the keeper of culture, the bulwark of the Church, and the cornerstone of the nation. Wow!! That pretty much says it all. And yet, there are those who want to change God's priceless jewel of blessing - the family - from his design to something of human design, from husband (man) wife (woman) and children, to something more in line with current cultural and societal tastes and standards. Again, go from riches to rags. Any change to God's design for family, his order of creation instituted in the Garden of Eden, is not an improvement, but sheer foolishness and a degradation and corruption of the Sanctity of Family.

The Sanctity of Family has been the bedrock of nations and civilizations since time immemorial. Again, the saying: "As the family goes, so goes the nation." Our Founders certainly revered family as the bedrock of the nation. George Washington pointed out that public life must be grounded on private morality that stems from the home and family. John Adams said that the foundation of national morality must be laid in private families, that children learn the meaning of morality, religion, and respect for law from the habitual fidelity of their parents to one another.

The United States Supreme Court, In the 1885 case of Murphy v. Ramsey and Others, stated the following in its high opinion concerning family:

> "Certainly no legislation can be supposed more wholesome and necessary in the founding of a free, self-governing commonwealth...than that which seeks to establish it on the basis of the idea of the family, as consisting in and springing from the union for life of one man and one woman in the holy estate of matrimony; the family is the sure foundation of all that is stable and noble in our civilization."

The secular progressive liberal radicalism in the Democrat party, along with its political correctness and other ungodly, un-American, and unhinged policies has led to a serious decline of parental authority, and with it, to the serious weakening of that stable and noble foundation and bedrock of society - the family. Secular progressive liberalism tells us that government and government agencies know more about raising children than the parents, that educators, school boards, and teachers' unions know more about what children should learn than the parents. This is utter foolishness, appalling arrogance, and extremely dangerous.

Secular progressive liberalism's ideology concerning politics, economics, cultural, and spiritual matters including life, marriage, and family, has become a major power broker within the Democratic Party today, and its Marxist/Socialist base sows the seeds for societal disintegration, cultural degradation, and the lack of genuine and beneficial social, political, and cultural progress. Also, its rejection of sound monetary policies and sensible budgeting pave the way for economic disaster. The survival of the Democratic Party as a viable, relevant, political party depends on its cleansing itself of secular progressive liberal radicalism.

Furthermore, if we as a people hold to the combination of equality of opportunity, righteousness and fairness in conduct, and an industrious work ethic, the nation cannot but prosper. But first, foremost, and above all, we must turn back to our Judeo-Christian roots which includes holding to the Supreme Court's 1885 description of marriage and family which I quoted above.

Finally, concerning family, the Lutheran Cyclopedia referenced in the foregoing, emphasized that new strains and stresses have been placed on the family by world-shattering changes to society such as the astounding increase of separation, divorce, broken homes, and child delinquency. Notice that this was written back in 1954, and the situation is much, much worse today. The family is a crucial part of the battle between the Church and the world. The home, family, and Church face challenges greater than ever before, and therefore need each other more than ever before. Moreover, a major problem today is that many churches and a number of denominations have compromised themselves and God's Word to secular progressive liberalism, and can no longer be trusted for solid, consistently truthful, Biblical teaching and guidance.

The churches that remain faithful to God's Word, to Jesus' teachings, and the Gospel of Salvation must take the lead in calling this nation back to its Judeo-Christian roots, back to the Sanctity of Life, the Sanctity of Marriage, and the Sanctity of Family. Government is not going to do it. As President Reagan said: "Government is not the solution; government is the problem." And it is logical that the Church should take the lead because it has the regenerating power of the Gospel of Christ and the Holy Spirit, the love and concern and promises of the Good Shepherd, and the teaching facilities and agencies to carry out a balanced program of family life guidance. It is totally futile to expect such a program from our corrupted public education establishment, although it would truly be a blessing if our educational leaders and all teachers would come to the realization of the disaster our public school system has become, change course, and again become the godly, pro-America, and superbly effective organization it was for the first 180 years of our 249 years as a nation.

The greatest weapon the Church has in this mighty endeavor is prayer. Spiritual pollution, whether in an individual, political organization, or nation, must be wiped away through prayer. Only prayer can bind Satan and open the way for the Holy Spirit to bring revival. Every Christian in the country ought to be lifting this country up in prayer every day, that the country be cleansed of the corruption of the Sanctity of Life, the corruption of the Sanctity of Marriage, the corruption of the Sanctity of Family, prayers for those in authority and leadership positions in the Church, Government, Education, and Society, that their hearts and minds be open and able to discern the spiritual and secular dangers confronting our country, and that they seek divine guidance and help in getting the country back on track, both spiritually and secularly. And also, similar prayer for the citizenry of our nation, that the indifference and self-interest priority of the many be replaced by concern over what is happening to the nation, and action to reverse it and restore its greatness again as one nation, under God, with liberty and justice for all.

Indifference is a form of hate. I mentioned before that we, the citizens, are at fault for the nation's slide into immorality and corruption in its government and institutions. As a free people, we elect our leaders, and so we deserve the leaders we get. Our Founders emphasized this and warned us to be very careful in our selection of leaders and exhorted us to elect leaders of faith, integrity, virtue, honor, and honesty.

Sir George Adam Smith, in *The Book of the Twelve Prophets,* 1899, made this astute observation:

> "The great causes of God and humanity are not defeated by the hot assaults of the devil, but by the slow, crushing, glacier-like mass of thousands and thousands of indifferent nobodies. God's

causes are never destroyed by being blown-up, but by being sat upon."

The same is true for national aspirations. Sometimes it is the apathetic and indifferent who are more responsible for a nation's moral collapse than those who are actually engaged in the evil of bringing about that collapse, or those who have failed in the responsibilities of leadership. A central reason for judgment and a nation's downfall can often be because of the silent majority, who are not evil by acts of treason or heresy, but simply at fault for having done nothing to arrest the slide into confusion and chaos and corruption occurring all around them in their nation's daily life. For many people, their attitude towards both faith and patriotism can be summed up by the following statement:

> "They are not guilty of unbelief but are equally not overwhelmed by belief."

In other words, they are lukewarm, and therefore ineffective. They are like the members of the church at Laodicia, a wealthy city in Phrygia during Roman times, which our Lord Christ addressed in Revelation 3:15-16 as follows:

> "I know your deeds, that you are neither cold nor hot. I wish you were either one or the other! So, because you are lukewarm - neither hot nor cold - I am going to spit you out of my mouth."

Ask any supervisor or leader and they will tell you that having employees or followers who are lukewarm in their motivation and loyalty is one of the worst personnel problems one can have. Notice that in the above passage quoted from Revelation, Jesus told them that He wished they were one or the other, either hot or cold. Hot, of course, would be those who were passionate in their faith in Christ, passionate in their loyalty to Him, and passionate in the mission of evangelism He had given them. Cold, of course, would be the opposite. Passionate in their denial of Christ, passionate in their resistance to Him, passionate in their attempts to prevent evangelism and the spread of the faith. Why would Jesus say He would rather have them cold than lukewarm? Wouldn't a lukewarm follower be better than a cold enemy? No! Jesus understood the ineffectiveness and sorry state of lukewarmness and the great value and effectiveness of passion for a cause. He knew that if a cold person could be turned into a hot person, all that passion would be at his disposal and directed towards the Great Commission He had given his followers - to take the Gospel of Salvation to all the world.

A perfect example of this was Saul of Tarsus, who became the Apostle Paul. No greater enemy of the Church and of Christ existed during the early days of the Church. Saul, a passionate Pharisee, did all he could to destroy the early Church. He agreed to the stoning of Stephen, the first martyr. He arrested Christians and put them into prison. It was on his way to Damascus, with letters from the Jewish ruling council empowering him to arrest any Christians he found there, that Jesus appeared to him in a vision. With his conversion to faith in Jesus as his Lord and Savior, Saul, the Pharisee with his coldness toward Christ and his Church, became Paul, the Apostle, with his hot passion now directed towards Christ, his Church, and the task of taking the Gospel to all nations. Consider this passion which Jesus now had at his disposal.

Paul took the Gospel throughout Asia Minor, present day Turkey. He took the Gospel to Thrace and throughout Greece. He took the Gospel to Italy, to Rome, and there is strong evidence that he took the Gospel to Spain. That's almost all of Europe. And at the same time, with his epistles and letters to the churches he had planted, he managed to write half of the New Testament of the Bible. The Apostle Paul is the perfect example of what the Holy Spirit can accomplish through one man totally committed to Christ.

Apathy and lukewarmness towards a situation is often a result of forgetfulness or indifference concerning the past. In the case of faith, it can be forgetfulness of God's Word, acts, and promises or indifference towards them. In the case of patriotism, it can be forgetfulness of our founding as a nation, tradition, heritage, and exceptionalism, or indifference towards them. A faith that is forgetful or indifferent concerning God's Word is a dying or dead faith. A people that forgets its past or is indifferent towards it is a nation headed for oblivion. And remember this: One of the primary goals of the secular progressive liberal radicals of the Democratic Party is to have us forget or become indifferent to our Judeo-Christian heritage and capitalist economy and replace them with a secular foundation and a socialist economy.

An appreciation of the past, an understanding of the present, and a vision for the future are absolutely essential for both an individual and a nation if they are to progress, prosper, and reach their highest good and potential with passion and perseverance. The future can never be divorced from the present, and the present cannot be divorced from the past. Recounting the past has the primary purpose of bringing it to bear on the present and the future. Present and future events can be illumined and better prepared for by reference to analogous events of the past. As the saying goes: "Those who ignore history are doomed to repeat its mistakes." In Psalm 11:3, the Psalmist asks:

> "When the foundations are being destroyed, what can the righteous do?"

The answer is fight, resist, and if it comes down to it, revolt. That is precisely what the Founding Fathers did against a tyrannical British regime. And that is what they recommended we do if the leadership of this nation becomes tyrannical, defying the Constitution, becomes absolutely partisan in its politics, becomes obsessed with achieving absolute, total power, and casts aside the common welfare and good of the people for political expediency and dominant political power for the indefinite future. We must constantly remind our elected officials, which many of them have a tendency to forget, that they are servants and not rulers, and that they work for us and not we for them.

Again, as I did in the beginning introduction to this book, I justify the extensive use of Scripture passages and theology in this book on the basis that I am addressing both political and spiritual corruption in the Democratic Party, and when it comes to corruption, especially spiritual corruption, we're talking about sin, and sin is theological in nature. Therefore, when making such a charge, one better have the theological facts in order to support and justify the charge, and that requires specific theological explanation and application, in other words, theological discussion in detail which I have attempted to do, and I make no apology for it. I conclude this chapter and this book with some notes of wise observations I have gathered over the years which I consider essential to a godly and honorable life. I only wish that I had followed them more consistently and without failure.

1. "What a person believes is not what they say they believe. What they believe is what they do!" As the saying goes, "Actions speak louder than words." In 1John 4:1, God, through the Apostle tells us:

    "Dear friends, do not believe every spirit, but test the spirits to see whether they are from God, because many false prophets have gone out into the world."

And in Matthew 15:8, Jesus said:

    "These people honor me with their lips, but their hearts are far from Me."

In other words, don't believe everything you hear, but test it to see if it's true. The primary authority to use for testing it is God's Word. Many false prophets, false pastors, false teachers, false politicians, are with us, and they can sound so convincing; yet they seek to deceive us. Consider the monumental number of lies told to the public (that's you and I) by the Democrats against President Trump during his administration and the two fraudulent impeachments, all of which turned out to be baseless and untrue. And no Democrat has apologized to Trump or the public (you and I) for putting him, and us, through such an ordeal that went on and on and on, which is simply additional evidence of the corrupt, dishonorable, ungodly, un-American, and unhinged nature of the current radicalized Democrat Party.

2. Prominent individuals and organizations can, and often do, use virtue and charity as a cover for greed or the lust for celebrity and power. This is most common among politicians, Hollywood celebrities, and corporate officials, and has been especially

prevalent among the Democratic Party membership during the past five or six years.

3. "If we compromise the truth, we lose our sense of sin." Another word for compromise is accommodation, and I think it was G.K. Chesterton who coined the phrase: "Accommodation leads to accommodation leads to accommodation." In other words, if we compromise the truth a little, which is sin, it leads to more compromise, which leads to more compromise, etc., etc., until we eventually lose our sense of the terrible nature of sin, and I would add, we lose our appreciation of truth, which would be devastating to one's life.

4. The critical need today is wise discernment, the ability to discern, even when others can't or won't, the logical outcome of a slide in morals and ethical behavior, and the courage to stand firm and give stability where otherwise there would be none. May God bless us with such leaders.

5. Concerning acceptance, a major subject in today's society, I really like the comment on acceptance made by Lewis Smedes, Professor of Psychology, Fuller Theological Seminary, who said:

   "All of us need a sense that God accepts us, owns us, holds us, affirms us, and will never let go of us, even if He is not too impressed with what He has on his hands."

6. When we are weak, God is strong. When we are confused, God speaks with clarity in his Word. When we fall down, God picks us up.

7. John Derbyshire in *The Gladness of Early Greece,* said the following:

   "It is the great conceit of our age that we are wiser than our ancestors were, but this is taking the conceit too far."

This perfectly describes the attitude of the secular progressive radicals in the Democratic Party.

8. Christianity alone, among the belief systems, is reasonable, rational, and logical, for Christianity alone addresses and resolves the fundamental problem of human society, which is sin. And Christianity alone provides the answer to sin - a Savior -Christ the Lord. Therefore, Christianity is the only key that fits the lock of existence, life, death, and afterlife.

9. There is an on-going struggle between Judeo-Christian morality and secular progressive liberalism. Secular progressive liberalism tends to renounce Judeo-Christian morality in favor of a world in which human rights have replaced human duties and responsibilities. Alexis de Tocqueville's comment is appropriate to this subject when he said:

   "Habits formed in freedom may one day become fatal to that freedom."

That is, when so-called human rights are used to turn freedom into approval, support, and license for immoral behavior in contradiction to Judeo-Christian morality, along with attempts to convert a capitalist society into an entitlement society, freedom itself and our Democratic Republic are endangered. That is precisely the situation we find ourselves in today with the culture war against the secular progressive radical liberalism of the Democratic Party. It was also the rationale behind Benjamin Franklin's response to the woman who, after the Constitution was adopted, asked him: "Mr. Franklin, what have you given us?" And Franklin answered: "A Republic, if you can keep it!"

10. Concerning self-esteem, which is another major item in the secular progressive politically correct lexicon, let it be known that, according to Scripture, it is only in Christ that we can truly love ourselves, because it is only in Him that we can be cleansed of the filth of sin because He alone paid the full price and suffered the full punishment of our sin so we can be forgiven. The only self-esteem we can lay claim to is that which we have In Christ, and it is a gift of God, totally without merit on our part.

11. Secular progressive liberal ideology fails due to its intellectual and logical incoherence. 57 genders? Really? Who are the morons who came up with this? And yet, there are so-called major universities and colleges that go along with this intellectual foolishness and logical absurdity, which begs the question that if they promote this foolishness and absurdity, what other radical liberal foolishness and absurdities are they teaching our children?

12. Failure of our legislators to be bound by the laws they themselves promulgate sharpens the distinction between ruler and ruled and is therefore anathema to a democratic republic society. Every citizen should have this memorized and refer to it frequently.

13. "When a nation decays, it begins in the home." Another lesson of history which we should have learned ages ago, but which we still manage to ignore. It also highlights the critical importance of halting and cleansing the corruption of the Sanctity of Marriage and the Sanctity of Family which is so prevalent in society today.

14. Living without faith is living without purpose and fulfillment. Faith and passion are the two essentials for a life of purpose and fulfillment. And passion for whatever God calls you to do, whether great or small. Keep the following wise advice of Rev. Dr. Martin Luther King in mind always:

    "If a man is called to be a street sweeper, he should sweep streets even as Michelangelo painted, or Beethoven composed music, or Shakespeare wrote poetry. He should sweep streets so well that all the hosts of heaven and earth will pause to say: 'Here lived a great street sweeper who did his job well."

On this subject of living our lives with faith and passion, let me give you another wise piece of advice from the Rev. Dr. Martin Luther King:

    "Everyone can be great…because everyone can serve. You don't have to have a college degree to serve. You don't have to make your subject and verb agree to serve. You only need a heart full of grace and a soul generated by love."

Great advice for all aspiring leaders.

15. Evil always dresses itself up as good, and the worst looks like the best. In other words, if it looks or sounds too good to be true, it probably is.

16. "Always do that which is right. This will gratify some people and astonish the rest." Mark Twain.

17. "My idea of patriotism is to act so as to make one's country live up to its own highest standards." Arthur Schlesinger.

18. "Don't be discouraged by failure. It can be a positive experience . Failure is, in a sense, the highway to success, inasmuch as every discovery of what is false leads us to seek earnestly what is true, and every fresh experience points out some form of error that we shall afterwards carefully avoid." John Keats.

19. "Words are the most powerful drugs used by mankind." Rudyard Kipling. Warning: Words can do incalculable damage as well as incalculable good.

20. "No man is fully able to command unless he has first learned to obey." Another piece of wise advice for aspiring leaders taken from a Latin Proverb.

21. "Watch your thoughts; they become words. Watch your words; they become actions. Watch your actions; they become habits. Watch your habits; they become character. Watch your character; it becomes your destiny." Motto of Milwaukee YMCA.

22. "Truth is inconvertible. Panic may resent it. Ignorance may deride it. Malice may distort it. But there it is." Winston Churchill,

23. "For everything that was written in the past was written to teach us, so that through endurance and the encouragement of the Scriptures, we might have hope." Romans 15:4. And therein is the only true hope, the Living Hope which we have in Christ.

24. And some final good advice on living from Dr. Anthony Esolen, Professor at Thomas Moore College, in his article entitled *Raising Children in the Age of Nothing*, published in the Lutheran Witness magazine, August 2017. I have added a few points of my own, as well as comments on his main points, and minor changes to the order, but the main points are his. And these are:

"Live in the fullness of reality but use the imagination to explore good and great things." It was Albert Einstein who said: "Imagination is more important than knowledge." "Play and work, eat and drink, with gusto and passion." "Marry, stay married, and express your love to your darling every day." "Read good books and talk about them." "Treasure the good friends God gives you and honor them." "Turn your eye upon the incredible beauty of God's creation, large and small, and let your soul be filled with wonder and magnificence." "Bend the knee often in prayer, bringing all requests to God and thanking Him for all He has done, and for all He is going to do to bring you and yours to your highest good in Him."

I close with a suggestion. In World War II, during the Japanese attack on Pearl Harbor, a Chaplain on board one of the warships being attacked was helping bring ammunition from the hold of the ship to the deck guns. He yelled encouragement to the sailors under fire with the words: "Praise the Lord and pass the ammunition!" It became a famous battle-cry of the war. I suggest that we adopt a battle-cry for our war against secular progressive liberal radicalism, the ungodly, un-American, and unhinged political ideology which, not all, but a large number of Democrats are using to attack our Judeo-Christian heritage and capitalist economy.

The first part of our battle-cry will be the same as that World War II battle-cry, and the second part the favorite toast of a beloved friend and squadron member who has gone to be with the Lord; namely, "Praise the Lord, and Confusion to the Enemy!"

Thomas Jefferson

James Madison

Benjamin Franklin

John F. Kennedy

Alexis de Tocqueville

George Mason

St. Augustine, Bishop of Hippo